To Bob –
with affection and
appreciation to a wonderful
person + good afriend.

Lou Dorf/Sman

DORFSMAN &CBS

By Dick Hess and Marion Muller

American Showcase, Inc., New York

Author's Acknowledgements

We would like to thank all the people who helped nurture this book to completion: Ann Hysa Dorfsman, Dr. Frank Stanton, Ted Andresakes, Ira Teichberg and Dick Jackson for contributing their personal memories, experiences and observations; Kyla Kanz and Dean Morris for their monumental and painstaking labors with the production; Beth Slone for her perceptive and intelligent editing of the manuscript; Karen Silver, Bonnie Rosenfeld, Debbie Lovell and Stephanie Sherman for their good-natured compliance with countless requests for assistance, materials and information, and of course, Ira Shapiro and Chris Curtis, without whom this book would not have seen the light of day.

—Dick Hess and Marion Muller

Distributed in U.S. & Canada by:
Rizzoli International Publications, Inc.
597 Fifth Avenue
New York, NY 10017
Rizzoli ISBN 0-8478-0864-5

For sales outside U.S. & Canada:
Hearst Books International
105 Madison Avenue
New York, NY 10016

Published by:
American Showcase, Inc.
724 Fifth Avenue, 10th Floor
New York, New York 10019
(212) 245-0981
TLX: 880356 AMSHOW P

Design by: Richard Hess
Assistant Designer: Dean Morris
Printed in Japan: First Printing
Typesetting by: Franklin Typographers
ISBN 0-931144-41-8
Library of Congress
Catalog Card No. 86-070866

to Ann, Elissa, Mitchell and Neil
who didn't have half as much fun as I did.

— Lou

Contents

I n the firmament of advertising designers, there have been a great many stars. But Lou Dorfsman, by any measure, is a giant. His work for CBS Inc., in particular, endowed the company with an image so scintillating and elite, it helped raise the world's consciousness on the whole subject of "corporate communications." His peers applaud him. Students study him. Dorfsman has been exhibited, published and honored internationally with just about every award invented by the graphic arts community. But with all the exposure, no one has ever crawled inside his head and examined this intricate mind at work, and that is precisely the purpose of this book.

Rather than just another accolade for Dorfsman, this book was conceived with others in mind — corporate executives and managers of small businesses, advertising managers and account executives, art directors and copywriters, professionals and students — everyone who is involved in, or who has some curiosity about, the world of advertising and design.

The ads, promotional pieces and design projects included here are by no means a complete archive of Dorfsman's work. Nor are they exclusively prize winners. The work was selected primarily to demonstrate how Dorfsman confronted advertising and marketing problems, how his ideas were hatched and nurtured, the logistics behind his design and media decisions, and the amazing absorption with details that is at the heart of his reputation for integrity.

Although some of the material goes back decades, many of the problems and their solutions remain timeless. The case histories of his innumerable projects reveal Dorfsman's mix of perceptive business sense, intelligence, wit, inventiveness, tenacity, and superb taste. But for anyone who thinks Dorfsman rocketed to stardom on a swift and smooth trajectory, this story will also recount some of the obstacles, frustrations, hassles, politics, and maneuvers that are the day-in, day-out business of the business.

The details of the evolution of each project were drawn from countless hours of conversation and taped interviews with Dorfsman himself. Insights into his working habits and personality were elicited from artists and writers who have worked with him, his wife who lives with him, and from the authors' longtime personal knowledge and observations. But to give Dorfsman his proper place in the world of corporate graphics, the comments of certain people bear special weight.

William S. Paley, founder of CBS, Chairman and Chief Executive Officer for 50 years, and lifetime trustee of the corporation, said this of Dorfsman:

"CBS has a corporate commitment to excellence in design and Lou Dorfsman is the one whose genius has translated that commitment into reality. Deservedly, he has become a legend in the annals of commercial design. He combines a lively creative flair with an innate, sure sense of style and superb taste....The special 'CBS style' that he has created reflects, to a large extent, what I like to think of as the company's personality....I am very proud of the way he has defined CBS visually. I doubt that anyone else could have done it as well."

Dr. Frank Stanton, President Emeritus of CBS Inc., was President and Chief Operating Officer of CBS from 1946 to 1973. During those years he and Dorfsman established a philosophy and a visual image for the company that reached for impeccability. They also developed a mutual admiration that continues to this day. In 1978, when Lou was awarded the prestigious American Institute of Graphic Arts medal, Stanton made the presentation and summed up Lou's contribution to CBS with:

> "Everything Lou Dorfsman touched was made better for his efforts… whether it was a television studio set, a matchbook cover, a book, a booklet, a cafeteria wall, a paper cup, an annual report or an annual meeting, Lou has done it with taste and style and integrity."

Tom Wyman, who succeeded Paley as Chairman of the Board and Chief Executive Officer in 1980, came to CBS after serving in the top echelons of a number of major corporations. He spoke with firsthand experience when he made this observation:

> "The tone of most enterprises is set by a surprisingly small number of people. For CBS, Lou Dorfsman has been one of those — his elegant footprints surround us, and that has been our extraordinary good fortune. His career stands as eloquent confirmation that there is an important home for taste, style and the elements of fine design at the heart of worthy and successful commercial institutions."

From outside the CBS family, David Levy, Executive Dean and Chief Administrative Officer of the Parsons School of Design, sums up his assessment of Lou succinctly:

> "Lou is the ultimate in graphic design; his work is a reflection of his profound intellect, intuition and elegance."

But perhaps the most awesome compliment to Dorfsman comes from Dick Hess, noted designer, illustrator and instigator of this book, who said:

> "I did not go to art school; much of what I learned about this craft, I learned by studying Dorfsman. In developing the material for this book I was amazed to discover how greatly I am indebted to his example."

On the strength of his own illuminating encounter with Dorfsman's work, Dick Hess conceived of this book as an edifying experience for others as well. It isn't intended as a textbook, a how-to book or a holy bible of graphic design. But it is a documentation of the belief that advertising and commercial communication can be intelligent, market-wise, entertaining, informative, and at the same time scale the heights of sophistication in design.

—The Authors

Professionally, Lou Dorfsman has been a lot of people in his 40-year career: art director, designer, ad man, teacher, lecturer, consultant, advisor. He is also a trustee and board member of a number of schools and professional organizations, and ambassador-at-large to the international graphic arts community. But behind all those titles is the man himself, who directs and flavors every role he plays.

Any attempt to commit Lou Dorfsman to paper is like filming fireworks; you can record the event, but it's no substitute for the crackling live performance. An encounter with Lou is a very physical experience. He is tall, virile-looking and trim (a description that should please him as he worries about his waistline and keeps in shape with regular Sunday morning swims). He's an affectionate, demonstrative man. He greets visitors — men and women alike — with a warm bear hug and an infectious grin from beneath his generous mustache. With a hasty swipe at the pile of papers on his office couch, he clears a space and invites you to settle in; his eagerness to talk is palpable. Pick a topic — world affairs, science, sports, the arts, the advertising business — Lou is informed, perceptive and exceedingly articulate about it. He can sound erudite and Ivy-League-eloquent when it suits him. But Lou is at his best when he's not polishing his act. Take him off the dais, away from the microphone and lectern, and you hear the true Lou. His speech reverberates with graphic metaphors, nuggets of wit, pungent insights and outrageous language. You laugh a lot when you listen to Lou. His humor runs the gamut from gentle ridicule of his own foibles to searing sarcasm reserved for less fortunate victims. The truth is, this big, good-humored Teddy Bear can turn grizzly with his wit. He has been known to chew people out, make "chopped liver" (his own words) of their efforts, and leave a trail of shredded egos in his wake.

As it happens, the small sign outside his office door is a profound clue to the man inside. It doesn't bear his imposing title, "Vice President, Creative Director for Advertising and Design, CBS Inc." It reads simply, "LOU WHO?" It's a playful little sign that tells you Dorfsman is secure enough about his position to joke about it, and to forgo the pomp and trappings that normally accompany such prestigious titles. In fact, this arbiter of good taste for all the rest of CBS Inc. sits in an office that looks like the day after Armageddon. Papers overflow his desk and chairs, tear sheets flap from the bulletin board and memos cling to his lampshade. A stack of books, proofs and display samples in his closet is an avalanche-about-to-happen. It's obvious that momentous decisions have been made in this office. But the humble "LOU WHO?" sign betrays another aspect of Dorfsman. In spite of his obvious success and international fame, he has never quite obliterated the image of himself as "just a nobody kid from the Bronx."

Like the sign on his door, Dorfsman is a study in contradictions. He has a strong social conscience and is concerned about personal ethics clashing with business imperatives. Though he is troubled by the huckstering aspects of the advertising business, he unquestioningly loves the eternal problem-solving it requires. While he has often lamented that there were few heavy thinkers to help him in his projects, to hear him talk it becomes clear he truly relishes embracing a job and doing it all himself. And though he snipes privately at certain "empty suits" in the organization, in public Dorfsman is a trustworthy, loyal, reverent boy scout where CBS's image is concerned.

Considering his prodigious accomplishments, it surprises most people to discover that Lou is an irremediable worrier. "In fact," his wife Ann assures us, "Lou isn't really happy *unless* he's worrying." In spite of the adulation and authority he enjoys, he agonizes about his work. At one moment he presents a picture of indomitable self-confidence. In the next, he turns humble, questioning and self-deprecating. He has tortured himself, writers, designers and illustrators with revisions and alterations. He presses people to their limits of ability, patience and endurance. And after all the wrangling and perfecting, he'll wonder out loud if the results are really good, carefully pre-empting outside criticism by casting the first doubts himself.

Dick Jackson, a freelance writer who collaborated with Lou on a number of extra-curricular projects, reported a typical encounter. Meeting up with Lou on the street one day, Jackson congratulated him on his newest campaign for Dansk. Jackson described how Lou shifted around, uncomfortable with the compliment, and offered an apologetic, "Yeah, the ads look nice, but I'm not sure they sell any merchandise." Such self-derogation flabbergasted Jackson, because on the strength of those ads, he had just purchased a thousand dollar's worth of Dansk tableware for his home. Dorfsman, the sophisticated ad man, was genuinely amazed to hear such news.

T his same unexpected diffidence and humility pervades Lou's personal life as well, and explains how he came to own an expensive little MG auto. It seems that while visiting London sometime back in the late '60s, Lou was caught in one of those traditional afternoon showers. To get out of the rain, he ducked into the nearest shelter, which turned out to be an MG showroom. Now Lou, by his own admission, is a pushover for a British accent. "A guy talks British to me, and I immediately figure him for a 200 I.Q.," he volunteers. Well the salesman talked "British," the rain continued relentlessly, and by the time it stopped, Lou had hung around the showroom so long, he was embarrassed to leave without buying a car.

Even for a cavalier spender, which Lou is decidedly not, an MG is a heavy price to pay to cover an awkward situation. And the incident points up another aspect of Dorfsman's complex psyche. He is an appreciator of excellence. He has a penchant for perfection. But he wants it at bargain prices. Personally, he satisfies his cultivated taste in clothes with impeccable selections from Saks Fifth Avenue's end-of-season clearance racks. For CBS, its multi-million dollar advertising budget notwithstanding, Dorfsman strikes hard bargains with suppliers. The perfectionist in him spares no investment of energy or time; sometimes he'll travel great distances just to *feel the paper* for a job. Conversely, he derives exquisite pleasure out of saving the company twenty bucks! He once went so far as to get his own press pass to shoot photos of NFL football games for his newspaper ads. "Why *pay* for photos that you can take yourself?" he reasoned.

Lou attributes his aversion to extravagance to growing up during the Great Depression. The kid who knew the value of hand-me-down clothes grew to be a man who delights in his ingenuity for getting extra mileage out of design projects. He has incredible vision for designing elements that can be cloned for multiple uses.

Obviously, you can extricate the kid from the Depression, but you can't always get the Depression out of the kid. The hard-times mentality never quite released its grip on Ann and Lou Dorfsman who grew up, went to school and were married in those harrowing years. When they were finally able to make the move to the affluent Great Neck community on Long Island, they confounded the neighbors who came by to welcome them. Dressed in their old work clothes, Ann, cleaning windows, and Lou, clearing leaves out of rain gutters, were mistaken for the hired help. The Dorfsman children were the spoilers of the neighborhood. Not only did they rake leaves, mow the lawn and carry their weight of other household chores, they also managed to walk away with top scholastic honors in their school.

But if the Dorfsmans' work ethic surprised the neighbors, the Dorfsmans also intrigued them with the taste and craftsmanship displayed in their home. Ann, early on, dismissed the paper hanger who was messing up her flocked wallpaper and proceeded to hang it herself. Since then, no painter, paper hanger or workman of any skill has done a job in their house if Ann can do it herself, including laying BX cable to electrify the garage. Not only does it save money (which pleases Lou) and waiting time (which pleases Ann), but she has found enormous pleasure in mastering the required skills. Lou keeps his nose very clear of these household design and decorating projects. "Especially handling electricity," he exclaims, "for Godsake, you can get killed!" "So he leaves it to me!" interjects Ann, with more triumph than disdain.

While Lou absents himself from decorating projects, the Dorfsmans have a mutual interest in antiques, and together they have amassed an impressive collection. It is Lou's particular pleasure to go to work on a neglected piece of furniture and restore its beautiful old patina. Not long ago they bought an antique chest of drawers for some $750. Under 90 years of gunk and old varnish were inlays of six exotic woods and keyhole escutcheons made of mother-of-pearl. Lou attacked the chest. He scraped, sanded, varnished and burnished with meticulous care, laboring over the piece every weekend for ten months. When it was done, he surveyed the finished chest and, with typical self-mockery, quipped, "So now it's worth $780!"

Considering his zest for stripping old furniture, it's no surprise to see that Lou attacks advertising and design problems in much the same way. He has a special gift for zipping through "garbage" — extraneous issues and information — and cutting through to the beautiful bare essence of things. It makes life incredibly challenging for his staff. One writer summed up the experience in two words: "exasperating" and "exhilarating." Lou wrangles with headlines, dissects words, digs deeper and deeper, searching for just the right solution. And just when you think you've nailed it, he starts all over again with yet another angle to consider. Unless you can crawl inside his head, you're never really at the same level of a problem that he is. Worst of all, at the eleventh hour he is likely to come up with precisely the right headline and copy approach himself — a somewhat demoralizing thing for a designer to do to a writer.

Still, there are those exalted moments when writers see their ideas come to life more brilliantly than they envisioned, because of the logic, clarity and elegance he brings to the visual presentation. It is also a great comfort to writers that Dorfsman is not one of those designers who regards copy as a necessary evil. He has far too much respect for ideas, words and meaning, ever to make text illegible or subvert meaning for the sake of esthetics.

Like the writers, designers on his staff report the same extremes of experience. He presses them, eggs them on to do better. He directs them with a scribble on the back of an old envelope…with harrumphing and facial grimaces…with arms waving like semaphores. Some rise to his challenge and flourish; some don't. As one devoted longtime associate put it, "I was in awe of the guy's brilliance when I first came to CBS, and I still am. But not everybody can take it here. If your ego is totally invested in your work, you may have to move out or be crushed." All things considered, working with Lou can be a tearful, terrifying experience for some but a terrific education for others.

The Dorfsman family at Lou's induction into the New York Art Directors Hall of Fame, 1978. L. to R., daughter Elissa, Lou, son Neil, wife Ann. Son Mitchell (right) resides in California.

Dorfsman, like most movers and shakers, has bucked authority, ruffled feathers, and stepped on egos in his time. But it was always in the interest of getting his best work done that he made himself heard on programming, research, sales and marketing plans, as well as advertising and design. He never settled for ready-made solutions. He insisted on asking the questions and finding his own answers. "Of course," he explains, "you hope and pray that everyone else involved will have the grace, insight and taste to let you do a good job. But in every large company there are dozens of underlings who can be difficult (without the credentials to warrant it!); still you have to be nice and show them respect."

Such outspoken pronouncements and Lou's undisguised impatience with mediocrity may have offended people along the way. But Dorfsman redeems himself with his superb talent, his intelligence, his soul-searching, and his total lack of pretense. He is an ad man who shuns words like "creative"… "concept"… "images," and speaks plainly about ideas, words and pictures. He has taken brave new approaches to the field of advertising design. But probably his most enduring contribution has been his integrity and impeccable taste which has inspired a higher level of work and helped give "advertising" a respectable name.

No book about Lou Dorfsman can be complete without some mention of his lifetime relationship with Herb Lubalin, noted graphic designer and typographer. Four times, Lou reached the point of resigning from CBS to join Lubalin in a studio of their own. Once they even progressed to the point of arguing about whose name should take precedence on their logo. Herb suggested the studio be called *Dorfsman & Lubalin*, because Dorfsman was already famous. Lou declined the honor and opted for *Lubalin & Dorfsman*, because the partnership was Herb's idea. Needless to say, the argument was academic. Lou could never quite break his ties with CBS, and the partnership never happened. But Lubalin and Dorfsman remained an inseparable team in all their other activities.

The Dorfsman/Lubalin entente started back in 1935 when they enrolled in Cooper Union, and it continued after graduation. They both married their Cooper Union sweethearts, shared a wedding day, a honeymoon, and their first apartment. They teamed up on vacations, anniversaries and professional trips. Lou and Herb were frequently joint lecturers, joint judges, joint teachers, and an irrepressible comedy team.

But close as they were in their personal relationship, they were poles apart in personalities, physical traits and orientation to their work. Herb was slight of stature, reticent, generally uncommunicative about his philosophy of work, except when engaged as a panelist or lecturer. With regard to personal matters — feelings, fears and fantasies — he was deafeningly silent. Lou, by contrast, is tall, vigorous, expansive about his work and ideas, and disarmingly introspective about himself. In the 40-odd years of their relationship, Lou had two unresolved goals: one was to engage Herb in a conversation about "people and feelings;" the other was to get Herb to initiate a conversation on any subject. He failed at both. Once on a trip to California, where they were traveling to judge a graphics exhibition, Lou vowed that he would not utter a word unless Lubalin spoke first. To Lou's everlasting distress and amazement, they spent the entire transcontinental flight in silence.

If Lubalin was taciturn with words, he was paradoxically verbose with a pencil. He moved swiftly and silently over his tracing pad, spewing out multiple versions of a design, without so much as a flicker of doubt or hesitation. By contrast, Lou mulls and chews, reflects and reviews, discusses and dissects ideas over and over again before he commits a single squiggle to paper. Lou envied Herb's capacity to turn out volumes of impeccable work with ease and concluded that Herb was incapable of making a bad design. Lubalin never tortured himself with concerns about readership, audience motivation or questions such as, "What makes effective advertising?" He believed that if you did something exciting, people would pay attention.

Lou operates on the principle that the idea is paramount. He puts the designer in him on hold until he knows what buttons to push to engage his audience. As a feature story about him in *Communication Arts* put it: "Dorfsman has no style." Far from being a pejorative statement, it defines his strength as an ad man. There are no design clichés or Dorfsmanisms that stereotype his work. For him a project starts with studying the client's problems, understanding his business, figuring out what has to be said and how best to say it. Most often the words are in his head before the picture — a strange sequence of events for an art director! All the design decisions about layout, typography, illustration, etc., follow from the idea.

They might have made an extraordinary team — Lubalin, the prodigious designer, and Dorfsman, the formidable thinker. Their unconsummated partnership had become a joke they shared with the advertising and graphic arts community, but the possibilities of such an alliance ended when Lubalin died in 1981. Still the legend lingered on. It is typical of Lou's wit and unconstrained sentimentality that in his memorial service tribute to Herb he concluded with these words: "I feel sure that we will meet sometime in the future and at last pull off our business partnership. And when we do…we're going to redesign the hell out of heaven."

(Overleaf) Throughout their careers, Lubalin and Dorfsman teamed up as judges of graphics shows and guest lecturers at professional seminars. They also established themselves as an irrepressible comedy team.

A Kansas City illustrator recorded his vision of the Dorfsman/Lubalin team arriving for a visit to the Kansas City Art Institute.

Lubalin and Dorfsman at the ceremony inducting Lou into the New York Art Directors Hall of Fame, 1978.

Whenever the gurus of the advertising and design world assemble to hold seminars, judge shows, hand out medals or honor a member, one question invariably surfaces: "What's kept Lou Dorfsman at CBS all this time? (Over 40 years, in fact.) It's a question Dorfsman often raises himself. Most high-powered creative people have moved about from agency to agency, studio to studio — won their awards, established their reputations and finally set up shop for themselves. The fact that Dorfsman didn't follow this game plan had everything to do with the salubrious climate he found at CBS when he arrived in 1946 and that pervaded the company for decades afterwards.

Far from being the mythical "anonymous" corporation, CBS bore the imprint of a number of highly visible personalities. For starters, there was William S. Paley. As a young man Paley had a sharp head for business, a taste for adventure and energy to spare. In 1927 he brought all those assets to bear on a small ailing radio network called United Independent Broadcasting. For an investment of half-a-million dollars, he acquired controlling shares of the broadcasting company, its 16 affiliated stations and a record division. It was a runt of an organization compared with the giant RCA/NBC operation which had, in addition to a successful radio manufacturing division, some 50 affiliated stations in its grip. Paley found the competitive challenge invigorating. In the short span of three-and-a-half months, he tripled the number of his affiliated stations by offering attractive new contracts. The expanded broadcast coverage beefed up the capital worth of the company which he re-christened "The Columbia Broadcasting System."

But pure aggrandizement was never Paley's sole pleasure. He had an equally hearty appetite for the good life. He loved to travel. He sought out gourmet food, fine art and sparkling companions from cafe society and the cultural world. His taste for "the best of everything" didn't stop at the door of his home, but extended into his business in all its manifestations.

Dr. Frank Stanton   William S. Paley

In lining up programs for CBS, he was an aggressive and masterful showman. He pursued the most desirable and prestigious talent for his network. Some he discovered. Some he lured from Hollywood and NBC. In the '30s and '40s, CBS sponsored such notable stars as Will Rogers, Jack Benny, Kate Smith, Bing Crosby, Frank Sinatra, Benny Goodman, Paul Whiteman, Guy Lombardo, Glenn Miller, Duke Ellington, and the Dorsey Brothers.

But beyond satisfying the popular tastes in entertainment, Paley wanted to identify his network with a higher level of art. In 1930, CBS Radio made broadcast history by transmitting the first concert by what is now called the New York Philharmonic. In the drama department, CBS sponsored Orson Welles' "Mercury Theatre of the Air," and initiated the "Columbia Workshop." This experimental radio drama program was never offered for sponsorship to keep it free of commercial intervention. It became a showcase for such literary lights as W.H. Auden, Dorothy Parker, William Saroyan, Irwin Shaw, Stephen Vincent Benét, and others of such caliber. Another prized CBS property was the gifted dramatist, Norman Corwin, who won an appreciative following with his innovative radio plays.

During World War II, CBS Radio had the undisputed outstanding news staff, broadcasting directly from the fronts in Europe and Asia. Listeners who could not tell you the names of their own Congressman were intimately acquainted with the names and voices of Edward R. Murrow, William Shirer, Eric Sevareid, Charles Collingwood, Robert Trout, Cecil Brown, Larry LeSueur, and others. They were more than household names; these CBS newsmen became world-famous authorities.

Later, when television took its place in the corporate scheme, CBS sought the same balanced program mix. Through the years they offered the popular entertainment shows — "I Love Lucy," "The Ed Sullivan Show," "Gunsmoke," "The Carol Burnett Show," "The Mary Tyler Moore Show," "All in the Family," "The Waltons," "Lou Grant," and "M*A*S*H." But this light fare was fortified with serious documentaries, news specials and image-building dramatic presentations, such as: "See It Now," "60 Minutes," "Face the Nation," a steady stream of "CBS Reports," "The Body Human," "Requiem for a Heavyweight," "The Autobiography of Miss Jane Pittman," "A Tale of Two Cities," "I, Leonardo," ...not to mention sports specials and educational and dramatic shows for children.

Dynamo though he was, Paley was never a one-man operation. While he busied himself buying talent and selling air time, he delegated responsibility to others to run his company. His flair for acquiring the best of everything extended to key people for his organization. One such find was Paul Kesten. Paley hired him in 1930 to head the Research and Promotion Department. At the time, Kesten was only 31, but already had ten years of advertising experience under his belt. Kesten was a close match for Paley in his enthusiasm and energy where CBS was concerned. Paley admired his elegance and taste "along with the touch of majesty with which he presented the image of CBS." Paley's confidence in Kesten was well placed. Aside from the man's own accomplishments in promoting CBS, he was responsible for bringing other people into the organization who continued to enhance it.

As a sales promotion strategist, Kesten relied heavily on research. In 1935, he came upon some cognitive studies done by a young man pursuing a doctoral degree in Psychology. The work intrigued Kesten who perceived that the research findings might be useful in promoting radio. He sent for the young psychologist and was so favorably impressed, he fervently encouraged him to accept a job at CBS as head of Research. The young man was Dr. Frank Stanton, who in no time at all became Kesten's protégé. Stanton's intelligence, diligence and grace in dealing with people were quickly discerned. As Kesten's administrative activities at the network expanded, Stanton took over his position as head of Promotion.

In the mid-1940s, when it was obvious that television was no longer an experiment, but a major industry, Paley felt it was time to reorganize the company for more effective use of its personnel. He wanted to concentrate on television programming and scouting for talent, and expected to turn the presidency and day-to-day operations of the company over to Kesten. To Paley's distress, he learned that Paul Kesten was seriously ill and couldn't undertake such a burdensome job. But there was no doubt in Kesten's mind who could substitute for him. And so with Paley's approval, on January 9, 1946, Dr. Frank Stanton was named President of CBS.

If Stanton's reserved demeanor was the antithesis of Paley's expansive personality, Stanton out-Paley'd Paley in his concern for dignity and style in CBS-related activities. During his 30-year reign as President and Chief Operating Officer of CBS, he was a patron of excellence. His own broad vision and fastidiousness spurred creative people to do their best work. His eloquence and diplomacy in dealing with clients, affiliates and government agencies made him a highly respected spokesman, not only for CBS, but for the entire broadcasting industry.

In the pioneering days of television, there were also a number of other exceptional people in the CBS fold — newsmen, writers and administrators — who helped nurture an image of the company as a dynamic, imaginative organization. To the public, CBS was visible through its programming. To Lou Dorfsman, other fledgling art directors and old pro's, the name that was synonymous with CBS was Bill Golden.

Bill Golden joined the CBS Art Department, as an assistant, in 1937, and became an art director three years later. Although his career at CBS ended prematurely, (he died suddenly in 1959), his contributions to graphic design were profound — the most visible of which is his CBS "eye." Golden had come to CBS from the art department of *House & Garden* magazine. There under the tutelage of Dr. M.F. Agha, the noted Condé Nast Art Director, he was educated in the elegant and polished ways of a master, and he brought that orientation to CBS. Golden treated each advertising and design project as if it were fine art. He commissioned such painters as Ben Shahn and René Bouché to illustrate CBS ads and promotional material. He paid excruciating attention to typography. He was a purist when it came to materials. Golden's talents won him innumerable awards from the Art Directors Club of New York. Twice he was named among the ten best art directors by the National Society of Art Directors. He was elected to the Board of Directors of the American Institute of Graphic Arts. He was not only a star in the

Paul Kesten   Bill Golden

communications field, he was also honored in 1958 with an exhibition at the White Museum of Art at Cornell University.

And so it happened that, with Paley's showmanship, Kesten's and Stanton's sagacious and imaginative management and Golden's fastidious graphic design, CBS became visible to the world as a very glamorous and classy corporation.

No wonder that Sgt. Louis Dorfsman, lying on his Army cot in Dallas, during World War II, flipping through *Art Directors Annuals*, was smitten with the work he saw coming out of CBS. Then and there he made up his mind: "CBS is the place to work!"

From its modest beginnings, CBS has expanded into a multi-faceted, $5 billion corporation. Aside from its vast broadcasting function, its record divison, Columbia Records, grew to be the world's largest producer and distributor of recorded music. CBS Inc. also expanded its operation into publishing music, magazines, textbooks, educational materials, computer software, video cassettes and disks, and theatrical films. In all their activities, CBS designers felt the mandate to operate in the same high style ordained by the management team of Paley and Stanton. "You couldn't escape it," according to Dorfsman. "The sense of eliteness permeated the building and everything that emanated from it. It was in our genes!"

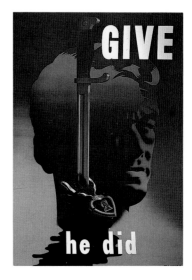

1. Sergeant Dorfsman's posters took first and second prize in a National Army Arts Contest, 1945. First prize poster.

Dorfsman's beginnings

Actually, Lou never dreamed of becoming an artist or designer in any sense. He grew up in the Bronx, went to local public schools and graduated from Roosevelt High School in 1935. His mother had high hopes he would become a doctor someday, and Lou in fact had a strong leaning toward science. He had his heart set on enrolling at New York University and majoring in bacteriology. But in 1935 the country was in the midst of the Great Depression. "The annual tuition at NYU was a big $300," Lou explains. "I don't know for sure whether my father really didn't have the money or just wouldn't spring for that much bread, so I had to consider other options." One possibility was to join his father in his sign-painting business, which Lou promptly rejected. The other was to apply to The Cooper Union for the Advancement of Science and Art. It was a highly respected, selective institution. It also had the decided attraction of being absolutely free. Since Lou liked to draw and the price was right, he took the entrance exam which, to his surprise, he passed. It was the end of his mother's dream of Louis Dorfsman, M.D., but it was the start of something neither imagined.

Looking back at his years at Cooper Union, Lou can't recall that he was particularly interested in the Advertising Design courses. He was intrigued with Architecture, Decorative Design, Painting, and Lettering. More memorable still were the hours he spent away from classes altogether — up at the Apollo in Harlem, listening to the jazz greats of the era. And most important of all, were the friends and lifetime attachments formed at CU — to Ann Hysa who became his wife, and to Herb Lubalin, his lifelong friend.

As far as Lou is concerned, his preparation for his career in advertising design came from the 11 jobs he held before, during and after school and from his experience in the Army. While still a student at Cooper Union, Lou worked part time at a Trans-Lux movie theatre, painting signs for $18 a week. He also worked on-and-off for a number of small display shops which gave him his first taste of the exhibit business. The most auspicious of these jobs was with an outfit called Display Guild, heavily involved in producing exhibits for the 1939 World's Fair. The job was high in excitement, but low in pay — a mere $8 a week — but, even then, Lou recognized an opportunity and a challenge he couldn't resist. He gave up the more lucrative Trans-Lux job, transferred from Cooper Union day school to night school, and went to work full time in the exhibit business.

It turned out that the job at Display Guild as assistant to the art director, Bob Maguire, was truly a "higher education" of a special caliber. Maguire was an industrial designer who in later years distinguished himself as one of the creators of the Ford "Thunderbird." But to Lou, he was a teacher, advisor, father, and mentor on a broad range of topics. He taught Lou all about friskets and airbrush, about architectural and structural design, and about the engineering of exhibits. He also enlightened Lou as to the social and political implications of the "Little Orphan Annie" comic strip. To this day Lou warms to the memory of Bob Maguire and still feels a real affinity for the exhibit business. He savors the smell of paints and glues and recalls with nostalgia the joy of sanding, sawing and airbrushing. His experience and ingenuity about the construction of displays, in fact, is in evidence in a number of unique CBS projects.

2. Second prize poster.

In 1940, the newlywed Dorfsmans and the newlywed Lubalins decided to share an apartment to save on expenses. Lou was nervous about Herb's ability to kick in his share of the rent. He prevailed upon his boss at Display Guild to give Lubalin a job, which he did, for the munificent salary of $5 a week. In a very short time, Lou was informed by his employer, "Tell your friend he has no talent for this work and he should find himself something else to do." Lubalin was fired and went on to seek his fortune in two-dimensional design.

Lou continued in the display business, feeling very macho with the airbrush, until 1943, when he was inducted into the Army. He was stationed with an engineering unit in Louisiana which was scheduled to go overseas. A final physical, however, revealed he had a punctured eardrum which disqualified him from active duty. As luck would have it, the Eighth Service Command in Dallas had just circulated a request for an exhibit designer. That Lou was discovered and offered the job was a remarkable coincidence, as the Army did not generally have a record of such felicitous matching of personnel and positions. Lou was shipped to Dallas, where he spent the remainder of his Army career designing posters, displays and traveling exhibits. When the Army announced a National Army Arts Contest, Lou submitted several of his posters and, to his delight, won first and second prize. "But," he reports with his typical sardonic humor, "my luck the war ended and the posters were never produced."

When Lou returned to civilian life, it was Lubalin's turn to help him find work. Lubalin, who had been sidetracked from military service because of a broken jaw, was already a full-fledged art director at a small New York advertising agency. He magnanimously found work in his art department for many Cooper Union friends returning from service, and Lou was among them. At that time, Lou was a complete stranger to the world of print media: words like "photostat," "letterpress" and "offset" were enigmas to him. But just when he was getting the hang of it all, Herb decided he was bored with agency work. He wanted to strike out in a studio of his own, and he wanted Lou to join him in partnership. They put together a portfolio of their combined work, which consisted mostly of Herb's ads and Lou's posters and World's Fair exhibit designs, and went scouting for business.

3. An early airbrush illustration; a gift for his father-in-law.

Recalling the inspired CBS advertising and promotional material he had seen in the old *Art Directors Annuals*, Lou took the portfolio straight to CBS. Eventually the portfolio came to the attention of Bill Golden who was not interested in freelancers, but was impressed enough to offer a job in the CBS art department. Hearing this, Herb wisecracked, "Great, *we'll* take it!" To mitigate a potential crisis, Herb who had already received a tempting offer from a highly respected pharmaceutical agency, Sudler & Hennessey, decided to accept it. The job at CBS was Lou's for the taking. And the plan for the Lubalin/Dorfsman partnership was shelved for a while.

To quote Frank Stanton, "It was a very bright day in the history of CBS when Lou Dorfsman came to work in the old building at 485 Madison Avenue." According to Lou, on that day in 1946, he was heady with exhilaration, but a little weak in the knees. He was not only about to enter the temple of the revered Bill Golden, but he was to sit at the altar beside him.

Lou had reason for his trepidation. Because of his limited experience, he was not entirely comfortable in the area of advertising design. He was happy and secure working on exhibits, building models, designing posters and signs and "airbrushing the hell out of them." To add to his troubles, he was being paid the staggering salary of $125 a week. It seemed to him an awesome amount of money, especially because he felt inadequate for the job. Lou would have preferred a different scenario. He confesses that he would have been more comfortable if he were *underpaid*. "I would rather have been a good bargain. When you earn top dollar, someone's bound to look over your shoulder and measure your output against your draw. When you work at bargain prices, anything you do is gravy. It's a no-lose situation."

Nevertheless, he settled in at CBS as Golden's assistant, and started to learn his polished professional tricks. Coming from the pedestrian, mass-production little agency to CBS was such a contrast, "you could get the bends," quipped Lou. "At CBS, for instance, we didn't rough-in facsimiles of photos for a layout. We shot a photo or pulled one out of our files. We didn't scribble "Greek" into type blocks, we had type set and pasted it in position, even at the layout stage."

But with all this advanced experience in producing an ad, Lou did not yet know the answer to a question that had been gnawing at him: "How does an ad become an ad?.... How and where does it all start?" He had watched Lubalin at work. Herb was a machine; he churned out layout after layout — each one different, each a wonderful piece of design. Lou had watched Golden at work, maneuvering photostats and type with lightning moves, like playing the old shell game. But while Lubalin and Golden were superb at what they did, neither of them ever answered the basic question Lou asked. Golden's reassuring pat on the head and nonchalant, "You do it, Louie, by doing it," were very small comfort to him.

Maybe it was the repressed scientist in Dorfsman that made him dig and dissect and want to know the root of things. He was still ill at ease in his new position. To make matters worse, CBS employees had just been unionized, and Lou got the terrifying word that he was slated for a $28-a-week raise. It was the last straw. He wanted out, and once again he and Lubalin talked partnership. But when Lou spoke to Bill Golden about leaving CBS, Golden convinced him to hang in. It was the vote of confidence he needed.

About this time, in the early 1950s, television had come of age and nothing in the communications and entertainment world would ever be the same. CBS, like the other networks, was overwhelmed with the ramifications of the new medium. Programming, Production, Sales, Advertising and Promotion — every department was challenged to its limits. In order to give each one ample time to explore the vast new potential of television, it was decided to split radio and television into separate units — the CBS Radio Network and CBS Television Network. In the Advertising and Promotion Department, Bill Golden was freed to concentrate all his efforts on television. Dorfsman, who by now had made a substantial impression on top management, was offered the job of Art Director for the Radio Network.

Now here was a dilemma. On the one hand, Lou would have to separate himself from the glamour and excitement of the new medium, and from Golden, his hero and mentor. On the other hand, this was a golden opportunity of another sort. In the face of the TV explosion, radio was stumbling along — an orphan child. This was his chance to be that "bargain" art director; anything that could be done to make radio look alive would be appreciated. Besides, it was an irresistible chance to test himself against great odds.

Lou likes to recall one of the most important lessons of his life, learned

4. One-column radio ads from the early '50s. Dorfsman has a special fondness for small space ads and a talent for investing them with enormous impact.

5. Photo taken for a story in *Interiors Magazine*, 1955, the first of many Dorfsman profiles in professional publications.

Variety

1
2
3
4
5
6
7
8
9
10
11
12
13
14
15
16
17
18
19
20
21
22
23
24
25
26
27
THIS ONE IS <u>NOT</u> ON CBS RADIO ~~28~~
29
30
31
32
33
34
35
36
37
38
39
40

In the current Nielsen ranking of all rated Monday-through-Friday daytime programs (2nd Report, April 1956)... all but one of the first 40 are on the CBS Radio Network. <u>39 out of 40</u>? Yes. And this extraordinary popularity has been going on for quite a while. A good thing to know when making media decisions involving radio's important daylight hours.

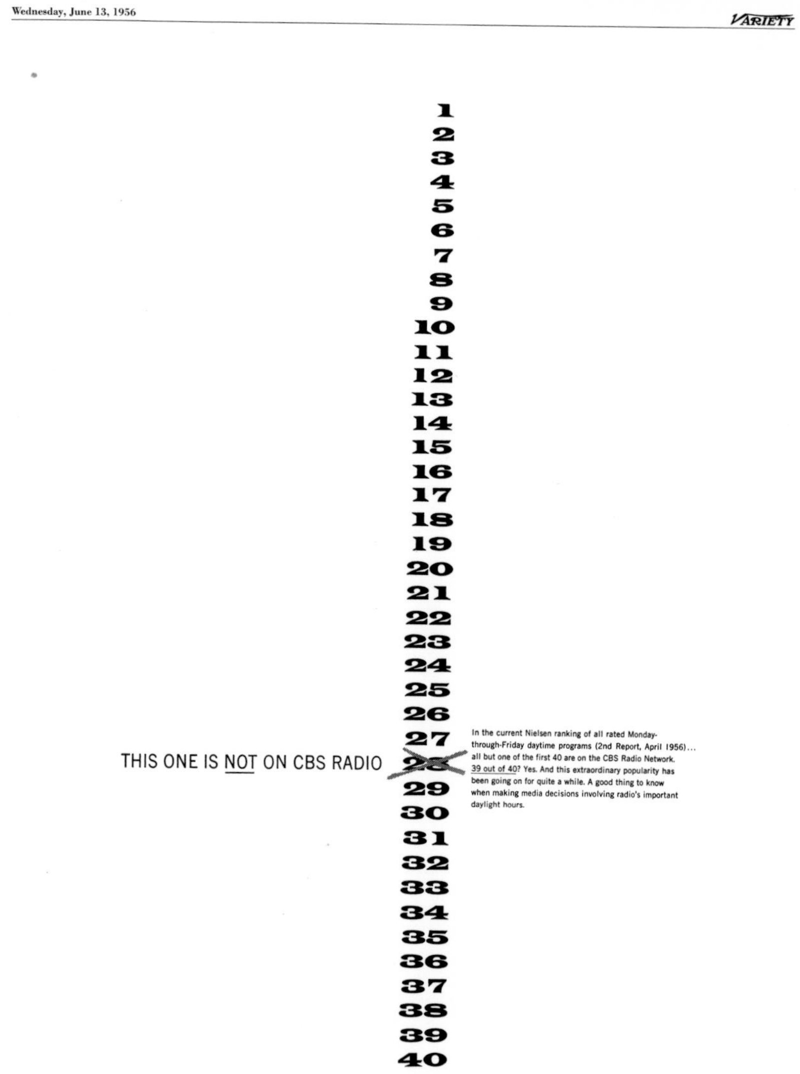

In a list of numbers from 1 to 40, 28 is crossed out, indicating that of the top 40 radio shows, only one — the 28th in popularity — is on another network.

6.

On a 1950's state-of-the-art radio, the dial is set at 88, and the tuning knob is gone, suggesting the loyalty of CBS's radio audience.

7.

8. A time clock, with punch cards bearing the names of CBS stars and hit shows, graphically presents the dynamic CBS "sales force" working for advertisers.

Variety Wednesday, March 18, 1953 Wednesday, March 18, 1953 *Variety*

The day they threw the knob away

THE CBS RADIO NETWORK
Where America Listens Most

7.

The pictures talk
Instead of graphs and charts, Dorfsman used engaging pictorial devices in these trade ads from the mid-1950's to demonstrate the pre-eminence of CBS Radio.

24

THEY'RE ALL BACK

...and out front with the customers

You might easily picture this time clock in stores all over the country.
And with the same names. For Benny, Bergen, Crosby, and company have
started a new fall season on CBS Radio....*There's no sales force like them*—
for selling more things to more people in more places....All year long, the
star attractions of CBS Radio build bigger audiences for *all* the network's
sponsors—offer the finest locations along the main stream of customer traffic—
assure the lowest cost....For this reason 25 per cent more time is sponsored on
CBS Radio than on any other network. And the time-slots still available
have all the "crowd" advantages of stores next to Macy's or Gimbel's....You too
can be out front with the customers on the **CBS RADIO NETWORK**

from a tyrannical old high school English teacher. The class was assigned to write a composition about the Bronx Park Zoo. Since Lou lived just a few blocks from the zoo, it held no magic for him anymore. "The zoo?" he remembers whining, "that's such a boring topic." In reply to which the old man jabbed his finger in Lou's face and blasted, "There are no boring topics — only boring people…like you!"

Lou never forgot that exchange. He has never since approached a project with the preconception that it was unexciting. On the contrary, the more hopelessly dull a problem threatens to be, the more intrigued and challenged he feels to find a fascinating solution.

Lou accepted the offer and moved to the Radio Network. But contrary to his expectations that he would be a member of a team working to keep radio vital, the mood at the radio network was gloom and doom. To be stuck in radio seemed a bum rap to people in the department. When Lou arrived, he found himself the subject of brutal scrutiny. Like the standup comedian in a nightclub, he felt all eyes on him. "So," they seemed to say, "do something… make us laugh…make a difference!" The pressure was on, but it was exactly the kind of challenge Lou relished. He wasn't certain how to proceed, but he knew one thing for sure — he wasn't going to make a big difference with just a pencil and a layout pad.

It turned out after all that, while working as Golden's assistant, Lou had learned an extremely important lesson about the origin of ads. He had observed that while he and Golden were sitting in their shirtsleeves scaling photos and cutting type apart, certain ivy-leaguers in three-piece suits were sitting upstairs in conferences making decisions about the very projects he and Golden were producing. It was obvious to Lou that he could do a more intelligent and meaningful job if he were "up there" where the problems were being discussed. This realization was the beginning of the do-it-yourself education of Lou Dorfsman, advertising man.

Lesson 1: Mind the client's business

The first objective Lou set for himself as Art Director for the Radio Network was to learn the business. CBS was not only his employer, it was his client. Lou stopped hanging out with his art department buddies at lunch time, and started to make lunch dates with the sales reps, the people in Programming and Research. He asked questions, and listened to their reports, followed Nielsen ratings, read the trade papers, and studied the competition. It became clear to him that the network was concerned not only with its immediate clients, the sponsors, but with a wide range of audiences: the listening public, the clients' advertising agencies, prospective clients, affiliated stations, government agencies, religious organizations, women's groups, racial and ethnic minorities, political parties, civil rights organizations, conservationsists… the list goes on. Not to be forgotten were CBS stockholders and CBS employees. It was incumbent on CBS to be responsive to all these sensitive groups, and at the same time to constantly send out signals about the integrity and pre-eminence of the company.

Lou did his homework and concluded that in the face of TV's explosive growth, radio might never regain its former robust health. But he believed it could be kept profitable.

9. Instead of a list of sponsors' names, this early trade ad for CBS radio used empty packing cartons to dramatize the famous brand-name manufacturers who advertised on the network. (Story on page 27.)

GENERAL**
AGREEMENT**

General Electric, General Foods, General Mills, General Motors – all agree it's sound strategy to be on the CBS Radio Network. Along with scores of other top-ranking national advertisers, they know that on CBS Radio, commercial salvos hit more listeners (47% more people listen per commercial minute than on any other radio network). And they hit them harder. (By its very nature, CBS Radio programming screens out the non-listening listener.) That's why, in the battle for the dollar, these generals make sure their campaigns are on the CBS Radio Network. Maybe what's good for them is good for you!

11. This 1955 institutional ad for CBS Radio drew a parallel between the bumblebee's success in flying, despite its poor aerodynamics, and the continued success of radio vis-à-vis television, despite the negative predictions. The drawing is by Robert Osborn.

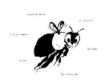

CBS RADIO NETWORK

10. Many of CBS Radio's
consistent advertisers
were big budget corpo-
rations whose names
began with "General."
This jocular ad reeled
them off.

12. An historic CBS Radio
ad on drug addiction.
The year was 1952.
The artwork is Andy
Warhol's, his first
commercial piece to
appear in print. The ad
won a Gold Medal
from the New York Art
Directors Club.

Accoring to Lou, once you know what the business is about, who your customers are and what's good for them, you don't need a set of rules or a pre-ordained philosophy to do effective advertising. Opportunities for ads are lying around waiting to be discovered. "And when you're tripping over one, you've got to be smart enough to pick it up and run with it," he admonishes.

As a case in point, he refers to his 1953 "Busy Market" ad (9), one of his early works. The idea came to him, one Saturday, while he and his wife were loading groceries into their car in the parking lot of their local supermarket. There in a corner of the lot, Lou spied a huge pile of trash from the market — cartons, cans, boxes, bottles. It was obvious that this was an active market. He also noted that the cartons all bore the names of well-known, successful brands. From this parking lot refuse pile came the flash of inspiration for a CBS Radio trade ad. CBS also had an impressive list of brand name advertisers. But instead of a boring list of client's names, he envisioned an ad showing a stack of their empty packing cases. The ad would make the point that many successful brands continue to spend advertising dollars on the CBS Radio Network.

On another occasion, while Lou was browsing through a list of CBS Radio advertisers, he was amused by the number of formidable clients whose names began with "General." There was General Electric, General Foods, General Mills, General Motors — all impressive names. From that list came Lou's whimsical trade ad, "General Agreement" (10). The message: If CBS Radio is good for all these big gun advertisers, it could be good for you, too.

In this way, Dorfsman found opportunities for ads in the most obvious places — in letters of endorsement from sponsors and listeners that had been tucked away in some executive's drawer... in statistics, misinterpreted or ignored. Sometimes even a negligible bit of information could be turned into a powerful argument. Lou likes to relate the genesis of the Pepsi Cola ad, "Be Sociable" (187): "I had just returned to work after a month's vacation and was all fired up for action. I made straight for the office of the V.P. in charge of Radio and asked him, 'What's new? Anything come up while I was gone?' He told me business was lousy... nothing of interest had come through. It was hard to believe. 'Not a single piece of new business?' I persisted. Then he grudgingly allowed that Pepsi Cola had bought some time — nothing to get excited about, he warned me, because they had also bought NBC, ABC and MBS. There was, however, the small satisfaction that 40% of the total budget was going to CBS."

As a wise old philosopher once observed, "There's no such thing as reality, only our perception of it." What this experienced, intelligent vice president perceived as a negligible piece of information, Lou seized as an opportunity for an important trade ad. By remarkable coincidence, he learned from a friend at the Pepsi-Cola advertising agency that Pepsi's new consumer campaign was built around the slogan, "Be Sociable." Lou made an immediate connection. He conceived of a photo of a bottle of Pepsi-Cola with four straws in it, surrounded by microphones of all four radio networks. With the caption, "Be Sociable," the ad telegraphed the information that Pepsi-Cola had included all the major radio networks in their advertising plans. The copy went on to reveal that CBS was getting the major share of the budget, proving that the successful Pepsi management knew the value of radio advertising in general, and of CBS Radio in particular.

The thrust of Dorfsman's ads for CBS Radio was to convince advertisers that network radio was still alive and well. Personally, Lou was also coming alive in his role. He had the feel of what advertising was all about. Not just pretty ads, not just tasteful typography and pictures, but solid facts presented in dramatic, provocative form. He was obviously successful. In his first year as Art Director for the Radio Network, he won a number of gold medals from the New York Art Directors Club and a lot of respect from the CBS administration. He was promoted from Art Director to Creative Director and up the ladder to Vice President for Advertising and Promotion for the Radio Network. When Bill Golden died suddenly in 1959, Dorfsman was immediately moved into the job of Creative Director for the CBS Television Network, and subsequently was elevated to Vice President and Creative Director of the entire Broadcast Group.

Lesson 3: Assume responsibility

It's possible Dorfsman has a special kink in his brain for recognizing opportunities for ads. But he is quick to advise that it doesn't amount to a bag of peanuts if you don't have the wherewithal to set your plan in motion. "Now, life can get complicated," he explains. "You want authority? You have to know what you're talking about. You have to be willing to sit in meetings for hours on end. You have to care about research and budgets. You have to fight for your ideas with cogent arguments. You have to earn the confidence of the people in top management." And Lou repeats over and over again that "Without a perceptive, intelligent, tasteful guy like Frank Stanton at the controls," he could have papered the walls of his office with all his brainstorms. Nevertheless, the presentation is always crucial. Even the most astute, receptive audience requires a properly packaged idea. "You don't have to produce a finished piece of work. You can omit the cosmetics," advises Lou, "but you must be able to show that the project answers a need, how it will work, what it will cost, to whom and how it will be distributed."

With all his savvy in these matters, Lou concedes that CBS was no Shangri-la. Not every brainchild of his flourished. Some never even saw the light of day. But there were a few projects in his radio and TV experience that demonstrate the importance of learning to identify opportunities and then having the strategy to see them through. One favorite project was the Football Book.

In the early '60s, CBS-TV had an exclusive, enviable contract with the National Football League to broadcast all scheduled Sunday games throughout the country. It was an extremely prestigious property for CBS, but the contract was running out. It was obvious to Lou that NBC and ABC were going to make a bid for the franchise. Football was big business. People who mattered to the networks — business executives, advertising people, station managers of affiliates, government people — all cared about football. It was nice wholesome action programming, too, so from every angle, the NFL contract was worth keeping.

Because of his connection with CBS, Lou managed to obtain a press pass to shoot his own photos of the New York games for his newspaper ads. One Sunday, out on the field with his camera, he was knocked off his pins by a sidelines play. It also knocked some sense into his head. "Why am I fooling around with this two-bit photography," he thought, "when there's the makings of a major promotion here!" Lou knew there was an impressive story to tell about the technological feat of broadcasting seven different games in seven separate areas of the country. It was a story that would glorify CBS, interest football fans, make points with advertisers, and give the NFL a lot of exposure.

Monday morning, Dorfsman went straight to Jim Aubrey, the then President of CBS-TV, and outlined his plan. He proposed that CBS produce an elegant coffee-table type book covering a Sunday afternoon in the life of the National Football League. It would cover all seven games played on a given Sunday of the season. Lou recommended that two thousand copies of the book be given to Pete Rozelle, President of the NFL, to distribute to his organization. There was no doubt in Lou's mind that NBC or ABC could woo Rozelle with more money, and that CBS might have to match their offer to renew its franchise. But the quality of the book Lou had in mind would surely make Rozelle think respectfully about CBS's initiative and style. Other copies of the book would be distributed to CBS affiliates, to clients, to advertising agencies, to Congressmen, to schools and public libraries. It

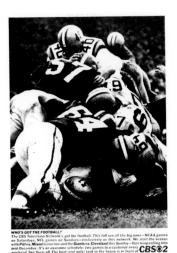

WHO'S GOT THE FOOTBALL?
The CBS Television Network's got the football. This fall see all the big ones—NCAA games on Saturdays, NFL games on Sundays—exclusively on this network. We start the season with Pitt vs. Miami tomorrow and the Giants vs. Cleveland this Sunday—then keep rolling into mid-December. It's an awesome schedule: two games to a customer every weekend. See them all. The best (and only) seat in the house is in front of **CBS◉2**

13. A newspaper ad for CBS/National Football League broadcasts. To impress NFL management, and to head off competition from other networks for the valuable NFL franchise, Lou planned his dazzling Football Book. (Story on this page.)

14. Another newspaper tune-in ad promoting CBS/NFL broadcasts. Dorfsman got extra mileage out of the photos in this ad by cloning them for an on-air promotion (146) and the Football Book (250).

How to watch football

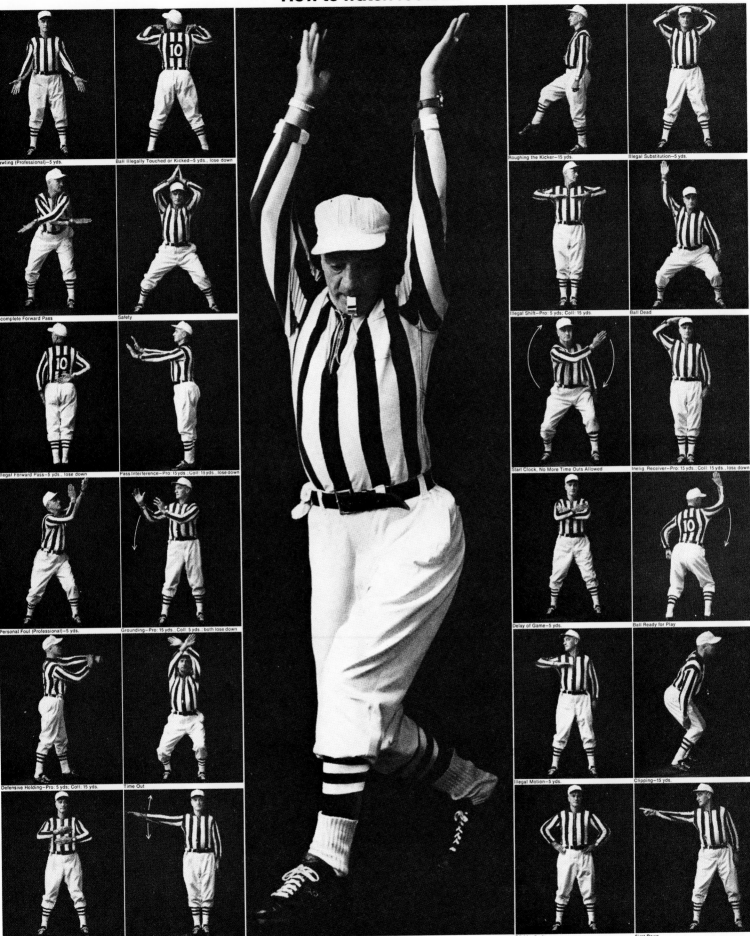

Crawling (Professional)—5 yds.

Ball Illegally Touched or Kicked—5 yds., lose down

Incomplete Forward Pass

Safety

Illegal Forward Pass—5 yds., lose down

Pass Interference—Pro: 15 yds.; Coll: 15 yds., lose down

Personal Foul (Professional)—5 yds.

Grounding—Pro: 15 yds.; Coll: 5 yds.; both lose down

Defensive Holding—Pro: 5 yds.; Coll: 15 yds.

Time Out

Illegal Procedure or Position—5 yds.

Personal Foul (College)—15 yds.

Touchdown or Field Goal

Roughing the Kicker—15 yds.

Illegal Substitution—5 yds.

Illegal Shift—Pro: 5 yds.; Coll: 15 yds.

Ball Dead

Start Clock, No More Time Outs Allowed

Inelig. Receiver—Pro: 15 yds.; Coll: 15 yds., lose down

Delay of Game—5 yds.

Ball Ready for Play

Illegal Motion—5 yds.

Clipping—15 yds.

Offside—5 yds.

First Down

Dyed-in-the-wool football fans always keep one eye on the ball and one eye on the referee. For the next 14 consecutive weekends they will keep both eyes on the CBS Television Network, where they will see exclusive coverage of the world's best football played by America's leading college and professional teams. Tomorrow they will see Florida vs. Georgia Tech in the season's first NCAA Game of the Week. Sunday, in one of five regional games, the Giants begin NFL play against the Colts. Altogether, this season we will present 24 NCAA and 94 NFL games in various regions throughout the nation. Clearly, the way to watch football is to

watch the CBS Television Network ⊙2

would be an all around educational and recreational contribution in addition to a major business promotion.

Aubrey presented the plan to Pete Rozelle, who loved the idea. He cleared the way for Dorfsman to send photographers into team locker rooms. From a friend at *Sports Illustrated,* Lou got the names of newspaper sports photographers in each city where a game was scheduled. He engaged them and sent each one a four-page letter with detailed instructions of the shots he wanted — locker rooms, scoreboards, long shots, close-ups, the offense, the defensive action, the line, the quarterbacks, the referees, the hot dog vendors, the stands. They were instructed to send him just the negatives, along with the local Monday newspaper account of the game so he could identify the action and the players. From the negatives, Lou ordered and edited the prints. The CBS house staff wrote the text. Picture captions were composed by an ex-football player, which provided color and authenticity. The book was a huge success. It was perceived as a gift, rather than a promotion. Every recipient was delighted, and the CBS/NFL contract was renewed.

While Dorfsman makes no claim that the Football Book saved the franchise, (the new contract did have a higher price tag,) he is quick to point out that efforts of that nature definitely enhance the reputation of a company, which is a highly desirable goal. He also emphasizes that such a promotion would probably never have been initiated by persons outside the company, as they would not have been privy to CBS/NFL contract negotiations. It fortifies his conviction that advertising people must be in on a company's business to do an effective job.

Dorfsman has countless success stories to demonstrate the scope of his involvement in CBS promotions. His all-time favorite is his campaign to save "The Waltons." As Lou tells it:

"We have·this TV show, "The Waltons." According to Nielsen, nobody's watching. It's opposite "Flip Wilson" on NBC, and we're getting clobbered. They tell me we're losing $25,000 a week on the show. It's the early '70s… the country is crazy. Kids are tearing up the campuses. It's a kid society. Agencies are hiring 13-year-old creative directors. There's a whole upside-down craziness… with pot… and violence… and along comes this very sweet, very civilized, very decent program. It's set in Depression time, and it's full of old-fashioned values — family, work, love, caring. Kids say, 'Yes sir, Dad'…. 'May I help you, Mother?' ….'Please'…. 'Thank you'….All that nice warm stuff.

"But the show is dying… dying in the ratings, and we're about to blow it off the air. This bothers me, because it seems to me it's a nice wholesome program, and the network mix should include one of these. It's good for the people; it's good for the country; it's good for peace and quiet, and it has good historical context. And frankly, I'm personally square enough to like it! I had a gut feeling that the show hasn't had a chance to catch on, even though it got terrific raves from the critics. I want to save this show.

"One evening, I'm watching the show with my youngest kid, Neil. He's about 15 or 16 at the time…hair down to his butt…dressed in the proper attire of the day — torn blue jeans…dirty sneakers — a real standout student, though. I see he's watching the show intently, and I think I also see some tears welling up in his eyes. During the commercial break, I turn to him and ask casually, 'You like this stuff, Neil?'

"'Yeah,' he mumbles.

"'So how come you never want to listen to *my* Depression stories?' I complain.

"'Well,' he goes on, ignoring my grievance, 'all the kids in school watch it. Tomorrow, they'll be talking about it.'

"Well, I had just done my in-depth research with my kid. In those days, kids seemed to be at the cutting edge of programming, and he confirmed what I had felt all along. The show needed a chance to succeed. The next day I called Bob Wood, who was then president of the TV network, and laid out a plan I'd thought out to build an audience for the show."

First, Lou asked for close to $70,000 for a spread in *TV Guide.* He also wanted a big on-air campaign featuring all the wonderful critical comments about the show. In effect, he wanted to tell the TV audience, "This is a beau-

15. The ad that saved "The Waltons" series from extinction. Deceptively simple, it was designed with the precision of an engineer. (Story on this page.)

This program is so beautiful, it has to die.

That was, as you will see, the strange verdict pronounced by many television critics about a new series, "The Waltons."

The audience reaction has been unusual, too. Little children get all smiley and weepy about it, the way they do for things like My Friend Flicka, Little Women, and the Cookie Monster stubbing his toe.

But from there on up in age and sophistication, overt emotions disappear. To be replaced by little smiles of recognition. An occasional gulp. Red eyes.

And in grown men, funny little sounds and fumblings in the dark, designed to hide the fact that a man is doing something as "unmanly" as being moved by a tender, sentimental story.

We at CBS would like to tell you what "The Waltons" is all about, but it won't be easy. Because everything we tell you can turn you off, if you relate it to similar programs with similar themes.

"The Waltons" is different. Not because it isn't "with it" and it isn't cutesy. Which it isn't. Not because it isn't exciting. Which it is. But because it's an honest attempt to portray a particular kind of American family during a particular time in history.

The Waltons are a large family. Seven children, the eldest eighteen, the youngest six. A mother and father. A grandmother and grandfather. Even a dog. Not a heroic Lassie dog. Not a funny, mangy dog. A dog dog.

And it's about the 1930's. Depression days. In the Blue Ridge Mountains of Virginia. The family is poor. One of the kids plays the harmonica. And it's all about how they all face life.

And that's what makes the Waltons special. *The kind of life they face.*

It has the feel of truth. The look, the texture. You can believe that there were people like this who led lives like this during times like these.

You can believe that maybe this was really how it was to grow up in tough country during tough times. How it really was to be part of a big, loving family.

It's about people who love each other, and love others. About people who care for their aged as well as their young.

And it's funny, too, because it's about a sprawling family of bright, vital individualists.

But it isn't puppy-cute. It isn't pat. And each program doesn't tightly package a moral, like a fortune cookie.

Though there is a moral, overall. Life can be tough. It can also be beautiful. Not easy. Beautiful.

"The Waltons" is on Thursdays. Opposite that funny man, Flip Wilson. And the exciting action show, "The Mod Squad."

It will remain alive until the end of this season, because some people here at CBS believe that there are enough of us around — even in this super-sophisticated day and age—who can still respond to some old-fashioned notions like respect, and dignity, and love. Who aren't embarrassed by an honest lump in the throat.

If there are enough of us, "The Waltons" may even fool the critics and live next year.

Watch "The Waltons" tonight, for a change. It may bring out the best in you.

It did in us.

Save "The Waltons"

See them tonight at 8:00 on Channel 2.

tiful show; if you don't watch it, you'll be missing out on a good thing, because unless there's better viewer response the show will be cancelled."

He didn't get the appropriation for *TV Guide,* but settled instead for a page in *The New York Times, The Washington Post* and *The Los Angeles Times.* He carefully picked these papers to impress upon business people, affiliates, government and the Hollywood community that CBS cared about values as well as about business. He also arranged to trade air time for space in *Time* magazine and *Newsweek.* Then he put his ad together.

The ad (15) was a composite of glowing critical comments, with a headline, excerpted from one of the reviews, which read: "This show is so beautiful, it's going to die." Designwise, the ad was no dazzler. Lou didn't want that. He wanted to avoid the esthetic niceties and make the ad look like a cause — a "Save the Children" kind of appeal. The copy, written by Peter Nord, was clean and straightforward. The photo of the cast looked like a snapshot out of an old family album. The ad was signed, "Save the Waltons." Lou had to do battle to omit the CBS signature, but he prevailed.

According to Lou, the ad changed his life. He was never really certain how to measure the effectiveness of advertising. Now he had concrete results. CBS was inundated with letters and petitions bearing thousands of signatures. They came from school children, from local station listeners, and from the readers of *Time* and *Newsweek.* "The Waltons" remained on the air and by the end of the season was the number-one CBS-TV show.

Dorfsman observed, honestly, "Maybe, given time, the public would have caught onto the show anyway. But the point is, to initiate a catalytic ad like that, you had to be an insider. You had to know the projected plans for the program and have the leverage to turn them around. Such responsibility goes way beyond art directing."

Lesson 4: Define the company's character

In the 40-odd years that Dorfsman has been associated with CBS, he has risen from staff artist to Vice President and Creative Director for Advertising and Design for CBS Inc., with a variety of interim titles and responsibilities. As a staff artist and art director, he did his stint at the drawing board. As a creative director, he initiated projects and supervised the planning and production of thousands of ads and promotional pieces. As a designer, he has had his hand in defining CBS's appearance in print and its physical environment. But however lofty his title, he was never above involving himself in those minute details of a job that spell the difference between "pedestrian" and "perfect."

Much as Lou reveled in advertising problems, he was in his element when he became immersed in the graphics for the new CBS building. It was no secret that not everybody in the CBS hierarchy was thrilled with the new home. In the '60s, when New York City was in danger of becoming one solid wall of aluminum and glass, the black granite monolith was a shocker; "Black Rock," people called it. Once, in those early days, a cab driver deposited Lou at the door of the building with the parting sneer, "Here you are... Buchenwald!"

But just as Frank Stanton had stuck by his choice of the elegant Eero Saarinen design, he was equally determined about the character of the interior and exterior graphics. Dissatisfied with the plans submitted by the architectural firm, he decided to handle the job in-house. He turned the project over to Dorfsman who once more pronounced Frank Stanton, "the dream client." It was a fastidious operation all the way. For Lou, there was not only the joy of the unity he was able to achieve, but also the economies he affected through his knowledge and ingenuity.

When the building was just a hole in the ground, instead of the usual plywood fence with peepholes for "sidewalk engineers," Lou elected to wrap

16. The CBS building at 51 West 52nd Street in New York City is unique architecturally and historically. It was Eero Saarinen's first skyscraper design, and also his last project before he died. In keeping with CBS design consciousness, Frank Stanton (president at the time) nurtured every detail with vigilance. After searching the quarries of the world, the desired granite was finally found and imported from Canada. For the finish, special equipment was fabricated to achieve the matte black color and enhance the natural rough texture of the stone. The building, once mockingly, but now endearingly dubbed, "Black Rock," has won awards from the American Institute of Architects, the New York Chapter of the AIA, the New York Board of Trade and the Municipal Art Society of New York.

NEW HOME OF CBS

a clear plexiglass wall around the excavation. Loudspeakers placed at intervals informed pedestrians about the future home of the company and provided periodic CBS news reports. As the building rose on its foundation, the plexiglass wall had to be replaced with a protective walkway. Veteran display designer that he was, Dorfsman's adrenalin flowed at the prospect of usable exhibition space. He came up with a plan that turned the normally depressing passageway into a pleasant, entertaining thoroughfare, and a smashing promotional opportunity for CBS, as well.

From his experiences at the 1939 World's Fair and other exhibitions, Lou became a great believer in audience participation. He had 30 illuminated panels fabricated, each equipped with a small alcove for a telephone. The panels provided space for visual material; the telephone receivers, when lifted, delivered a relevant recorded message. The panels were installed along the walkway, and they became the vehicle for three different exhibits (21-23).

The first installation recalled broadcasts of notable news events from 1927 to 1963, the years of CBS's life span at that time. The second exhibit, scheduled to coincide with that summer's presidential nominating conventions, celebrated past presidents and reminded listeners to tune in CBS convention coverage. Finally, in autumn, the third exhibit was devoted to promoting CBS's fall programs. Lou ordered blow-ups of the Hirschfeld caricatures he had commissioned for his newspaper ads. These were installed in the illuminated panels, and the telephone recordings carried messages from the featured stars reminding the listener to tune in.

Eventually, this walkway exhibit was dismantled and stored away. But out of sight was not out of mind for Lou. The thought of perfectly good, expensive display material lying fallow prickled his conscience. It didn't take long for him to hit on the idea of resurrecting the whole display for the New York Yankee baseball team, a CBS Inc. property at that time. He pulled all the panels and telephone receivers out of the warehouse and, with minor adjustments, turned the old exhibit into a brand new Yankees Hall of Fame (24), which was installed at the stadium. The panels contained photo blow-ups of Yankee heroes; their bios and statistical data were recorded on the telephone tapes. This kind of shrewd manipulation of design resources gives Dorfsman enormous pleasure.

While Lou is always invigorated when he saves a buck, he and Frank Stanton gave no quarter when it came to the tone and quality of design projects for the new building. The words "good enough" never crossed their lips. For the CBS logo outside the building, and for almost all the interior signage, Lou re-styled and hand-lettered the gracious old 17th-century typeface, Didot. As an auxiliary to the elegant CBS Didot, he chose a restrained sans serif face, now referred to as CBS Sans. Everything related to the building, from the eight-and-one-half inch bronze letters over the entrances to the cafeteria paper goods, was unified in the two CBS faces. Some 80-odd Swiss electric clocks were taken apart and fitted with new numerals and hands in CBS Didot. Cafeteria dispensing machines were masked off and repainted with CBS Didot lettering. Floor numerals, door numbers, directories, exit signs — everything read in CBS Didot and CBS Sans (25).

It was over the exit signs that Lou fought an exhilarating battle, though he almost met his Waterloo. A fire inspector, whose duty it was to make sure that exit signs met with fire department specifications, took one look at the fancy Didot lettering and said, "Nothing doing!" Fire regulations are very clear: the word EXIT must be eight inches high, straight up and down, no thicks and thins, and no serifs! But Lou was indomitable. He returned to his office, whipped out a hairline felt-tipped pen and carefully lettered EXIT, eight inches high. Back to the fire department he raced with his two signs. "Here," he said, flashing his alternate version, "just what your specs say: straight up and down letters, even thickness, no serifs! Now, if you were in a burning building, which sign would you rather have — this one with the skinny letters that follow your specs, or my nice clear one?" Lou won the argument, but the fire department specs have since been carefully reworded, and a caper like that will probably never happen again.

Two other design projects prompted by the move to the new building were especially satisfying to Dorfsman. One was the stationery. The other was the cafeteria wall.

Like anyone moving to new quarters, Frank Stanton decided it was time

17. Window washer cleaning the plexiglass fence installed around the CBS construction site. Instead of peering through knotholes sidewalk superintendents had an unobstructed view of the action.

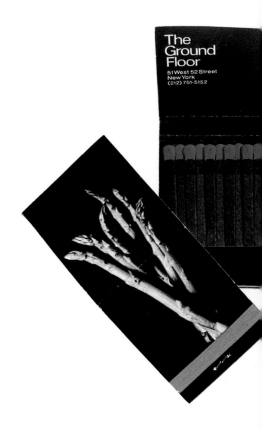

18. Figures on the roof of the protective walkway were dwarfed by the scale of the CBS logo. The mammoth clean and classic letterforms proclaimed the august character of the new neighbor on the block.

19. CBS design consciousness filtered down to the matchbooks designed for *The Ground Floor* restaurant. Dorfsman commissioned Irving Penn to shoot the still life photos. As a final touch, he color coded the match tips to the vegetables on the cover.

to clean the attic. He wanted all the old printed materials and supplies reviewed, excesses trimmed away, so they could start in the new building with a clean, unified look. One area that desperately needed rethinking was the stationery. To study the problem, Lou ordered a sample of every memo pad, letterhead, envelope, mailing tube, and label sent to his office. He was not prepared for the inundation. "I was up to my navel in cartons," he described. Not only did each division have its own version of CBS stationery, every executive and executive assistant had his own personal letterhead, memo pads and envelopes. There was variety in sizes of letterpaper, in weights, in rag content, engraving…and so on. Considering the frequency with which people moved around within the organization, keeping up with so much personalized stationery was a staggering expense, to say nothing of the storage problem.

Dorfsman, with Stanton's approval, made some quick and drastic decisions. To cut down on the number of letterheads he concluded that nobody below the rank of vice president should have personalized stationery. (Since Lou was not yet a vice president, he felt he could recommend this measure with impunity.) Instead of the variety of weights and sizes, he standardized down to two sizes in a lightweight 20-lb paper with a 25% rag content. Both he and Stanton preferred lightweight paper on esthetic grounds. They estimated that the savings on paper alone, multiplied by the million-and-a-half letters mailed annually, would save the company hundreds of thousands of dollars a year. With no small satisfaction, Lou figured how many times over he had earned his salary with that one move. By standardizing the weight and rag content of all his paper, he was able to gang-buy his supplies and worked out a deal to have the paper watermarked with the CBS insignia instead of the paper company's. A very classy touch.

The paper question settled, he then proceeded to redesign the letterheads for each division of CBS in a cohesive format. Large mailing envelopes were also standardized to a customized uniform gray with black Didot lettering. For wrapping materials, he specified custom kraft paper of the same gray with black string. The results were economical and elegant. Dorfsman's Law in matters of esthetics is to spend where it shows; save where it doesn't matter. To carry the CBS design consciousness to its ultimate conclusion, every box of stationery comes packed with a typewritten sample letter which designates the exact format to be followed for every communication that leaves the building. It is specific, even to the dot where the salutation should begin (26-32).

During the years that CBS was settling into the new building at 51 West 52nd Street in New York City, Dorfsman was not only involved in the details of graphic design, he was also curator of most of the art that was installed in corridors and offices. He purchased paintings and prints and supervised their distribution and installation. He confesses that he and Stanton were in such a fever over the esthetics of the building, they'd hold clandestine meetings on Saturdays, stalk the corridors and offices to see if the screws in the door hinges were all lined up, and that nobody had polluted their offices with snapshots of their grandmothers. "Unless," Lou conceded, "it was an Avedon portrait." If that kind of vigilance seemed extraneous, it was the price they were willing to pay to maintain CBS's legendary style.

Of all the design projects that Lou contributed to the new building, the one that stands as his magnum opus is the cafeteria wall (39). When Frank Stanton and interior designer Florence Knoll Bassett contemplated the empty, still incomplete cafeteria, they were stymied about what to do with a 40-ft. blank wall. All the predictable ideas were mentioned — a photo mural of the city, maps, etc. At this point Lou joined the meeting and reminded Stanton of something Lou had given him as a birthday gift — an old job case, filled with wooden letterforms and copper engravings. Lou suddenly envisioned the wall as an expanded job case, but instead of filling it with unrelated, isolated characters, it would be a collage of words related to food. He visualized the words as three-dimensional cutouts in a variety of faces, sizes, weights and depths, interspersed with culinary paraphernalia — pots, pans,

21.

22.

20.

Building an image
In the early 1960s, while the new CBS building was under construction, it was necessary to
erect a protective walkway for pedestrians. Instead of the usual dark, depressing jungle of stanchions,
plywood and planking, Dorfsman created a passageway that was an entertaining and functional exhibition space.

Thirty illuminated, illustrated panels, equipped with recorded messages, formed the basis for three successive CBS promotions.
The first was devoted to historic news broadcasts. The second promoted the summer's presidential nominating
conventions. The third previewed the new CBS fall schedule. (Story on page 34.)

23.

24.

24. When the walkway was dismantled, Lou conceived of setting up the exhibit in Yankee Stadium as a Yankees Hall of Fame for the then CBS-owned baseball team.

"I get a special kick out of cloning my own projects and extending their usefulness," Dorfsman volunteers. "I believe that understanding budgets and affecting economies is an enviable talent for a designer to possess."

25.

A face for the image

Dorfsman co-opted the elegant 17th-century typeface, Didot, and made it
CBS's own. He made some necessary adjustments in the letterforms for the sake of
modern reproduction techniques and rechristened the face, CBS Didot. This typeface is
the unifying graphic element of the building. The bronze letters over the entrance doors,
floor numbers, room numbers, executives names, mail chutes, fire alarm boxes,
clock faces and even the exit signs (over the protest, but final consent
of the NYC Fire Department) are all in CBS Didot.
(Story on page 34.)

CBS
Columbia Broadcasting System, Inc.
51 West 52 Street
New York, New York 10019
(212) 765-4321

CBS TELEVISION NETWORK
A Division of Columbia Broadcasting System, Inc.
51 West 52 Street
New York, New York 10019
(212) 765-4321

CBS NEWS
A Division of Columbia Broadcasting System, Inc.
524 West 57 Street
New York, New York 10019
(212) 765-4321

CBS RADIO
A Division of CBS Inc.
51 West 52 Street
New York, New York 10019
(212) 975-4321

CBS RECORDS
A Division of CBS Inc.
51 West 52 Street
New York, New York 10019

CBS ENTERTAINMENT
A Division of CBS Inc.
51 West 52 Street
New York, New York 10019

CBS
CBS Inc. 51 West 52 Street
New York, New York 10019
(212) 765-4321

CBS
CBS Inc. 51 West 52 Street
New York, New York 10019

CBS ENTERTAINMENT
A Division of CBS Inc.
51 West 52 Street
New York, New York 10019
(212) 975-4321

27.

CBS
Columbia Broadcasting System, Inc
51 West 52 Street
New York, New York 10019
(212) 765-4321

FLUSH

(DOT)

MAXIMUM WIDTH 5 3/4"

Dear Miss Secretary:

This is the format to be used with your new CBS stationery. Please prepare your letters in the following manner so that uniformity of style can be maintained throughout the company.

The salutation should be 3" from the top of the sheet (a printed dot indicates the proper position). The left-hand margin of the letter should align with the printed address at the top. Leave one space after the salutation, between each paragraph, and immediately preceding the closing.

Paragraphs are not to be indented. No line should be longer than 5 3/4"; an average length of 5 1/2" is most desirable. Whenever possible, words should not be broken at the end of a line. If the stationery is not personalized, leave three lines for the signature, then type the sender's name and title. Leave two lines, then type the addressee's name and address, followed by the date one space below. If the stationery is personalized, the same seven-line space between your closing and the addressee's name is to be maintained.

Your letter should not look crowded on the page. If it is longer than this one, continue the letter on a second sheet.

Your closing.

Signature

Sender's Name
Title

Addressee
Company
Company Address
City, State and Zip Code

Date

ONE LINE SPACE

ALWAYS 7 LINE SPACE   UNLESS STATIONERY IS PERSONALIZED

ONE LINE SPACE

MAXIMUM DEPTH

28.

26.

Stationery

The move to new corporate headquarters, with a new address,
prompted a revision of the company's stationery and mailing supplies. In the matter of
letterheads, Dorfsman discovered that democracy had gotten out of hand. From top executives
to minor assistants, everyone was operating with individualized letterheads
and paper of varying sizes, weights and rag content. He redesigned
stationery for all CBS divisions in a cohesive format.

40

29.

30.

31.

CBS TELEPHONE DIRECTORY / SEPTEMBER 1965

32.

Personal imprints were restricted to vice-presidents and up. Paper
was ordered in uniform size, weight and rag content. For the ultimate in
fastidious design, every box of CBS stationery is packed with a sample letter which demonstrates
the exact format to be used in CBS correspondence and includes a dot to indicate where
the salutation should begin (28). Envelopes and wrapping materials were
standardized to gray kraft paper and black string. (Story on page 35.)

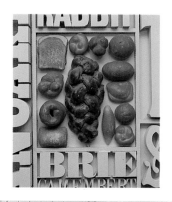

33.-39.

40.

<u>The cafeteria</u>
A blank wall, 40 ft. long and 8½ ft. high, begged to be filled and integrated into the space.
Dorfsman resisted the obvious — photo murals, maps, etc. — and opted to treat the wall like an
enlarged printer's job case, with a lockup of words and objects related to food.

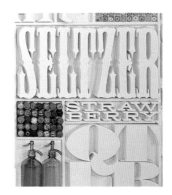

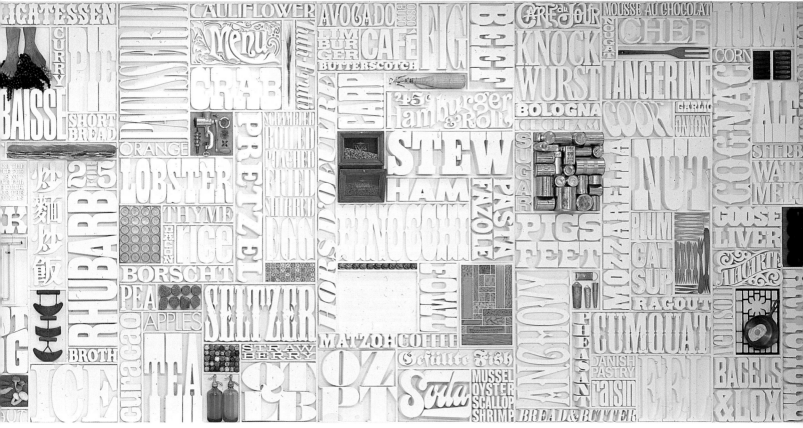

41. Even the paper goods in the cafeteria did not escape Dorfsman's commitment to unity. Plates, cups, sugar, salt and pepper packets — all are imprinted with "51/20 CLUB" (abbreviation for 51st Street, 20th floor) in CBS Didot. Words on food dispensing machines were also re-lettered in the Didot face.

41.

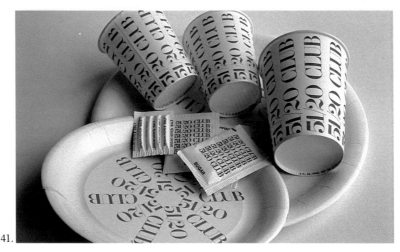

(For story see page 44.)
The wall was created in nine separate panels. Most words were
jigsawed out of wood, interstices filled with sculpted food items and culinary props, and
the entire assemblage was spray-painted in white enamel.

strainers, beaters, etc. and assemblages of sculpted foods. The wall was to stretch from floor to ceiling, span the entire length of the cafeteria and be spray-painted in white lacquer for a unified and stunning effect. Stanton was enthusiastic about the idea and gave Lou the nod to proceed with his plan.

Lou's experience in the display business made this potentially overwhelming project feasible. His first move was to design and produce a sample panel, four by eight-and-one-half feet. He recognized that the wall would have to be created in sections. Using his sample panel as a guide, he enlisted Herb Lubalin to work out the details of the remaining eight sections. Herb, by this time, had distinguished himself as a connoisseur of typography, and the job couldn't have fallen into more loving hands. Lou and Herb collaborated on the project, using typography and hand lettering. Lou designated the depths of words to create interesting shadow effects. With particular ingenuity, he also devised a simple means of hanging the panels so they are removable and appear to be seamless on the wall. The wall, complete with found and fabricated objects, as well as antiques filched from his wife's kitchen, is a monumental achievement. Lou prides himself not only on the idea and the design, but on the engineering and construction details, as well. It gives him particular pleasure, too, to recall that this mega-project — the "gastrotypographicalassemblage," as he calls it, was produced for a mere $14,000. It was recently estimated at a value 20 times his original expenditure — a credit to his experience and ingenuity in display design.

42. Dorfsman involved himself in all aspects of CBS business. To revive Walter Cronkite's slipping ratings, Lou conceived the idea of a guest appearance on the popular "Mary Tyler Moore Show." All parties were delighted with the results.

The total designer

Obviously, there's hardly an aspect of the visual communications business that has escaped Lou Dorfsman's attention. There is no one word to describe his labors on behalf of CBS. He shuns the word "designer" because it has the connotation of "cosmetician," a person who pretties things up. But he accepts the title "designer" if it implies the fullest sense of the word — master planner. That is the area in which he feels his talent lies. He has been an initiator of projects and an innovator. He was ahead of the field in creating environments for newscasters. He pushed to make weather reports a scientific learning experience. He was the first to use film for on-air promotions and TV spots for radio promotions. As far back as 1952, he was using *The New York Times* as a trade paper to influence clients, ad agencies and government policies. His long arm even reached into programming when he revived Walter Cronkite's slipping rating by engineering (with the help of publicist Sid Garfield) a guest appearance on "The Mary Tyler Moore Show."

To be sure, Dorfsman did not bat a thousand in getting his ideas approved. Among his favorite unfulfilled schemes for the TV network was his plan for an "on air" sweepstakes to induce audiences to tune in and sample CBS's new fall line-up. Another, was his proposal for a national election, in which audiences would cast votes for the pilot shows they wanted kept on the air. But topping the list of favorite rejects, was his institutional campaign idea for CBS, Inc.

In 1960, when the new building was still at the excavation stage, it occurred to Lou that most people had no idea of the diversity of CBS's activities. It was known mostly as a broadcasting company. "What a marvelous opportunity," he thought, "to let the public (and the stockholders) know what CBS is all about — the entertainment function, the record division, the publications, the electronics — all related to American culture."

Lou visualized a series of ads with the construction site as a stage set. The gist of the campaign would be: on this site a building was being constructed, dedicated to information, education and entertainment. As the building progressed from floor to floor, each ad would demonstrate a specific

43. Roughs for his pet building-under-construction campaign, rejected but not forgotten. (Story on this page.) Dorfsman does only the roughest, most rudimentary sketches of his ideas. He generally communicates his concepts with comped photo images and actual dummy type blocks. Most often he presents his ideas verbally, accompanied by inimitable facial and hand gestures that only his longtime associates have become expert at interpreting.

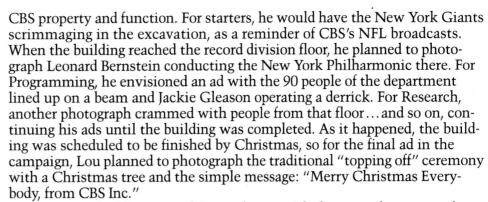

CBS property and function. For starters, he would have the New York Giants scrimmaging in the excavation, as a reminder of CBS's NFL broadcasts. When the building reached the record division floor, he planned to photograph Leonard Bernstein conducting the New York Philharmonic there. For Programming, he envisioned an ad with the 90 people of the department lined up on a beam and Jackie Gleason operating a derrick. For Research, another photograph crammed with people from that floor...and so on, continuing his ads until the building was completed. As it happened, the building was scheduled to be finished by Christmas, so for the final ad in the campaign, Lou planned to photograph the traditional "topping off" ceremony with a Christmas tree and the simple message: "Merry Christmas Everybody, from CBS Inc."

Sweet as the idea was to him, and even with the staunch support of Frank Stanton, Lou could not get the campaign budget approved. It remains a memory, albeit a fond one. Which proves there's no Utopia for designers, not even at CBS.

Dorfsman sums it all up

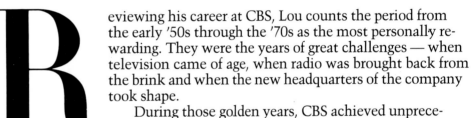

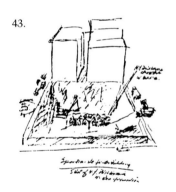

43.

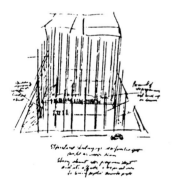

Reviewing his career at CBS, Lou counts the period from the early '50s through the '70s as the most personally rewarding. They were the years of great challenges — when television came of age, when radio was brought back from the brink and when the new headquarters of the company took shape.

During those golden years, CBS achieved unprecedented heights in its advertising and design work. There were two reasons, according to Lou. The first was Frank Stanton, Lou's modern day Medici, who provided an incomparable, benevolent and supportive atmosphere for creative work. "Stanton was the fantasy client. You never had to sell him on a good idea; he could see the possibilities before you finished your sentence. And he made wonderful, intelligent design judgements of his own," Lou emphasizes.

The second reason for CBS's luminous reputation in advertising and design was that "everything was handled in-house. In the CBS Broadcast Group, we operated our own self-contained advertising agency and design studio. We produced our own ads, specified the media, and were responsible for all our own packaging, displays, interior design and architectural constructions. Measured by our billings, in 1977 for instance, the Broadcast Group's Advertising and Design Department would have ranked as the 11th largest agency in the United States."

Lou presses the point that as an insider he was able to keep tight control over the quality and unity of design in everything that bore the CBS insignia. More important, he was in a better position to function as a problem-solver than someone outside the organization. He was intimately acquainted with all aspects of the Broadcast Group's business. He had access to developments concerning the company that enabled him to respond quickly and appropriately with ads, promotions and special projects. Dorfsman doubts that anyone outside the company could have the perspective, or would invest the time, to dream up speculative projects not solicited by CBS.

Of course, not every "insider" in an organization has the appetite and acumen to perform like Dorfsman. Paradoxically, even when he's an "outsider" working on a freelance project, Lou operates like an insider. He digs into research, marketing problems, media decisions — all the hard gritty facts about a client's business — and manages to find an elegant solution for every problem he embraces. This volume of work is testimony to the fact that Dorfsman is one of those rare stars that streaks across our horizon only once in a lifetime.

Companies with tangible merchandise to sell can, for the most part, determine who their customers are, and when and where to advertise their products. Network advertising is far more complex. First, there are a multitude of diverse programs to market: there is entertainment in the form of dramas, sit-coms, musicals, variety shows, sports, comedy, children's programs, and movies; there are special educational programs and cultural offerings; and there are documentaries, news specials as well as the day-in, day-out, scheduled news broadcasts.

Not only must the network produce the right mix of programs to please its listeners, it must take into account its pluralistic audience: the clients and prospective clients who sponsor shows, their advertising agencies, and the network stations and affiliates that carry the shows. Beyond all those interested parties is a long list of vigilant "watchers" to whom the network must also be responsive: racial, religious and ethnic minorities, women's groups, political parties, opinion leaders in government and the academic community, environmentalists, and certainly the stockholders.

Like every program broadcast by the network, everything that appears in print or on the air in the way of advertising is subject to scrutiny by many interested parties. Every form of network communication must reach out to the intended audience without offending others. In addition, at CBS there was a concerted effort to make their visual presentations convey a sense of the pre-eminence of the company.

Dorfsman's total immersion in the advertising function was unique for an art director. He involved himself in the planning of ads, in media decisions, in marketing problems, as well as in the technical and design problems. All too often, art directors limit themselves to the purely visual aspects of a project. "But if you are in the visual <u>communications</u> business," Dorfsman advises graphic design students, "you have to ask yourself 'Why am I doing this design?' You're doing it to sell a product, a service or an idea! You can go home and paint or sculpt for yourself," he says, "but if you are in advertising, you must constantly keep in mind your clients' needs, the public's need and," he often adds, "my little old aunt in Brooklyn."

44. (Overleaf) Photograph of vintage CBS microphones, commissioned for the 1976 Annual Report, in celebration of the company's 50th Anniversary (319).

45. The telegraphic headline, billboard-like photo and brief copy communicate a sense of excitement and urgency. Even the unintrusive, tiny logo helps magnify the importance of the entertainment.

Variety

NEXT TUESDAY FOR AN HOUR
(NEXT SEASON-EVERY WEEK!)

Tuesday, March 19, 8:30-9:30 pm EST—JUDY GARLAND AND HER GUESTS, PHIL SILVERS AND ROBERT GOULET—on the CBS Television Network

CBS ⦿ PREVIEW

Innovative use of media
In 1962, when almost all television advertising was concentrated in
daily newspapers, Dorfsman proposed that CBS announce its new fall schedule in a
magazine supplement and distribute it through the major Sunday newspapers in markets where
CBS either owned stations or had affiliates. Such inserts had been used frequently
to advertise fashion and home furnishings merchandise,
but for TV programs, it was a bold new idea.

46. The elegant gravure supplement proved successful on a number of counts: it was economical to produce and distribute; reprints were made available to CBS stations for their own local promotions (the back page was left blank for their imprint); photo and copy elements were reusable for spin-off ads and promotions. Most important, the concentrated announcement had enormous impact and positioned CBS as the prime network for entertainment.

47. Inside spreads; one for each day of the week.

MONDAY

7:15 PM – CBS NEWS WITH WALTER CRONKITE Monday through Friday every week of the year, start your night with this concise, expert, up-to-the-minute roundup of the day's news.

7:30 PM – TO TELL THE TRUTH It keeps right on running all year long. The three distinguished, bearded men all claim to be a certain famous explorer, and obviously two of them are lying. But which two? It sounds easy, and yet five years have passed since the challenge was first raised, and the program's popularity never flags. Bud Collyer is host.

8:00 PM – I'VE GOT A SECRET *(new time, new series starts September 17)* Garry Moore, Betsy Palmer, Henry Morgan, Bill Cullen and Bess Myerson are the magic personalities who grace this light-hearted panel program. Dark, Freudian secrets are taboo, and what the guests are hiding, only Garry knows.

8:30 PM – THE LUCY SHOW *(Premiere October 1)* The name of this brand new series is probably its own best advertisement. Lucille Ball returns – Vivian Vance is second banana. Since Miss Ball is television's most precious gift to the select company of great clowns, this the best news since I LOVE LUCY.

9:00 PM – THE DANNY THOMAS SHOW *(new series starts October 1)* The great art of playing – and being – a good guy may be the secret of Danny Thomas' perennial appeal. Certainly the program that bears his name has deserved its many awards for the human qualities he portrays so well. It starts a new round of stories about the home-loving nightclub entertainer whose resemblance to the real Danny is more than coincidental.

9:30 PM – THE ANDY GRIFFITH SHOW *(new series starts October 1)* Just as Andy Griffith dazzled the sophisticates of Broadway and Hollywood, the famous slow-talking, fast-thinking Southern sheriff he portrays on television out-foxes the craftiest city slickers who pass through Mayberry. And this despite the rubious aid of deputy Don Knotts, whose fumblings and mumblings have won him an Emmy.

10:00 PM – THE NEW LORETTA YOUNG SHOW *(Premiere September 24)* No stranger to television, the poised and beautiful Loretta Young now makes her debut as a continuing character in her own dramatic series. Miss Young plays a talented magazine writer, the widowed mother of seven children, whose encounter with editor James Philbrook eventually sets the stage for complications both properly professional and deeply personal.

10:30 PM – STUMP THE STARS *(Premiere September 17)* Charades is the game, comedian Pat Harrington, Jr., is the master of ceremonies, and you can easily tell the talented players without a scorecard. If this sounds like your old favorite, PANTOMIME QUIZ, you are right. It is. Only better.

TUESDAY

7:30 PM – MARSHAL DILLON Every week of the year brings you an opportunity, well worth seizing, to relive some of the most stirring half-hour episodes in Dodge City's lawless past. James Arness is Dillon, and this series of rebroadcasts is the cream of the early GUNSMOKE crop.

8:00 PM – KAISER PRESENTS THE LLOYD BRIDGES SHOW *(Premiere September 11)* The once-glamorous profession of journalism may get a new lease on life when the nation meets Lloyd Bridges in the role of reporter Adam Shepherd. In the swashbuckling tradition of such international correspondents as Richard Harding Davis, Shepherd displays a nose for news, an instinct for danger and an unerring eye for feminine beauty at all times.

8:30 PM – THE RED SKELTON HOUR *(Premiere September 25)* The news here is that Red will be "double-exposed" this season, with a full sixty minutes to play in, instead of the previous half-hour format. More scope for one of television's most inventive clowns, whose characterizations have become part of American lore. With guest stars and "Discovery Corner," a showcase for new talent.

9:30 PM – THE JACK BENNY PROGRAM *(new day, new time, new series starts September 25)* Who ever heard of a television season without Jack Benny? Who ever heard of Jack Benny performing on Tuesday nights? This is indeed an extra-special year for television, as the world's funniest violin virtuoso moves to perk up Tuesdays. The country will just have to learn to get through Sundays without him.

10:00 PM – THE GARRY MOORE SHOW *(new series starts September 25)* Television's special kind of variety show at the peak of its form – affable, nostalgic, funny and perfectly presented. It takes a fearless performer to follow Skelton and Benny, but Garry does and it works. With Durward Kirby, and the regular troupe, and guests.

SATURDAY

7:30 PM – THE JACKIE GLEASON SHOW AND HIS AMERICAN SCENE MAGAZINE *(Premiere September 29)* One of the season's most eagerly awaited premieres, to be staged in the same full-hour review format that brought Jackie Gleason his first television triumphs. Needless to say, it will be a lavish, funny, fast-moving showcase for the versatile Gleason and his guests. Among other features, each program will take a satirical look at one aspect of the American scene, from a description of Washington affairs to a report from a Brooklyn bar.

8:30 PM – THE DEFENDERS *(new series starts September 15)* The most honored new television series of last season centers on the activities of a father-and-son team of trial lawyers, played by E. G. Marshall and Robert Reed. Created by Reginald Rose and produced by Herbert Brodkin, THE DEFENDERS consistently attracts television's foremost playwrights. The results are notable for their maturity and honest presentation of problems in the law.

9:30 PM – HAVE GUN – WILL TRAVEL *(new series starts September 15)* Richard Boone plays the role of the most cultivated gunfighter on the Old Frontier. Paladin, connoisseur of women, wine, music, art and hand-to-hand combat, is also a first-class amateur psychologist whose calling card is an invitation to entertaining adventure.

10:00 PM – GUNSMOKE *(new series starts September 15)* With GUNSMOKE still going strong, James Arness as Marshal Matt Dillon, Amanda Blake as Kitty, Dennis Weaver as Chester and the rest of the Dodge City crowd are household familiars. Why Westerns in general are so popular is a matter for philosophers. Why this is the most famous of all television Westerns is easy to understand – they just don't come any better.

CURTAIN GOING UP ON A NEW SEASON....

©1963 CBS, INC.

Same concept, new technique

The 1962 magazine supplement announcing the new season's offerings
proved so successful, Dorfsman repeated the idea in 1963. This time he engaged Hirschfeld,
the artist who for years has been the definitive caricaturist of film and theatre people, especially
for *The New York Times*. The artwork endowed the supplement with a drama page editorial
look, and helped identify CBS with show business and stars. As with the 1962 supplement,
the 1963 edition became the source of spin-off and tie-in ads for daily newspapers.

MONDAY

Advertisement   Advertisement

⊙2
10:00-11:00 PM WCBS-TV
THE DANNY KAYE SHOW
Your world is brighter this season
because Danny takes over for an hour
each week at CBS, The Stars' Address!

1. CBS EVENING NEWS WITH WALTER CRONKITE A new expanded series of half-hour news broadcasts Monday through Friday which, in addition to presenting a concise summary of the important news of the day, will include on-the-spot reports and expert analyses of world events by CBS News domestic and foreign correspondents.
2. TO TELL THE TRUTH—7:30 PM (new series starts September 9) Everybody thinks he can tell who is fibbing and who is not when host Bud Collyer presents three contestants. It is not so easy. Two of the contestants are imposters who pretend to be what the third contestant really is.
3. I'VE GOT A SECRET—8:00 PM (new series starts September 9) Blasting off with Garry Moore, you could hardly ask for a livelier gang of inquisitors than Bill Cullen, Bess Myerson, Henry Morgan and Betsy Palmer. By now they are all expert in extracting confidential information from the most tight-lipped guest.
4. THE LUCY SHOW—8:30 PM (new series starts September 30) When Lucille Ball and Vivian Vance started this new series last Fall, everybody knew what would happen—and it did! The show was an immediate smash and remained one all season long. These two zanies have established a permanent corner on the nation's funny bone.
5. THE DANNY THOMAS SHOW—9:00 PM (new series starts September 30) Technically, Danny is the head of his delightful family supported by Marjorie Lord and Rusty Hamer. But by the time the show ends he's apt to turn out low man on the totem pole.
6. THE ANDY GRIFFITH SHOW—9:30 PM (new series starts September 30) Behind the good-humored, slow-talking face of Sheriff Andy Griffith there's a powerful arsenal of guile. The fellow who speaks loudly and carries a small stick is Deputy Don Knotts.
7. EAST SIDE/WEST SIDE—10:00 PM (premiere September 23) George C. Scott, one of the most compelling personalities in the American theatre, stars as a hard-hitting, but compassionate social worker. A new hour-long series centered on the human conflicts of a great city. Produced by David Susskind.   **THE STARS' ADDRESS IS CBS⊙**

TUESDAY

Advertisement   Advertisement

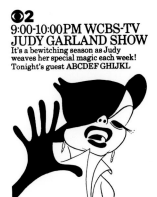

⊙2
9:00-10:00PM WCBS-TV
JUDY GARLAND SHOW
It's a bewitching season as Judy
weaves her special magic each week!
Tonight's guest ABCDEF GHIJKL

1. MARSHAL DILLON—7:30 PM The greatest danger for a frontier peace officer comes not so much from gun fighters as from ordinarily law-abiding citizens who are provoked to violence. But James Arness, as the Marshal, together with Dennis Weaver, Milburn Stone and Amanda Blake are a match for whatever comes along each week in these compelling rebroadcasts of the best of the half-hour GUNSMOKE series.
2. THE RED SKELTON HOUR—8:00 PM (new time, new series starts September 24) When Red expanded his half-hour program last season to a full hour, all that happened was that everybody started laughing twice as much and kept it up all season. This season all that will happen is they'll start laughing a half hour earlier. America's King of Clowns has never been in funnier fettle—which is just about as funny as you can get.
3. PETTICOAT JUNCTION—9:00 PM (premiere September 24) A new and entirely different series created by the same Paul Henning whose BEVERLY HILLBILLIES proved to be last season's smash comedy hit. Bea Benaderet stars as a widowed proprietor of a rural hotel on the spur line of an old railroad. Everything is somewhat chaotic except her three daughters: each is a masterpiece of beauty and the moving force behind the railroad and its passengers. With Edgar Buchanan.
4. THE JACK BENNY PROGRAM—9:30 PM (new series starts September 24) If a new entertainment medium ever supplants television, you can be sure of one thing: its leading comedian will be a 39-year-old man who will walk across the stage, remove his glasses and stare fixedly at the audience. His name will be Jack Benny and he will be instantly recognized as the most durable and invariably funny entertainer in history.
5. THE GARRY MOORE SHOW—10:00 PM (new series starts September 24) Garry's amazing versatility cuts across all aspects of show business—as a performer, a discoverer of talent, and a provider of entertainment. One of last season's exciting innovations was the occasional appearance of a brilliant new comedienne named Dorothy Loudon. This season she will be on regularly with Garry, Durward Kirby and the rest of his talented troupe.   **THE STARS' ADDRESS IS CBS⊙**

SATURDAY

Advertisement   Advertisement

⊙2
8:00-9:00PM WCBS-TV
ED SULLIVAN SHOW
Television's top showman presents
ABCDEFG HIJKLMNOP QRSTUVWX
ABCDEFGH IJKLMNO PQRSTUV

1. THE JACKIE GLEASON SHOW—7:30 PM (new series starts September 28) One of the marks of a great entertainer is his ability to attract, nourish and surround himself with similar talent. And the great Gleason is no exception. Last season marked his own triumphant return to television, with the June Taylor dancers, Frank Fontaine and guest stars all of whom worked together to capture and hold the hearts of the television audience. Needless to say, Jackie and his troupe—as well as some new surprises—are back again in a full-blown musical comedy hour that dazzles the eyes week after week. It's all "awa-a-a-y we go" comedy.
2. THE NEW PHIL SILVERS SHOW—8:30 PM (premiere September 28) One of television's greatest comic inventions was a staff sergeant named Ernie Bilko. The man whose inspired clowning endowed this character with flesh and blood now returns to the network in a civilian role which given every promise of surpassing his former creation. Phil Silvers, one of the top bananas of all time, will be seen as a factory foreman whose schemes for self-enrichment are usually self-defeating.
3. THE DEFENDERS—9:00 PM (new time, new series starts September 28) Last Spring it was honored as television's best drama, with best dramatic writing, best dramatic direction, best film editing. And E. G. Marshall received a highly deserved award for the best "acting in a series." He'll be back again ably assisted by his young partner Robert Reed in this distinguished series created by Reginald Rose with Herbert Brodkin as executive producer.
4. GUNSMOKE—10:00 PM (new series starts September 28) Explaining the phenomenal popularity of the Western has become one of the most popular academic indoor sports. No single program has been as widely discussed by television critics and social scientists as GUNSMOKE. And for good reason. It is by far the most challenging and provocative of all Westerns, as well as the most popular. But its reality defies all analysis, for it is compounded of the superb performances of James Arness, the star, and the notable quartet of Dennis Weaver, Milburn Stone, Amanda Blake and Burt Reynolds.   **THE STARS' ADDRESS IS CBS⊙**

49.   50.

48. Cover of 1963 magazine supplement.   49. Inside spreads.   50. Small space newspaper spin-off ads.

51. The old Jules Verne vintage engraving intimated the science fiction nature of the program. The other illustrative elements — the trajectory of the rocket and the arc of the moon in the upper left — directed the reader to the headline and down through the text.

52. Which name would be the bigger attraction: Moses or Burt Lancaster? By subtle use of typography, they received equal billing. "Moses" was set larger than "Burt Lancaster," but subdued by a screen so that both names read with equal importance. The daring juxtaposition of an ancient subject with a contemporary split-screen photo technique energized the page.

53. The poster-style treatment of this ad implied an event of artistic significance. The contrast in size and scale of the juxtaposed photos heightened the drama; an example of deft maneuvers with stock photos.

51.

52.

Announcing the "specials"
Aside from its regularly scheduled programs, CBS offers one-time-only "specials." To accentuate the uniqueness of each of the broadcasts, Dorfsman consciously avoided uniformity in the ads. Each event was treated in a graphic style that reflected the specific content and mood of the program. The ads were not immediately identifiable as CBS ads, but bore the look of editorials. Even the CBS logo surrendered its identity and conformed to the typography of the headline in each ad.

53.

THE NEW YORK TIMES, THURSDAY, JUNE 14, 1962

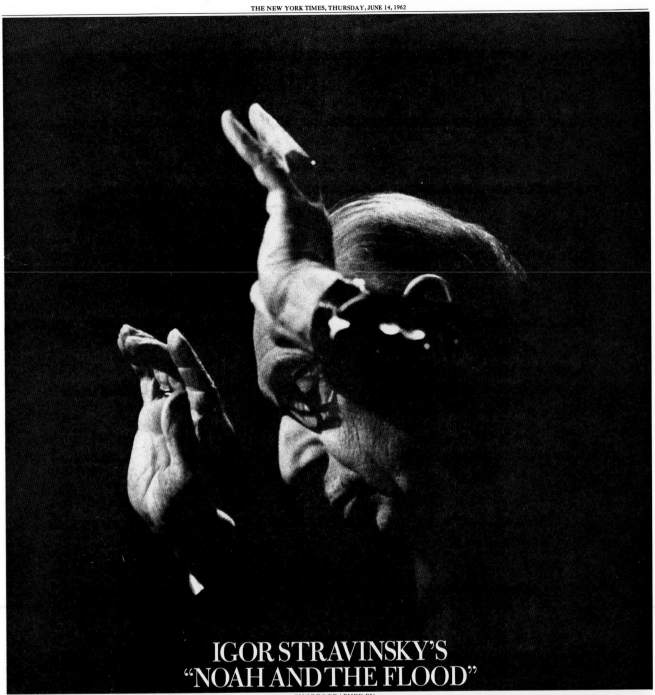

IGOR STRAVINSKY'S
"NOAH AND THE FLOOD"
CHOREOGRAPHED BY
GEORGE BALANCHINE

An original dance drama based on the familiar Biblical theme, with Laurence Harvey, Sebastian Cabot,
Jacques d'Amboise, and Elsa Lanchester; performed by the New York City Ballet, and produced by Sextant Inc.
A Breck Golden Showcase presentation. Commissioned by the CBS Television Network.

WORLD PREMIERE TONIGHT 9:00 TO 10:00 CBS◉2

Ingrid Bergman appears tonight on the CBS Television Network in a hauntingly powerful 90-minute drama of romance and betrayal: "Twenty-Four Hours in a Woman's Life." Also starring Rip Torn. TONIGHT 9:00 TO 10:30 CBS ◉2

54.

CBS LOVES LUCY

54. Ingrid Bergman was not anxious to sit for a special costume portrait for this ad, but Dorfsman felt that no stock photo would characterize the nature of the program. He dipped into his budget and wooed her with a Richard Avedon photo.

etted, illuminated face emerging from the background, and the arms extended toward her audience, epitomized Garland's style in concert. The open hands lead into the copy block which, set in reverse, maintains the unity of the ad.

55. Judy Garland's picture for this ad came out of a CBS library of stock photos. The silhou-

56. This quintessential Lucy mug shot from the CBS photo library was a perfect illustra-

TWO BIG TELEVISION "SPECIALS" TONIGHT ON CBS ◉2

Judy sings! and sings! and sings! in a shimmering hour filled with her favorite songs and her unquenchable talent. And as if Judy alone weren't enough, she also dances, jokes, and cavorts with two great guest stars, FRANK SINATRA & DEAN MARTIN on THE JUDY GARLAND SHOW 9 TO 10:00 CBS ◉2

55.

Presenting the stars
Some performers are guaranteed drawing cards.
But viewers can also be enticed by the
theme or mood of a show. Communicating
such information in an ad is not always
as simple as Dorfsman made it look,
especially when time and budget limitations
often forced him to work with stock
photos. Dorfsman's choices and decisions
about scaling, cropping, silhouetting
and combining photos, made them look
made-to-order for each ad.

he was Lucy Ricardo, and she made America laugh…no, roar… r the first time on October 15, 1951.

Twenty-five years later, Lucille Ball is the world's best-loved dhead. The astonished…and astonishing…eyes, the endless legs, the beautiful, sexy, funny, marvelous goddess of innocent bedlam are world-wide phenomena. Around the clock and around the globe, at almost any hour, someone somewhere is in front of a television set having a ball with Ball. She has, in fact, become an international art form. And like all good art forms, she deserves retrospective.

This Sunday from 8 to 10 pm we present "CBS Salutes Lucy…the First 25 Years." It is a gorgeous tribute to a gorgeous woman. Fifteen of the world's eatest entertainers will join her, including many of the people she as worked with. There'll be laughter, reminiscences, and replays f some of the funniest of her funny moments. And there'll a special introduction by CBS Chairman William S. Paley.

We at CBS are proud to have been home to Lucy for l the years of her television life. Like everyone else, we are guilty f having chuckled, giggled, laughed and roared at the lady for e last quarter of a century. With affection and infinite respect, e want the world to know that we, too, love Lucy.

These two hours are our way of showing it.

56.

tion for the ad announcing the 25th anniversary of the "I Love Lucy" show.

skyline. The combined photos summed up the contents and character of the program.

57. Elizabeth Taylor made her first appearance on TV as a hostess on a tour of her native London. Instead of the usual sultry movie star image, Dorfsman presented her with ambassadorial dignity silhouetted against a photo of the London

58. Despite the Carnegie Hall setting, it was clear from the photo that this was to be no long-haired performance. Julie Andrews, in ten-gallon hat, was not going to behave like Mary Poppins, and Carol Burnett promised to be her zany self.

ELIZABETH TAYLOR IN LONDON / TONIGHT 10-11 CBS ◉ 2
In her first appearance on television, the noted actress brings to the screen a fascinating mosaic of the people and places that make her native city unique among the capitals of the world. In color and black and white with script by S. J. Perelman.

57.

"Julie and Carol at Carnegie Hall" starring Julie Andrews and Carol Burnett Tonight 10 to 11 CBS ◉ 2

58.

RUSSIANS: SELF IMPRESSIONS

On the principle that the life of a nation is reflected in its literature, the Public Affairs Department of CBS News offers a revealing insight into the character of the Russian people tonight at 7:30 EST in a special full hour broadcast based on the works of five famous Russian authors.

As host on the program "Russians: Self-Impressions," Prof. Ernest J. Simmons, noted authority on Russian literature, presents a social and historical commentary on the dramatic presentations. "In this program," he declares, "we seek an insight into the often enigmatic character of the Russian. . . . To gain that insight into the Russian as he is, we must try to understand the Russian as he was . . . to know something of the world he grew out of and revolted against."

This world is sharply revealed in scenes from Gogol's classic story "The Overcoat" and Chekhov's drama "The Cherry Orchard." They disclose the poverty and decadence of much of Russian life in the 19th century; while a pervading sense of injustice and futility is reflected in other vignettes from Dostoevsky's "The Brothers Karamazov" and Turgenev's "Fathers and Sons." In introducing the concluding scene from Pasternak's "Dr. Zhivago," Professor Simmons declares—"As with us all, when the social structure crumbles, the only order in the world is to be found in the love one human being can have for another."

A brilliant cast starring Jo Van Fleet, Kim Hunter, Sam Wanamaker, George Voskovec and Joseph Buloff portray the principal characters in the five dramatic sketches.

In employing the literature of the past to illuminate the present, CBS News offers still another example of its many-faceted effort to explore all possible resources that can give meaning to our times. Other instances of this same effort can be seen in the clarification of social and economic issues on CBS REPORTS; in the pages of recent history turned back on THE TWENTIETH CENTURY; in the march of events broadcast each week on EYEWITNESS; and, in fact, in the regularly scheduled daily news reports. To watch them is to gain deeper understanding of the world we live in.

CBS TELEVISION NETWORK ●

The illustration for the "Russians", done by Milton Glaser in 1963, is still the subject of a friendly feud between Glaser and Dorfsman. Glaser preferred his original version, a virtuoso drawing which he considered esthetically superior to this one. Dorfsman, however, rejected it because he felt it lacked clarity. The final illustration is the result of numerous arguments and revisions, a circumstance that has happily not compromised their friendship.

59.

59.

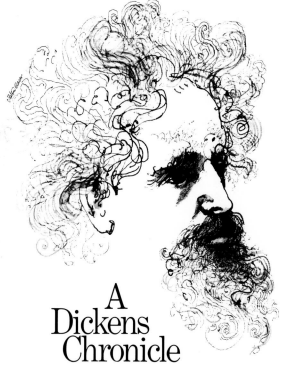

A Dickens Chronicle

No single individual conjures up the world of 19th Century England as vividly as Charles Dickens—a world of cosy inns and roaring fires, of grinding poverty and social injustice.

Tonight at 7:30 EST, CBS News brings this world to life in a compelling broadcast in which episodes from the novelist's tormented personal life are presented in dramatic counterpoint to some of the celebrated creations of his soaring imagination.

Dominating the screen is the memorable figure of Mr. Pickwick's famous manservant—Sam Weller—who alternates between presenting fellow characters from the various novels and providing the biographical background to scenes from Dickens' family life. You are happily bewildered by the plump and garrulous Mrs. Nickleby expounding her fuzzy notions. You are shocked by the browbeating schoolmaster, Wackford Squeers. You are touched by the foolish optimism of Mr. Micawber: "until something turns up I have nothing to bestow but advice." You are delighted by the innocence and warmth of Mr. Pickwick himself as Sam Weller introduces him to Weller, Sr., "the old 'un" over a glass of brandy.

And in between this colorful parade of characters you enter the Dickens household at various stages—in his childhood as the son of a father imprisoned for debt; in the days of his courtship as a young, romantic writer; and in the crowning years of his success as one of the greatest literary figures the world has produced. As he himself wrote: "My whole nature was so penetrated by the grief and humiliation of such considerations (his father's imprisonment) that even now, famous and caressed and happy, I often forget in my dreams that I have a dear wife and children....even that I am a man...and wander desolately back to that time of my life."

Performed by a distinguished cast starring Clive Revill as Sam Weller; Robert Stephens as Dickens; Rosemary Harris as his wife, Kate; and Douglas Campbell as Mr. Micawber, tonight's broadcast offers a unique viewing experience for the entire family.

The influence of great men on their times is no less of a reality than the latest news report of a fire, an act of Congress, or a labor dispute. In tonight's broadcast CBS News reaches into the realities of a past century to illuminate its customs, manners and conditions, just as it reaches into today's international realities and tomorrow's technological realities to present an interview with Chancellor Adenauer, a military expedition in Southeast Asia, a space launching from Cape Canaveral. To a resourceful and enterprising news organization all reality is its province.

● CBS NEWS

60.

The Impact of Drawings

Since newspapers are saturated with photographs, Dorfsman occasionally likes the sudden change of pace and impact of drawings. Also, there are times when photographs are not available, or readers would not recognize the characters from photos anyway, as in the case of Dostoevsky, Gogol, Turgenev, Chekhov, and Pasternak (59) and Charles Dickens (60). A drawing, more than a photograph, can infuse a character with a legendary quality, as in the Gershwin portrait (61). "Besides," Dorfsman admitted, "when everybody is zigging, I like to zag."

Rialto Ripples
Kongo Kate
That Certain Feeling
Do It Again!
Someone To Watch Over Me
Concerto in F
Fascinating Rhythm
Oh! Kay!
But Not For Me!

Love is Sweeping The Country Swanee
I Got Rhythm An American in Paris Maybe
'S Wonderful My One and Only Treat Me Rough
I'll Build A Stairway To Paradise Somebody Loves Me
Rhapsody in Blue Clap Yo' Hands Do Do Do Liza
The Man I Love Strike Up The Band Love Walked In
Soon I've Got A Crush On You A Foggy Day Mine
Cuban Overture Who Cares? Summertime By Strauss
Nice Work if You Can Get It I Got Plenty O'Nuttin'

They All Laughed
Changing My Time
Lo-La-Lo
Funny Face
Shall We Dance
Bidin' My Time

THE GERSHWIN YEARS

The CBS Television Network presents a 90-minute musical extravaganza with Richard Rodgers as host—starring Maurice Chevalier, Florence Henderson, Ron Husmann, Julie London, Frank Sinatra and Ethel Merman...Produced by Leland Hayward.

8:00 TO 9:30 TONIGHT ON CBS ● CHANNEL 2

WHAT A SEASON OF SPARKLING SPECIALS!

Dramatic specials…variety specials…comedy specials…specials in animation, music, documentaries—more of all kinds will appear on CBS Television for the 1976-77 season than ever before.

On this page are a few of the specials in the CBS schedule. Another 60 or more include "Goldenrod," a dramatic love story of the rodeo circuit in Western Canada…"The Attempted Defection of Simas Kudirka," a tense drama based on a Soviet seaman's life-and-death leap to freedom…"Monte Carlo Circus Festival"…Peggy Fleming with "Holiday on Ice" at Madison Square Garden…The Grammy Awards. And many more.

Program specials are a CBS specialty. They open up television to the widest array of talent, to the oldest and newest forms of entertainment. They create a season within a season, adding sparkle, endless variety and change of pace.

They're all in addition to the exciting new series starting on the CBS Television Network this fall, and to continuing program favorites.

"They Said It with Music: Yankee Doodle to Ragtime": A truly all-star cast and two glittering hours of song, story, and graphics. The tracing of the nation's character through its music.

"America's Salute to Richard Rodgers": Gene Kelly and Henry Winkler co-host a stylish all-star, two-hour tribute to the nation's best-loved composer.

Beverly Sills and Carol Burnett star in a variety hour of magnificent sound and comedy. "Sills & Burnett at the Met."

Bing Crosby stars in a stunning new variety special—as well as in the Crosby family's annual Christmas celebration.

Nadia Comaneci, the incredible star of the '76 Summer Olympics, performs miracles of gymnastics in a spectacular entertainment odyssey through her picturesque homeland. "Nadia: From Rumania With Love."

Shirley MacLaine, versatile movie star and Emmy winner of last year's Best Variety Special, performs through an hour of dazzling comedy, dance, and song.

"Minstrel Man": starring Glynn Turman in a story of two brothers, born into the minstrel tradition and determined to live and work in dignity. A powerful dramatic special with music.

Jane Alexander plays a well-to-do woman who reaches outside her conventional life to help emotionally disturbed children. A moving two-hour drama: "Circle of Children." Co-starring Rachel Roberts.

"Lucille Ball's 25th Anniversary Special": An all-star retrospective of one of the greatest comedy careers in history. A major television event.

Charlie Brown. The return of the whole irresistible troop of the Charles Schulz characters in new—and in many of your favorite—animated specials.

ON CBS

62.

60

CBS PRESENTS FEBRUARY
Or how come such a cold month has so many hot specials?

Saturdays Feb.1, 8,15, 22. CBS Golf Classic. 4-5 pm. Warm up for spring each Saturday as top contenders pair up to vie for $225,000 in prizes in a match-play series.

Sundays Feb. 2, 9,16, 23. NHL Hockey. 2:30-5 pm. The fastest men in the world hot up the ice each Sunday as CBS Sports follows their drive for a crack at the Stanley Cup.

Tuesdays Feb. 4 and 18. 60 Minutes. 10-11 pm. CBS News' every-other-Tuesday magazine covers an extraordinary range of subjects: on February 4, a visit with the Duke and Duchess of Windsor as they try to sell Harry Reasoner their million-dollar home near Paris.

Sunday, Feb. 9. A Midsummer Night's Dream. 9- 11:15 pm. A weaver turned donkey and a fairy queen bewitched into loving him are just two of the mismated mortals and playful spirits who add mischief—and fun— to the Royal Shakespeare Company production of the Bard's "sweet comedy."

Saturday, Feb. 15. Fisherman's World. 1-2 pm. Gypsy Rose Lee, Garry Moore, Sam Snead and other celebrities are cast in a new role.

Tuesday, Feb. 18 Australia: The Timeless Land. 7:30-8:30 pm. A National Geographic special brings a sweeping panorama of the land down under—from cosmopolitan cities to the continent's great untamed core.

Tuesday, Feb. 25. CBS Playhouse: "The Experiment." 9:30-11 pm. A love story of the Now generation that poses timeless questions about the price of success. Barry Sullivan heads a cast in which the younger generation is represented by Tisha Sterling (Ann Sothern's daughter) and M. K. Douglas (Kirk's son).

Friday, Feb. 28. The Flight of Apollo 9. 11 am.* For ten days CBS News will cover every phase of this next critical step in our progress towards a moon landing. *Launch time approximate.

Double Feature: Thursday, Feb. 20. He's Your Dog, Charlie Brown. 7:30-8 pm. Snoopy gets ideas above his station and the Peanuts Gang may lose their star shortstop.

Looking Back. 8-9 pm. Andy Griffith and guests including Janet Leigh, Don Knotts and Tennessee Ernie Ford take a fast, funny look at the charms of the Thirties.

CBS ②

The total effect — there's a lot of excitement on CBS-TV.
Despite the variety of illustration techniques, the typography unifies the page. All picture captions are set in the same typeface and size. The logo repeats the typeface of the headline, sandwiching in all the disparate elements and keeping the page under control.

THE GOLDEN AGE OF GREECE 6-7 PM Tonight in a unique television broadcast, King Paul and Queen Frederika of Greece review their country's historic contributions to civilization symbolized by that great monument of human aspiration, the Parthenon. Surrounded by its soaring columns, the King and Queen discuss the design of the famous structure with CBS News Correspondent Eric Sevareid, demonstrating how its noble proportions reflected the social, political and artistic ideals and way of life of the Age of Pericles, the forerunner of modern democracy. Produced by Perry Wolff, tonight's on-the-scene broadcast is the second in a CBS News series of specials entitled THE ROOTS OF FREEDOM.

THE HERITAGE AND THE PROMISE

LINCOLN CENTER DAY 8-9 PM Just one year ago Lincoln Center for the Performing Arts opened its doors to express "the enduring values of art as a true measure of civilization." Tonight a first-anniversary broadcast, with Alistair Cook as host, will display the arts of the ballet and the musical theatre. Members of the New York City Ballet, directed by George Balanchine, will perform excerpts from ballets by Stravinsky and Bizet. Another portion of the program introduced by Richard Rodgers will tell the story of the American musical stage, through the singing of a notable cast with Sally Ann Howes, Robert Merrill, Veronica Tyler, David Wayne, special guest star Miss Ethel Merman. ●2

This one ad announced two CBS cultural programs scheduled for the same evening: a documentary on "The Golden Age of Greece" and a broadcast celebrating the first anniversary of Lincoln Center. By juxtaposing an ancient Greek temple and the architecturally derived Lincoln Center building, Dorfsman made a visual equation between the culture inherited from Ancient Greece and the cultural offerings to come from Lincoln Center and CBS.

When an associate of Dorfsman discovered a 1927 newspaper story about CBS's first broadcast from the old Metropolitan Opera House, Lou did not let the promotional opportunity slip through his fingers. On September 27, 1966, exactly 39 years after that first broadcast, he ran this ad congratulating the Metropolitan Opera on its move to its new home at Lincoln Center. The ad confirmed CBS's longtime commitment to cultural programming.

Just seven notes on a startling blank page of music may seem like reckless use of expensive space. Here, it is an irresistible visual device for drawing readers into the text. The copy in this ad celebrated the opening of Lincoln Center's Philharmonic Hall and CBS's continuing involvement in broadcasting and recording concerts by The New York Philharmonic.

Promoting the cultural image
The opening of Lincoln Center for the Performing Arts in New York City provided CBS with numerous opportunities to broadcast concerts, ballets and operas. It also created opportunities for promoting CBS's image as a major disseminator of culture.

We have a more than passing interest in the transformation of the grand old lady of Thirty-ninth Street into the debutante of Lincoln Center. For while the Metropolitan Opera inaugurates its new home we will be celebrating an anniversary.

CBS went on the air 39 years ago, on September 18, 1927, and the Met was with us on our opening night as we presented the first broadcast of an American opera, "The King's Henchman," by Deems Taylor.

In the years since then CBS has brought America the voices of virtually every great star from the world of song. We have helped to foster public interest in fine music generally through millions of records and thousands of hours of radio and television broadcasts. Down the years CBS has commissioned over 300 works by the world's foremost composers. And, in developing the Long-Playing® record which can reproduce an entire opera on two or three discs, we have transformed the very nature of recorded music.

They have been busy and rewarding years since that opening night. And now there is another opening: the Metropolitan Opera at Lincoln Center. It is with special joy that we salute a great musical institution in its beautiful new home. Bravissimo!

COLUMBIA
BROADCASTING
SYSTEM

Notes of triumph

All that music is, and probably ever can be, starts with these seven sounds. In different combinations they have lulled children to sleep, serenaded women, sent men off to war.

Bach used them to praise God. Brahms turned them into a famous lullaby. Beethoven built them into nine transfiguring symphonies that echo the depths of man's hopes, joys and fears.

Tonight these same notes celebrate the triumph of an idea—the opening of the new Lincoln Center for the Performing Arts. As part of the ceremonies the New York Philharmonic Orchestra under Leonard Bernstein will present its first concert in its new home, Philharmonic Hall.

Attended by a brilliant audience of 2600 people, the concert equally represents the triumph and magic of electronic communication. For it will be broadcast over the CBS Radio and CBS Television Networks, where it will be heard and seen by more people than have attended all the performances of the orchestra in its 120 years of existence. And it will be permanently recorded for posterity by Columbia Records.

In recent years the Columbia Broadcasting System has commissioned over 300 original works for broadcast—many of them by the world's foremost composers including Igor Stravinsky, Aaron Copland, Benjamin Britten and Darius Milhaud. Its association with the New York Philharmonic Orchestra has extended without interruption over 32 years through 1124 radio and television broadcasts. Since 1940 Columbia Records has been the exclusive recording organization for the Philharmonic. And in 1948 CBS Laboratories revolutionized the recording industry by developing the famous long-playing record which could reproduce a complete symphony on a single disc.

CBS takes pride in helping to usher in a new era of pleasure and inspiration for Americans through its nationwide television and radio broadcasts of tonight's inaugural ceremonies at Lincoln Center from 9 to 11 pm EDT. Be sure you are looking and listening.

THE COLUMBIA BROADCASTING SYSTEM

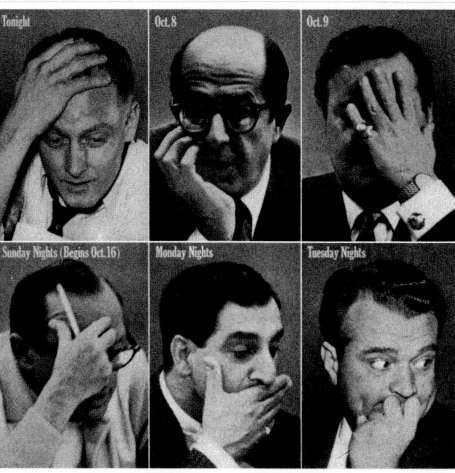

Tonight

Oct. 8

Oct. 9

Sunday Nights (Begins Oct. 16)

Monday Nights

Tuesday Nights

The immediate purpose of this ad was to announce Danny Kaye's first appearance on TV. But, by including other CBS funny men, the ad engendered additional support for Kaye and for CBS comedy, as well. The unexpected serious expressions conveyed to prospective advertisers and to the public that CBS comedy programming was thoughtfully planned, and carefully researched; it was serious business. The ad reinforced CBS's dominance in the field of comedy.

67.

THE BUSINESS OF BEING FUNNY

Obviously the business of being funny is no laughing matter. But hard as it is to come by, there will be more comedy on the CBS Television Network this year than ever before. In fact, three out of every ten hours in our evening schedule will be given over to laughter. For in our view nothing is as satisfying for every member of the family as a good laugh.

During this month alone, for example, you'll see four hilarious hour-long programs in which Art Carney will demonstrate his versatility as the world's greatest lover; Jackie Gleason will emerge as America's Number 1 Salesman; Phil Silvers will conjure up a mad musical satire on show business;

and as a special treat—on October 30—the inimitable Danny Kaye will make his first television appearance in a full hour of dazzling comedy.

You will be laughing twice as often at Jack Benny, who will be back every Sunday. You'll again be seeing Danny Thomas, the most popular practitioner of "situation" comedy, and Red Skelton, the most exuberant and durable clown in television.

Also in store are eight brand new and, we think, very funny series that will bring into your home the talents of other great performers: THE ANDY GRIFFITH SHOW, ANGEL, BRINGING UP BUDDY, MY SISTER EILEEN, OH THOSE BELLS, PETE AND GLADYS, THE

TOM EWELL SHOW, and starting tonight, CANDID CAMERA, with its engaging host Arthur Godfrey.

And, of course, you can look forward to such favorites of last year as THE ANN SOTHERN SHOW, DENNIS THE MENACE, DOBIE GILLIS, FATHER KNOWS BEST, and HENNESEY, not to mention the many zany skits of THE GARRY MOORE SHOW and a special musical satire, "Step on the Gas," to be seen this month on THE UNITED STATES STEEL HOUR.

Here are 22 reasons why there will be more laughter in these parts than ever before. And why for the sixth straight year the nation's biggest audiences will watch the programs of **CBS**◉

Oct. 30

Serious about comedy
These ads demonstrate two Dorfsman imperatives: grab hold of every promotional opportunity and milk every advertising dollar for its full value. Each of these ads started with a specific message which he extrapolated into a larger one to position CBS as "the network of comedy stars."

68.

When Dorsfman heard from an associate that Goodman Ace, a recognized giant among comedy writers, had privately raved about CBS's "Mary Tyler Moore Show," he did not let the unsolicited endorsement slip away unrecorded. He used it to promote all of the CBS comedy shows, and to impress other comedy writers, directors and players (especially in the Hollywood community) with CBS's leadership in the field.

The design of the ad looks simplistic. There is more text than picture. (Lou knows when to let esthetics take a back seat to a good story.) The headline, photo, postscript pictures of other CBS stars, and the "hahahaha" tell the whole CBS story, even if the ad isn't read in its entirety.

THE NEW YORK TIMES, THURSDAY, MARCH 1, 1973

When the dean of American comedy writers says something is funny, it's funny.

For something like forty years, Goodman Ace has been the comedy writers' comedy writer. Name the funny man, and the chances are that Goodman Ace put funny words in his mouth.

So if he says something is funny, you got to figure it's funny. And this is what he said about CBS's Mary Tyler Moore Show:

"A show with a finely honed group of players, so believable and hilarious that during the six days they're not on the air, I find myself fighting a desire to phone their TV studio in Minneapolis to ask Mary, Mr. Grant, Rhoda, Murray and Ted Baxter how things are going. Mary Tyler Moore is not TV's traditional 'girl who lives next door.' But you wish she did."

And Time magazine, which doesn't usually get all choked up about situation comedies, said this:

"Someone should write an ode to Mary Tyler Moore, whose show seems to get better with every passing week. Now in its third year, the series has taken the brass of the usual situation comedy formula and transmuted it into something resembling gold."

The Mary Tyler Moore Show is just one in a long line of CBS comedies that have made us beyond argument (which isn't to say that we won't get an argument) the top banana of the three television networks since the earliest days of humor on the tube.

For argument's sake, let's just take Saturday nights on CBS these days. Starting in a neat little home in Queens and ending in a big shambles in Hollywood, all we do is work your funny bone.

For openers, there's the top-rated show on all television, a little number called All in the Family. Take away its groundbreaking themes, its precedent-shattering dialogue, its psychology, sociology, philosophy, and all the other heavy stuff, and what you've got is one funny television show.

From Edith, Archie and the kids, we go to Bridget Loves Bernie, which mainly proves that all the world loves two lovers. But just listen to how much they love these two lovers. This year, the three networks brought out 23 new shows. Two of them—just two of them—burst into the top ten. Both from CBS. Both comedies. And Bridget Loves Bernie was one of them. (The other one was the indomitable Maude, whom you can catch on Tuesday night, sailing into battle with her heart on her mink sleeve, her political position fixed, and her mouth at full speed ahead.)

Next, we're off to Minneapolis and the aforementioned lady with the voice that lives on the edge of panic—Mary Tyler Moore.

Whereupon Bob Newhart gets on the line to show us that (A) a psychologist who shares a secretary with a dentist can't be all bad, and (B) Newhart's maybe even funnier off the phone than on.

Next, exploding onto our screen is... Carol Burnett. Mostly tearing things to shreds. Like traditions, pomposity and an occasional piece of furniture. And becoming even more popular while she's at it.

Now we didn't put you through all this just to get you to watch CBS some Saturday night. But just for laughs, why don't you watch CBS this Saturday night? You'll see for yourself that when we say something is funny, it's funny.

And you'll see enough to keep you smiling right up to the eleven o'clock news, and the report of that low pressure area heading your way, bringing with it heavy rains, and you have to take the dog out, and you know you left your umbrella in the office. (Research sources available on request.)

65

Jack Benny's twentieth 69
year on radio was
acknowledged with
this ad, as quietly
comical as the star
himself. Until Benny
appeared on TV, his
face was not familiar to
most people, but the
sound of his hapless
violin playing was
recognized instantly.
What better I.D. for
the comedian than
the violin with
the broken string?

JACK BENNY Maestro of the microphone...genius of easy laughter
...faithful keeper of the violin, the Maxwell, and the all-Benny dollar.
He helped make radio a voice heard everywhere—and comedy
a new art in radio. His unfailing example of taste and showmanship
guides a new generation of artists. Today, his 20th year
on the air is a double anniversary—in a showman's career and in
a nation's entertainment. To the joy and pride of radio,
with the joy and pride of CBS Radio—CONGRATULATIONS

69.

Suiting the message to the medium
Dorfsman struck incisively at the inherent difference between television and radio in these
ads. Each ad is appropriate to the star and to the medium in which he appeared.

THE NEW YORK TIMES, FRIDAY, SEPTEMBER 28, 1962

Jackie of all trades

He has yet to play Hamlet. But don't knock the idea. For this is a man of multiple and monumental talents that have carried him to the pinnacle of fame in the entertainment world. Tomorrow night at 7:30 pm Jackie Gleason returns to the CBS Television Network in a brand-new full hour blazing musical comedy and variety program with special guest star Art Carney, Sue Ann Langdon, Frank Fontaine, the June Taylor dancers and his customary bevy of beautiful girls. Be sure you're watching. You'll see a phenomenon of showbusiness.

THE JACKIE GLEASON SHOW: THE AMERICAN SCENE MAGAZINE TOMORROW NIGHT FROM 7:30 TO 8:30 ON CBS◎2

Key to success: He first won nationwide acclaim nearly a decade ago on the CBS Television Network where his comic genius kept 40 million people fascinated every Saturday night as he pranced across the screen shouting "And awa-a-a-y we go!" (A). Few will forget his remarkable gifts for characterization in the series of celebrated sketches that include the blustering bus driver in "The Honeymooners" (B). They can be seen again in his new motion picture "Gigot" where he plays the part of a downtrodden deaf-and-dumb janitor (C). Last year his flair as a dramatic actor earned him an Academy Award nomination for his portrayal of Minnesota Fats in "The Hustler" (D). But this, too, came as no surprise to television viewers who had seen him in *Playhouse 90's* production of Saroyan's "The Time of Your Life" (E). In still another movie soon to be released, Gleason will play the part of the insidious fight manager in "Requiem for A Heavyweight" (F) which also had its origin on the CBS Television Network. Two years ago he wrote, narrated and conducted the score of the hour-long television musical "The Secret World of Eddie Hodges" (G) and the year before starred on stage as a small town reporter in the Broadway hit "Take Me Along" (H). He is a songwriter and orchestra leader with more than 30 top-selling record albums under his belt (I). He shoots golf in the 70's and is a companion of the great pro's (J). He is his own television and movie director (K). And tomorrow night—who knows what new talents he will reveal (LMNOPQRSTUVWXYZ)!

70.

67

With this announcement, CBS Radio opens the mass circulation of night-time, network radio to advertisers with limited budgets. Also, to large advertisers for special promotions.

RED SKELTON, star-showman, star-salesman — and his 13 million listeners — are now available on a one-time basis. The cost: appreciably less than a color page in a mass magazine.

Here's how a one-time budget now fits big-time radio:

QUESTION: How?

ANSWER: Red Skelton's regular half-hour show — one of the "top ten" in all radio — will be on the air for 39 consecutive weeks, starting October 3. Each mass-market broadcast will be sold to a single sponsor (but a sponsor will not be limited to a single broadcast).

QUESTION: How will advertisers use the show?

ANSWER: To say something special with *impact* — as explosive as the laughter of Skelton's listeners.... Here is mass radio uniquely produced to launch a new product — kick off a drive — announce a contest.... Here also is the perfect opportunity for the split-timing and commanding attention that many advertisers need for peak-selling seasons and holidays: Christmas, White Sales, Mother's Day, Father's Day, Straw Hat Time, June weddings and graduations. (Skelton ad libs over our shoulder: "For Thanksgiving, we can sell bogs and bogs of cranberries.")

QUESTION: Any merchandising tie-ins?

ANSWER: Displays and mailings will flash the appeal of Skelton's personality, tieing-in program, product, and purse at the sales counter.

QUESTION: What's the time of broadcast?

ANSWER: During a peak listening hour — 9:00 to 9:30 p.m., Wednesdays. Between the big-audience attractions of Dr. Christian and Bing Crosby.

QUESTION: How many stations in the Skelton line-up?

ANSWER: Stations accounting for 91.4 per cent of the entire CBS Radio circulation are available for clearance.

QUESTION: How many listeners will Red Skelton deliver on an average program?

ANSWER: Year-in, year-out, Red Skelton in front of a microphone is a human, fun-making magnet. Last season, he drew an average weekly audience of more than 13 million people.

QUESTION: How much does the show cost?

ANSWER: $23,500 — including time, talent, and merchandising. To give this price a yardstick: For $23,500, you can tap a mass audience and listener-loyalty that took an annual investment of more than $1,500,000 to build.

QUESTION: How will sponsors be scheduled?

ANSWER: Solely on a first-come, first-to-profit basis.

QUESTION: Are there any other answers?

ANSWER: Just a reminder: *To say things that get things started... or to give a peak-selling season a higher peak than ever, RED SKELTON is your boy....* For a program date best suited to your needs, call your representative at...

THE CBS RADIO NETWORK

LIKE TO HAVE A PIECE OF SKELTON?

71. The segmented photo graphically introduced to advertisers the new merchandising scheme of sponsoring segments of an expensive program. In the 1950s, this was a departure from the practice of selling a valuable property to a single advertiser.

<u>Three ways to see Red</u>
This retrospective of Red Skelton ads illustrates Dorfsman's flexibility in shifting approaches to the same subject. It also reveals how he responded to marketing imperatives and the visual vernacular and social themes of the times.

◉2
8:00-9:00 PM WCBS-TV
THE RED SKELTON HOUR
Have a hilarious hour with television's
Clown-Prince! Tonight's guest stars:
ABCDE ABCDEFGH ABCDEFGHIJK

72.

73. A tune-in ad with
Hirschfeld illustration
cloned from the 1963
supplement.
(See page 53.)

RED IS BEAUTIFUL.

And screamingly funny.
   With tonight's guests, Walter Bren-
nan and The Lettermen. And in weeks
to come with Martha Raye, Ed Sullivan,
Gary Puckett and the Union Gap, John
Wayne, The Baja Marimba Band, Liza
Minnelli, Godfrey Cambridge, Burl Ives.
Plus many, many more.
   Isn't that a beautiful way to see Red?
"The Red Skelton Show"
8:30 TONIGHT CBS◉2

74. A 1960s tune-in ad.
The headline echoes
the popular "black is
beautiful" slogan of the
'60s. The layout and
typographic treatment
reflect the prevailing
Minimalist movement
in the arts of that
period.

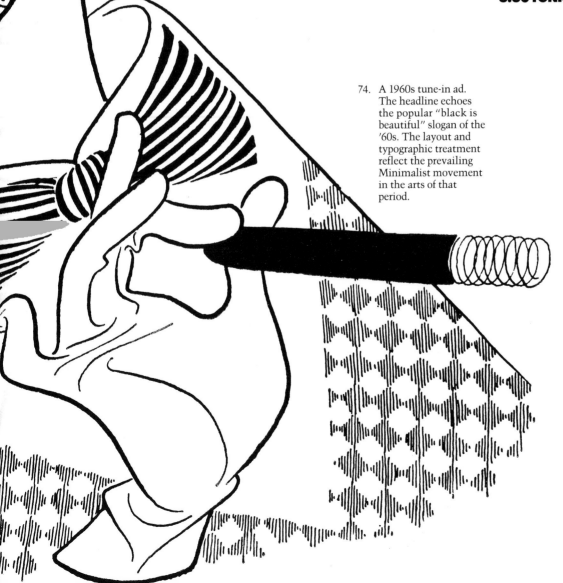

Because they enjoy the use of public airwaves, radio and TV stations are obliged to pay their dues and devote a portion of their broadcast time to news and matters of public interest. Although such programs are not generally high-audience shows, (CBS's current 60 Minutes is a notable exception), CBS went all-out in the area of public information — to maintain its desired image as a responsible public institution.

Starting back in the days before World War II, CBS lined up a news team that was the undisputed leader in the field. Their direct-from-the-front broadcasts during the war, their intrepid domestic reports and their elevated intellectual style set the standard for the entire industry. Through the years a succession of CBS reporters and analysts maintained the network's reputation and authority, and CBS News enjoyed a virtual monopoly in the field for decades. Also, CBS shows like "See It Now," "Face the Nation," the unforgettable 1954 "Army McCarthy Hearings," "CBS Reports" and a series of educational documentaries fortified the company's prestige.

But when television exploded as an advertising medium, the demand for prime time exceeded the supply. Networks had to do some serious juggling to balance profitable high-audience entertainment with less profitable educational and cultural offerings. As a result, the entire television industry came under blistering attack. In 1961, Newton Minow, the chairman of the Federal Communications Commission, chastised the industry for underestimating the intelligence of its viewers, programming lightweight, mindless entertainment and turning the public airwaves into a "vast wasteland." (Mr. Minow, still vigilant, currently exercises his concern as a board member of CBS, Inc.)

At that time, Dorfsman saw it as part of the Advertising Department's responsibility to counter the negative image and impress opinion leaders in Washington, as well as in the educational and religious communities, that CBS took its public obligation to heart. His ads had to reflect the intelligence and concern of the network. But he also knew he had to make news and information programs sound entertaining and urgent enough to attract listeners and sponsors. Every piece of advertising and promotion was geared to entice the audience and, at the same time, to make CBS appear as a veritable university of broadcasting.

75. The CBS News Team at a presidential nominating convention. The booth, designed by Dorfsman, made CBS eminently visible to convention participants and the TV audience.

Collision at Columbia, Backfire at Berkeley, Strife at Sorbonne, Disruption at Duke, Opposition at Oxford, Semantics at San Francisco, Turmoil at Tokyo, Conflict at Chicago, Revolt at Rutgers, No nonsense at Notre Dame.

WATCH THE WORLDWATCHERS CBS NEWS

What's got the students of the world in such a turmoil? We saw it start four years ago at Berkeley. And we've been working to define and illuminate the problem ever since. (With broadcasts like *The Berkeley Rebels, The New Left, Sixteen in Webster Groves,* and many more.) In 1969 we've stepped up our efforts. Last week you may have seen our hour-long broadcast, *The College Turmoil.* In late May and June we'll bring you a special series, three full hours titled *Generations Apart.* The failure of understanding between young and old can make you cry. Or rage. Or turn to a news source that offers less heat, more light.

76.

The "Worldwatchers" campaign

From the mid-'60s to the mid-'70s, the world was in a state of social and political convulsion. There were campus riots, race riots and international incidents. News reports were full of strange names. Battles were being fought in unpronounceable places. It was all troubling and perplexing.

The words for this series of ads were derived from newspaper headlines. With clever word play, repetition, alliteration, puzzling abbreviations, and arresting typography, the ads provoked curiosity and readership.

Dorfsman also coined a name for the CBS Network News Team, "Worldwatchers," and designed a symbol — a jigsawed globe resting in a newsman's hands. The take-apart globe and hands appeared in newspaper ads and in on-air promotions (176), intimating that CBS newsmen could take the world news apart, study it and put it back together for the viewer.

WHITE VS WHITE
WHITE VS BLACK
BLACK VS BLACK
BLACK VS WHITE
WHITE VS YELLOW
YELLOW VS YELLOW
YELLOW VS BROWN
BROWN VS BROWN

WATCH THE
WORLDWATCHERS
CBS NEWS

Our world seems racked by divisions. Color is only one.
The gap between rich and poor, some say, is deeper.
Between young and old, more frightening. CBS News has been
studying such collision points for a long time. In broadcasts
like Who Speaks for Birmingham? in 1961; Black Power—
White Backlash in 1966; the seven part series Of Black America
in 1968. We've called your attention to The Hippy Temptation and
The Policeman's Lot. To Vietnam: The Hawks and The Doves.
And right now we have more than 25 new projects in work.
At a time when what divides us can destroy us, it just isn't good
enough to rush the news to you when things happen.
So we go out after the facts and background you need.
It's a continuing effort. Toward understanding.

ABM, NLF, DMZ, SAM,
LEM, HEW, DEW, FCC,
LSD, DNA, HRA, UAR,
HUD, FTC, CIA, AMA,
ABA, OEO, FDA, SDS,
SOS!

WATCH
THE
WORLDWATCHERS
CBS NEWS

How do you make sense of this confusing world of abbreviations, codes, symbols?
To millions of Americans, CBS stands for the broadcasters who spell it all out most
meaningfully. Watch CBS News and you understand the excitement of a breakthrough like
DNA. (Walter Cronkite did it on The 21st Century.) Watch CBS News and you see why LSD,
SDS and ABM can all rock the country, can examined on CBS Reports, 60 Minutes, and other
CBS News Hour broadcasts.) Every week we bring you more hours of regularly scheduled
news than any other network. Because every week there's more you need to know.

Nixon watches Kosygin.
Kosygin watches Mao.
Mao watches Ho.
Ho watches Ky
(Who watches Thieu).
Nasser watches Dayan.
Dayan watches DeGaulle.
DeGaulle watches Nixon.
Cronkite watches Everybody.

WATCH
THE WORLDWATCHERS
CBS NEWS

Almost everybody watches Cronkite. CBS Evening News with
Walter Cronkite is now in its 22nd straight month of audience leadership.
For good reason. For dozens of good reasons. The whole team of
correspondents we call Worldwatchers. Men like Eric Sevareid in
Washington. Peter Kalischer in Paris. Charles Collingwood in London.
Men like Dan Rather, a President watcher. Marvin Kalb, a diplomat
watcher. Daniel Schorr, a city watcher. They know what to look for. And
how to impart it with clarity and meaning. Keep your eye on CBS News.
And watch Cronkite watch Nixon watch Kosygin watch Mao....

Innovation:Washington.
Initiation:Paris.
Indication:Saigon.
Intensification:Hanoi.
Indoctrination:Peking.
Inflammation:Prague.
Indignation:Moscow.
Imputation:Tel Aviv.
Implication:Cairo.
Intervention:U.N.
Installation:GrandForks.
Investigation:Moon.

WATCH
THE WORLDWATCHERS
CBS NEWS

There's a new combination of world events every time you turn around. What's vital is
now and why they connect. For this kind of understanding, millions of people turn to
CBS News. Sometimes you get it in two minutes from Eric Sevareid. Sometimes in an hour
like Hunger in America. Sometimes in a three-hour series like The Cities. It can take all this
and more to show, for example, the direct connections between hunger, welfare, the urban
crisis, inflation, and U.S. commitments abroad. In a world where so much is happening,
it's insight that makes the information meaningful. And lets you see things whole.

77-80.

73

Tonight television's most distinguished documentary series, CBS REPORTS, presents one of its most ambitious undertakings—a special 90-minute broadcast recapturing the sights, sounds and emotions of the greatest military invasion in history through the eyes and words of the man who shouldered the full responsibility for its outcome—the former Supreme Commander of the Allied Expeditionary Force, Gen. Dwight D. Eisenhower.

A year in preparation, tonight's broadcast shows General Eisenhower retracing the steps which launched the Allied armada against the French Coast just twenty years ago tomorrow. It records his vivid recollections and personal anecdotes supplemented by authentic films taken at the time of the invasion and gleaned from sources around the world.

Accompanied by CBS News Correspondent Walter Cronkite, himself a war correspondent at the Normandy beachhead, General Eisenhower begins his journey near Portsmouth, England, launching site for the invasion. Standing before the original map in the "most secret room in the Allied world," he details the invasion strategy as well as the time and tides which determined June 6, 1944, as D-Day.

Across the English Channel, the General's tour of battle sites includes Pointe du Hoc, the first objective from the sea; a German observation bunker overlooking Omaha Beach; and the hedgerows where the Allied breakthrough was temporarily halted. In a moving conversation with the General, the wife of the wartime Mayor of Ste. Mère Eglise recalls the events as American paratroopers dropped from the night to liberate the first French town.

The journey terminates in the American cemetery at St. Laurent with General Eisenhower's poignant reflections on D-Day and the need for lasting peace.

D-DAY PLUS 20 YEARS
EISENHOWER RETURNS TO NORMANDY

A 90-MINUTE SPECIAL BROADCAST: CBS REPORTS TONIGHT 8:30-IOPM ⊚2

The photo on top reveals the turbulent scene at Normandy Beach on D-Day. Below, General Eisenhower and Walter Cronkite survey the peaceable, deserted site 20 years later. The ad promises an authentic review of the event by the General and the CBS newsman who "were there." 81

81.

Film technique for newspaper ads
For these CBS documentaries, Dorfsman developed a format related to the split screen and quick cut used in film making. By positioning two contrasting photos side-by-side, he encapsulated the contents and drama of the shows.

82. The photo of the ocean is almost three times the size of the desert photo. The graphic relationship not only dramatizes the subject of the documentary, it promises startling insights into the paradox of thirst in the presence of oceans of water.

75% OF THE EARTH'S SURFACE IS WATER – BUT THE EARTH IS DYING OF THIRST!

In today's world of three billion people, two out of three are unable to get enough water. With the population growing at the rate of 50 million each year, scientists say the world must find a way to solve this crisis.

The reasons for the crisis — vast desert areas, pollution, waste, mismanagement and politics — are vividly brought home in tonight's presentation of "The Water Famine" by CBS Reports, which takes you from the arid lands of the Middle East to the California coast.

Among the most challenging solutions is removing the salt from sea water – a challenge that President Kennedy calls as important as reaching the moon. In revealing the techniques employed by science and industry to meet the world-wide water crisis, the CBS Television Network continues to clarify the crucial issues of our time. (Tomorrow night the CBS News program, Eyewitness, presents an on-the-scene report of the Communist Party Congress meeting in Moscow.)

CBS REPORTS:"THE WATER FAMINE"TONIGHT 10-11PM CBS◉2

82.

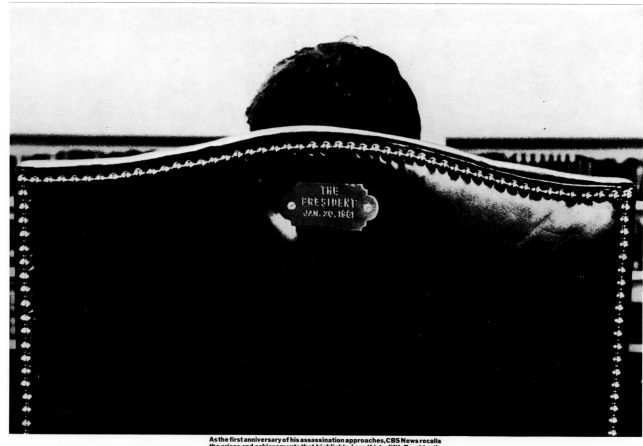

As the first anniversary of his assassination approaches, CBS News recalls the crises and achievements that highlighted our thirty-fifth President's quest for peace. The full-hour commemorative broadcast will present portions of numerous memorable addresses, including those at his inauguration, during the Cuban missile crisis, and following the signing of the nuclear test ban treaty. In recently-recorded narration, his closest associates reveal their personal memories of President Kennedy, contributing fresh insight to those history-making experiences they shared with him.

The Burden and the Glory of John F. Kennedy
Tonight 7:30-8:30 CBS News ◉2

Narrated by Hubert H. Humphrey, Dean Rusk, Adlai E. Stevenson,
W. Averell Harriman, McGeorge Bundy, Pierre Salinger,
Theodore C. Sorensen, Allen W. Dulles, Arthur M. Schlesinger, Jr.,
Dr. Jerome B. Wiesner, Walt Whitman Rostow

83. The documentary scheduled for the anniversary of President Kennedy's assassination was advertised with this haunting and provocative, rear-view photo. It defined the absence of the man and implied behind-the-scenes revelations.

84. Instead of a close-up portrait, Dorfsman did the unexpected and chose a long shot of President Eisenhower in casual conversation with Walter Cronkite. It reflected the universally held vision of Ike as the relaxed, communicative father-figure.

85. This candid, pugnacious close-up of Lyndon Johnson promised that his TV interview with Walter Cronkite will be a challenging confrontation. There is an immediacy and directness in the photo that guarantees some straight talk.

THE NEW YORK TIMES, THURSDAY, OCTOBER 12, 1961

TONIGHT 10–11 PM ON Ⓒ CHANNEL 2, CBS REPORTS PRESENTS THE PERSONAL STORY OF THE 34TH PRESIDENT OF THE UNITED STATES
EISENHOWER ON THE PRESIDENCY

The CBS Television Network brings you this unique broadcast mirroring the mind and personality of a man who as much as any other individual helped shape the massive events of the past two decades of history. For the first time millions of Americans throughout the nation will have an opportunity to see and hear former President Dwight D. Eisenhower reveal his candid assessment of many of the crucial events and issues of his administration.

In the first of an exclusive series of broadcasts he will discuss the question of Presidential disability and speak frankly about the dimensions of the McCarthy era and the Presidential candidacy of Richard M. Nixon. He will make known his concern over the growing military and technological forces at work in the nation. He will tell how he learned to live with the tensions of the Presidency and how we must all learn to live with the tensions of our times.

Filmed in the historic countryside surrounding the President's Gettysburg farm, this series of hour-long programs is a fascinating distillation of five days of informal conversation between Mr. Eisenhower and CBS News Correspondent Walter Cronkite.

THE NEW YORK TIMES FRIDAY, FEBRUARY 6, 1970

Last time he told Walter Cronkite that he would have beaten Nixon in '68, that he didn't intervene to keep the Democratic Convention in Chicago, that he wouldn't have accepted a draft for the Presidency, that he had rather serious questions in his own mind about being President.

What will he reveal to Cronkite tonight?
10 pm CBS News Ⓒ 2

LBJ: The decision to halt the bombing.

84.

85.

Depicting a president

The job of presenting a U.S. president in an ad raises questions beyond the quality of the photo. Is he recognizable? Does the photo capture the personality? Is it objective, or is it prejudicial? Will it please or offend the public? How will it reflect on CBS? Will the photo communicate the nature of the program?

In the actual broadcast, there are opportunities to present many facets of the person. In an ad, you get just one shot. Dorfsman's concern for CBS's image, and his own astute perceptions about the men involved, gave these ads their direction. The ads look like editorials, with no hint of commercialism. At the same time they present CBS as the host to an edifying experience.

For insertion Sunday, November 11, 1962
6 cols. x 223 lines :: 1338 lines
Position Request: TV Listings Page

Who makes the decision to use nuclear weapons? Who pushes the button? How long would an all out nuclear war last? Is use of nuclear weapons virtually automatic if war breaks in Europe? How long could the NATO forces hold in the event of Soviet nuclear attack? Is it true that manned bombers can't reach targets fast enough to evade Soviet anti-aircraft? At what point do you abandon conventional warfare and use tactical nuclear weapons? If nuclear weapons are in the hands of front-line units, does this not give away the power of decision you and the President want to retain? With fifteen fingers on the trigger (NATO countries) how can you arrive at a decision?

Tonight General Lauris Norstad, who faced these questions daily for the past six years as Supreme Commander of the NATO alliance, reveals some of the answers to these life-and-death issues in an exclusive interview on "The Twentieth Century." On the eve of his retirement General Norstad offers his estimate of how effectively the forces under his command could cope with a potential Soviet nuclear attack.

**"NORSTAD OF NATO"—TONIGHT
6 TO 7 PM CBS◉2**

86.

---

31 Million Americans Don't Even Know Whose Side We're On.

Incredible.

A nationwide survey* shows that one American out of four doesn't know whether the United States is supporting South or North Vietnam.

You can't blame it on a shortage of information. Newspapers, magazines, radio and television have been full of the Vietnam war day in, day out and week after week.

In fact, the shocking figure notwithstanding, the great majority of Americans can claim to be better informed right now than they have been at any other time in history. They read more and see more than ever before. The facts and issues are available whenever they go. Indeed, the news is as close as the switch on a television set—and that is exactly where most people turn to first for news.

It is that easy to be well informed.

On the CBS Television Network alone, CBS News reports world and national events in no less than 22 broadcasts a week.

In Vietnam, CBS Correspondents and cameramen fly the helicopter missions, wade the paddies, duck the mortars to show you what it's like at the front. In Washington, London, Moscow, Bonn, Rome, Paris, CBS News Correspondents buttonhole world leaders—so that you can know their views. Throughout the world over 1000 skilled specialists are on call around the clock so that CBS News can bring you the total picture of today's events—the unretouched truth in clear, concise reports.

The news is more than a job to these men. It's a mission. Men like Morley Safer, who has won six distinguished journalism awards for his reporting from Vietnam. Walter Cronkite, who has been called "the single most authoritative figure in TV news." Roger Mudd, Harry Reasoner, Charles Collingwood, Mike Wallace, Joseph Benti. The dean of news analysts, Eric Sevareid. And many more.

You can see why we are shocked that over 31 million Americans don't know North from South. We thank heaven for the many more millions who do.

You are, we hope, one of those millions who do. But think a minute. Just how much do you know about current events? Will you take the chance to find out?

Tonight, CBS News will conduct The National Current Events Test. We will quiz the nation's knowledge on Vietnam, China, NATO…, on the election results and the civil rights movement…, on inflation and Medicare and the new auto safety laws.

How Well Will You Measure Up?

Take The National Current Events Test Tonight At 10 In Color CBS News ◉2

*Opinion Research Corporation, December 1966

87.

Provocative questions and answers
The object of these ads was to arouse interest and create an audience for CBS's in-depth news specials. Each of the ads aimed to engage the audience with a different device.

His wife, his mother,
his best friend, his boss,
his fellow workers, the
boardinghouse keeper, the
police chief, the girls who
heard shots, the Governor,
the rifle range manager, the
bus driver, the cab driver,
the woman who saw
Tippitt shot, the clerk
who spotted the suspect,
the arresting officer...
will reveal today, as they
did before the Warren
Commission, what they
know of Lee Harvey Oswald
and the tragic events of
last November 22.

**Television's most complete
coverage of the background
and findings of the
Warren Commission Report
5-7pm Today CBS News◉2**

88.

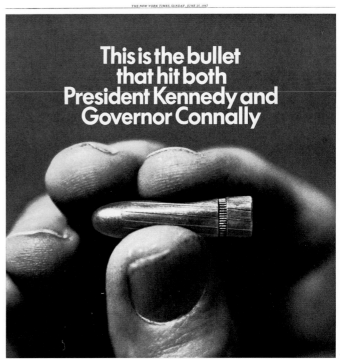

This is the bullet that hit both President Kennedy and Governor Connally

Or did it?

This bullet (Exhibit 399, now in the National Archives) lies at the center of one of the bitter controversies clouding the Warren Report on the assassination of John F. Kennedy. Did it, in fact, strike both the President and the Governor? And if not, could there have been more than three shots fired? Could there have been more than one assassin? Could there have been a conspiracy? And these are not the only areas of dispute. The damage done to the United States on that November day in 1963 did not end with the shots in Dallas. Because so many questions remain unanswered 43 months after this bullet was fired, our country is still beset by doubts, torn by all the wrangling over the Warren Report, confused by the conflicting theories and the awful rumors. CBS News, with a perspective sharpened by time, has spent more than six months investigating every major aspect of the report, going back to the evidence itself and many of the key witnesses, conducting new and enlightening tests, gathering new material on every vital question concerning the events surrounding the assassination. It will take four hours to present the findings of that inquiry. And, for the first time in television history, a network will devote a full hour on each of four consecutive evenings to the presentation of a single subject. Substituting understanding for confusion and meaningful analysis for shrill debate in one of the most troubled controversies of our time, they could very well be the most valuable four hours you ever spent with television.

**The Warren Report: A CBS News Inquiry in Four Parts
Tonight, Tomorrow, Tuesday and Wednesday at 10 pm in color CBS News◉2**

89.

86. The general in the ad looks worried. It's a disturbing picture because generals should radiate confidence. But General Norstad, Supreme Commander of NATO forces, has some troublesome questions about nuclear war that should also trouble the reader. The questions are articulated in the ad; the promise is they'll be answered in the broadcast.

87. A proposed ad to promote participation in the CBS Current Events Contest. The ad presented the shocking statistic that in the midst of the controversial Vietnam War, "31 Million Americans Don't Know Whose Side We're On." The ad suggested that the broadcast would clarify other important issues, as well.

88. The ad promises intimate person-to-person interviews, questions, answers, and revelations about the murder of President Kennedy. The copy, photo and name of the show are threaded together in one urgent message.

89. The headline states a fact, and then questions it. The program on the Warren Commission Report sounds like a mystery story, not a legal treatise. (Dorfsman went to the National Archives in Washington and held the actual bullet in his hand for this photograph. He never fakes the details if he can get the real thing.)

On Wednesday, July 20, for the first time in history, the United States Navy successfully fired the Polaris missile from an atomic submarine traveling beneath the surface of the sea. This test-firing under near combat conditions was the culminating point of a crash program to develop the nation's most effective deterrent weapon...a nuclear headed missile that is almost invulnerable to surprise attack.

The Polaris, with 140,000,000 square miles of ocean as its launching pad, needs no foreign bases. It requires no stationary firing facilities. It is actually a three-stage missile whose first stage is a 380-foot submarine that can go around the world on a core of uranium only slightly bigger than a golf ball. Its success is said to have been the most significant development in weaponry since the atom bomb itself.

Tonight, on its first program of the new season, CBS REPORTS will bring you the full story of the building of the Polaris, from the earliest experiments in a swimming pool, to the final underwater launching from the submarine George Washington. You will witness the successes and failures of this bold project which

required the simultaneous development of an extraordinary missile and a submarine capable of firing it while submerged.

"The Year of the Polaris" is more than an autobiography of a missile. It is a vivid, absorbing account of how decisions are made (and not made) in a democracy–an account of a daring undertaking that may affect every aspect of our defense and foreign policy.

Tonight and throughout the season CBS REPORTS, produced by Fred W. Friendly, will convey to the American people vital information of our times with unparalleled urgency and vividness. Its targets are the fateful issues and events that affect the lives of all of us. Its purpose is to use the full power of network television so that the nation will sit up, take notice and become involved in the critical problems of the present.

CBS REPORTS

THE YEAR OF THE POLARIS

WITH EDWARD R. MURROW

8-9 TONIGHT ON
CBS⊙CHANNEL 2

The United States' newest space team, Gemini astronauts McDivitt and White, embark on our most ambitious and complex step toward the moon. Their four-day journey holds such significance for future flights that it warrants the most extensive and authoritative coverage television can provide. CBS News will provide it. Reporting the launch from Cape Kennedy will be CBS News Correspondent Walter Cronkite, television's most expert space reporter. Following the launch, Cronkite will fly to Houston's Manned Spacecraft Center, control site for the remainder of the 98-hour flight, where he will

We'll keep our eye on McDivitt and White, you keep your eye on Cronkite and Wallace for complete coverage from countdown to recovery, starting tomorrow morning at 7

join CBS News Correspondent Mike Wallace. For four days, until the scheduled recovery in the Atlantic, they will provide live reports every hour during normal broadcast hours. And should events warrant during early morning hours, they will take to the air with additional live reports. Viewers are fast learning that the complexities of America's increased space activity are best reported and explained by CBS News. It is an excellent reason why, during the Grissom-Young Gemini flight this past March, more people kept an eye on the CBS Television Network than on any other network.

"Gemini Preview" tonight at 8
CBS NEWS ⊙2

90.

91.

CBS and the national adventure

For a series of CBS broadcasts about the United States' advanced technology in weapons and space explorations, Dorfsman established a totally journalistic approach. Some ads focused on the event, some on the people, some on the technology. In every case CBS was identified with the adventure as if it had been along on the voyage.

This morning at 9:32 am, Apollo 11 is scheduled to blast off on its epic voyage through space. A voyage that reaches its awesome climax next Monday, when Astronaut Neil Armstrong becomes the first man to set foot on the moon. In a single step, he thus completes a journey which has taken earthlings millions of years. And heralds the dawn of a new age.

Man has entered another realm.

The flight marks more than one milestone in history's span. For unlike other great discoverers of the past — giants like Copernicus, Newton, Columbus or Galileo — Astronaut Armstrong will share his moment of discovery with the world. Via television. Millions on earth will experience the moon's wonder.

You will experience its wonder.

CBS News coverage will be the most extensive ever devoted to a single planned news event. It includes 31 hours of continuous broadcasting on the two days spanning Apollo 11's landing and activity on the moon. Among the many world leaders who will participate is former President Lyndon B. Johnson in an exclusive interview discussing his role in the space program, and where it goes from here.

Walter Cronkite, the only major correspondent to cover every American-manned space launch from the suborbital missions of the '50s to the present, will again be anchorman. With him from lift-off and throughout the flight will be special analyst Walter Schirra and

space expert Arthur C. Clarke. Clarke, author of "2001: A Space Odyssey," predicted ten years ago that we would put a man on the moon "in the summer of 1969." Walter Schirra helped make that prediction come true; he is the only astronaut to fly missions on Mercury, Gemini and Apollo.

Here are some of the highlights of Apollo 11 coverage you will see on CBS News.

And only on CBS News.

Full-scale models of Command and Lunar Modules, manned by experts duplicating the actions of the astronauts, will help you to follow the flight in exact detail. The LM stands on an accurate quarter-acre studio model of the lunar surface.

In Downey, California, a walk-through model of the solar system, 40 feet in diameter and the only fully-operational model of its kind in the world, will be used to explain developments. As will remotes

from the Astrogeology Center in Flagstaff, Arizona.

At CBS News Headquarters in New York, on one of the largest sets of its kind ever built, a giant computer designed by the creator of Space Odyssey's HAL has been charged with thousands of pieces of space data. This unique expert will "talk" to Walter Cronkite. Answer questions about the flight in micro-seconds. Flash images — from diagrams to simulations of complex docking maneuvers — on a giant screen.

World figures will give their personal reactions to the voyage. Sir Bernard Lovell, Director of the Jodrell Bank Observatory and considered the world's foremost authority on radio astronomy, will give his views via satellite from Manchester. From London, Orson Welles, whose historic "War of the Worlds" broadcast 31 years ago presaged the space age, will be seen with Mike Wallace.

From Washington, D.C. From Disneyland. The Smithsonian. New York's Kennedy Airport. From cities like Phoenix and Wichita and Hartford and Seattle, CBS News will catch the faces and reactions of leaders and ordinary citizens alike at crucial moments during the mission.

From London, Tokyo and other major capitals of the world will come international reaction to the flight. Via satellite.

The next week may well be the most astonishing the world has ever known. Journey with us. And live it all.

The end of the beginning

Man on the Moon: The epic journey of Apollo 11
Coverage starts at 7am CBS News ◉2
If you can't watch, listen — on CBS Radio

92.

90. The sequence of photographs picturing the firing of the Polaris missile suggests that CBS cameras were on the scene. The copy guarantees that the broadcast will educate

listeners about this space-age nuclear weapon.

91. Astronauts James A. McDivitt and Edward H. White were featured as partners in space.

Newsmen Walter Cronkite and Mike Wallace were presented as their partners on the ground.

92. The close-up photo of the space shoes

suggests CBS's exhaustive coverage of the moon landing. Dorfsman regretted that he could not get his hands on the actual pair of space shoes used for the moon walk. But he

consulted with authorities at NASA and had a facsimile fabricated according to their specifications. The moon landing in the ad was re-created at a Long Island aircraft plant.

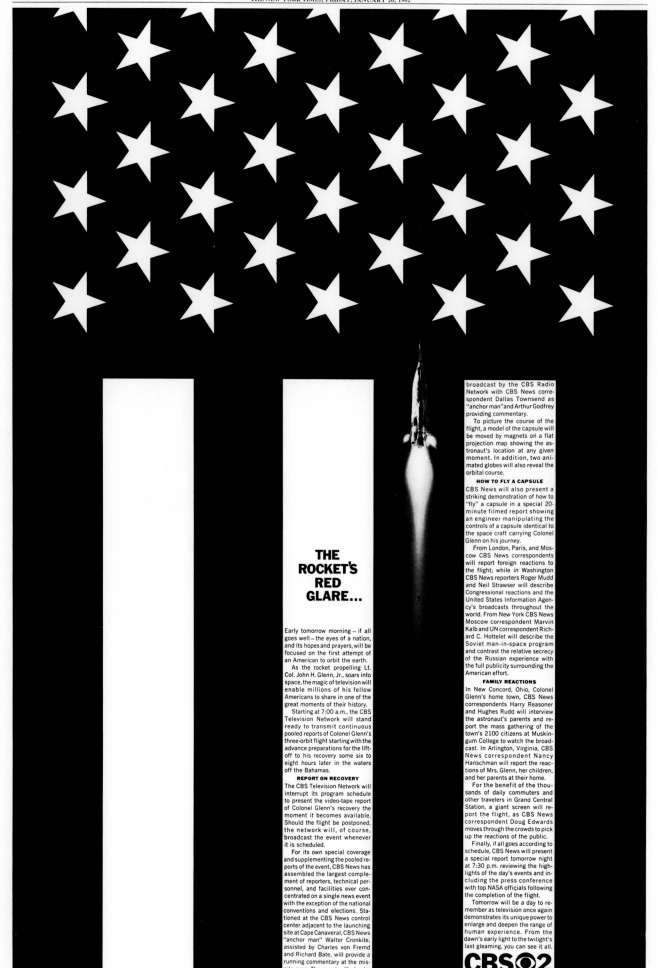

THE ROCKET'S RED GLARE...

Early tomorrow morning — if all goes well — the eyes of a nation, and its hopes and prayers, will be focused on the first attempt of an American to orbit the earth.

As the rocket propelling Lt. Col. John H. Glenn, Jr., soars into space, the magic of television will enable millions of his fellow Americans to share in one of the great moments of their history.

Starting at 7:00 a.m., the CBS Television Network will stand ready to transmit continuous pooled reports of Colonel Glenn's three-orbit flight starting with the advance preparations for the lift-off to his recovery some six to eight hours later in the waters off the Bahamas.

REPORT ON RECOVERY

The CBS Television Network will interrupt its program schedule to present the video-tape report of Colonel Glenn's recovery the moment it becomes available. Should the flight be postponed, the network will, of course, broadcast the event whenever it is scheduled.

For its own special coverage and supplementing the pooled reports of the event, CBS News has assembled the largest complement of reporters, technical personnel, and facilities ever concentrated on a single news event with the exception of the national conventions and elections. Stationed at the CBS News control center adjacent to the launching site at Cape Canaveral, CBS News "anchor man" Walter Cronkite, assisted by Charles von Fremd and Richard Bate, will provide a running commentary at the missile area. The event will also be broadcast by the CBS Radio Network with CBS News correspondent Dallas Townsend as "anchor man" and Arthur Godfrey providing commentary.

To picture the course of the flight, a model of the capsule will be moved by magnets on a flat projection map showing the astronaut's location at any given moment. In addition, two animated globes will also reveal the orbital course.

HOW TO FLY A CAPSULE

CBS News will also present a striking demonstration of how to "fly" a capsule in a special 20-minute filmed report showing an engineer manipulating the controls of a capsule identical to the space craft carrying Colonel Glenn on his journey.

From London, Paris, and Moscow CBS News correspondents will report foreign reactions to the flight; while in Washington CBS News reporters Roger Mudd and Neil Strawser will describe Congressional reactions and the United States Information Agency's broadcasts throughout the world. From New York CBS News Moscow correspondent Marvin Kalb and UN correspondent Richard C. Hottelet will describe the Soviet man-in-space program and contrast the relative secrecy of the Russian experience with the full publicity surrounding the American effort.

FAMILY REACTIONS

In New Concord, Ohio, Colonel Glenn's home town, CBS News correspondents Harry Reasoner and Hughes Rudd will interview the astronaut's parents and report the mass gathering of the town's 2100 citizens at Muskingum College to watch the broadcast. In Arlington, Virginia, CBS News correspondent Nancy Hanschman will report the reactions of Mrs. Glenn, her children, and her parents at their home.

For the benefit of the thousands of daily commuters and other travelers in Grand Central Station, a giant screen will report the flight, as CBS News correspondent Doug Edwards moves through the crowds to pick up the reactions of the public.

Finally, if all goes according to schedule, CBS News will present a special report tomorrow night at 7:30 p.m. reviewing the highlights of the day's events and including the press conference with top NASA officials following the completion of the flight.

Tomorrow will be a day to remember as television once again demonstrates its unique power to enlarge and deepen the range of human experience. From the dawn's early light to the twilight's last gleaming, you can see it all.

CBS◉2

93. This abstract version of the flag served a functional and psychic purpose. The white stripes provided copy space. The overall design provided the patriotic mood appropriate for the program.

94. The half-flag painted on the black man's face was a potent symbol of the unfulfilled citizenship of black Americans, the subject of the broadcast.

95. The succession of flags, coupled with the headline, made a satiric comment about the role of women in America. The ad was designed to arouse interest in a CBS-TV series on historical subjects.

THE NEW YORK TIMES, TUESDAY, JULY 7, 1969

First of a seven-part series

"Black History: Lost, Stolen or Strayed."

OF BLACK AMERICA

10 TONIGHT CBS NEWS ◎2

94.

THE NEW YORK TIMES, FRIDAY, MARCH 15, 1974

For 144 years, the hands that were good enough to sew our country's flags were not considered worthy to cast a ballot.

From 1776 to 1920, women had no say in government.

Betsy Ross was not allowed to vote. Neither was Dolly Madison. Or Martha Washington.

Or even Barbara Frietchie ("Shoot, if you must, this old gray head, but spare your country's flag," she said).

But voting wasn't the half of it.

Women were expected to keep their political opinions to themselves.

In one state, a man could legally beat his wife whenever he thought she needed it, provided the stick he used was no thicker than the local judge's thumb.

Women didn't win the right to vote until 1920. And things have been changing ever since.

Struggles like this still grip our attention.

So, as we approach our Bicentennial, we look behind us...to see how we got to where we are today.

CBS is doing just that.

In an exciting series of broadcasts entitled, appropriately enough, "The American Parade." And sponsored by Eaton Corporation.

The parade will be led by "We the Women," which will trace America's continuing — and sometimes bitter — struggle for women's equal rights.

"We the Women" will be followed by a dozen other Bicentennial perspectives on the Presidency, the Industrial Revolution, Slavery, the Armed Forces, the Winning of the West, Congress, Labor, and other aspects of our common heritage.

Next will be "Mr. President," which takes us from George Washington to Teddy Roosevelt, the first President of the 20th Century.

It will be followed by "The 34th Star." It will tell the story of Kansas, the 34th star in the Union flag — how it grew

from buffalo prairie through the coming of the railroad, the Indian and Civil Wars, the coming of the locusts, and the growth of cities.

In producing this series, CBS News thus takes a thematic, rather than a chronological approach to history, and allows it to be seen from a variety of new and different perspectives.

It is safe to say you and your family will learn a lot about America that you never knew before.

The American Parade

"We the Women"
The first in the series
premieres Sunday, March 17, 8-9PM.

CBS◎2

95.

Inventive use of a common symbol

The American flag is such a familiar symbol, it almost goes unnoticed. When Dorfsman injected the flag in a series of ads, it was done in such an unexpected way, it forced attention to itself and the ads in which it appeared.

You always said you wanted grandchildren.

And now your darling daughter has presented you with one that doesn't look like you. Or like her.

How do you handle it? What do you say when she tells you she has adopted a black baby instead of having a child of her own?

Ready for that kind of news? There's plenty of it around in this high-pressure, fast-changing, almost unrecognizable world.

Not just adoption across racial lines. Kids without marriage and marriage without kids. Teen-age divorce. Communes. Abortion. New attitudes, new ways, that are tearing up all the old ideas about sex, and love, and life, and family.

Bewildering, alien, frightening changes arrive faster and more unlooked-for every day. Especially in the big cities, where everything seems to happen first, change faster, and come harder.

How do you deal with it?

First of all, you've got to know what's going on. You can handle almost anything, but no surprises, please.

That's our job. The CBS Owned television stations in the big cities where the changes start. New York, Los Angeles, Chicago, Philadelphia, St. Louis. Digging into what's happening. Holding it up to the light. Examining it. Trying to see if it makes sense.

Our stations broadcast more than 800 hours a year of this kind of public affairs programs. Programs designed to eliminate some of the surprises. To cushion the shock of change.

Like the recent fifteen-part series in which our Chicago station probed today's marriage modes, so wedlock at 16 and divorce at 19 won't come as such a mystery.

Or a program our St. Louis station did on "VD and the Kid Next Door" that underscored one particularly worrisome aspect of changing times—VD, once considered an "adult" disease, and now most virulent among teen-agers.

An inquiry into the alienated lifestyles among today's youth called "Tomorrow's People"—which just won two local Emmys for our New York station—was designed to make it somewhat understandable when a youngster with all the promise in the world decides to chuck it and move into a commune.

A program called "V," in which our Philadelphia station showed one group of young activists actually working inside the system to change it. Successfully.

And what happens when daughter brings home a new, adopted, bouncing black baby—explored by our Los Angeles station in a program called "More Special Than Others," designed to ease the shock for grandpa.

So it won't come as a bolt from the blue. For him. Or his neighbors.

Change. You can see it coming on The Five CBS●Stations

96.

<u>Daring</u>
In an era of social revolution, CBS initiated a series of programs that spoke out about some traumatic problems facing the nation: the epidemic of divorce, school drop-outs, teen-age pregnancy, the spread of venereal disease, the breakup of families, babies born out-of-wedlock, and interracial adoption.

The plot to inform the people

Huddled in the empty vastness of San Francisco's Cow Palace are some of the most experienced, knowledgeable and expert journalists in television. When this picture was taken some 10 months ago they were formulating their strategy and tactics for the big day—July 13—when this huge auditorium will explode with a smoke-filled mass of banner-waving Republicans gathered in national convention to select their candidate for the next President of the United States.

The seated figure in the foreground is immediately recognizable to many millions of Americans who watch THE CBS EVENING NEWS WITH WALTER CRONKITE. They know him as one of television's most distinguished reporters who has tracked down and come back with some of the biggest stories of the past two decades…who does his own leg-work and meticulously gathers the facts and figures… who has covered every national convention and major election since 1952.

For the past four years Cronkite and his colleagues' have been plotting the coverage of the great political events of 1964. They have delved into the history of Presidential candidates, primary elections, party platforms, election campaigns and regional voting patterns until they know them virtually by heart. They form the nucleus of the CBS News Election Unit, part of a nationwide coordinated news organization of some 500 correspondents, reporters, political analysts and public opinion experts. In the weeks and months ahead they will present the most complete, accurate and informative pictures of the Presidential election process available to the television audience. If the scene above seems hushed and mysterious—wait till the political fireworks erupt on your screen in July. **●CBS News**

*(clockwise) CBS News Correspondent Walter Cronkite; CBS News Election Unit Editorial Director Bill Eames, Production Director Robert Wussler, Executive Producer Bill Leonard; CBS News Executive Producer Don Hewitt.

97.

Dramatic
There are more direct ways to tell the public that CBS will cover the presidential nominating conventions. But this mysterious photo of Walter Cronkite and CBS reporters seated in an empty convention hall planning their presentation, promised that the broadcasts would be comprehensive and memorable.

THE NEW YORK TIMES, WEDNESDAY, AUGUST 19, 1964

Trout.
Mudd.

What's in a name?

CBS News Correspondents Robert Trout and Roger Mudd will soon be perched 50 feet in the air in a glass-enclosed booth with an all-encompassing view of the Democratic Convention in Atlantic City. Trout and Mudd are a brand-new team with one of the most challenging assignments in television. They will be the anchormen for CBS News convention coverage, and, as a current saying has it, "With names like that, they'd better be good."

They are.

In teaming Trout and Mudd, CBS News combines the wisdom and experience of one of the most respected pros in the business with the wit and fresh insight of a poised young correspondent who has already made his mark. Trout, known as "The Iron Man of Broadcasting," has covered every political convention since 1936. Mudd recently gained national prominence when

his 67-day vigil on the steps of the Capitol, reporting the civil rights debate, was hailed as a landmark in television journalism.

Eric Sevareid—with his peerless ability to assess the issues and the issues behind the issues—will again play a key role. Stationed on the convention floor will be Harry Reasoner, Martin Agronsky, Mike Wallace and Charles Kuralt, whose objective, forthright reports are consistently refreshing and to the point. They are all part of a crack CBS News convention team set to bring you penetrating, comprehensive coverage of one of the major television events of the year.

And behind these names, this one: CBS News—broadcasting's most experienced news-gathering organization, dedicated to providing definitive answers to some of the most provocative questions of our time.

See for yourself
Starting Monday, August 24
Ⓒ CBS NEWS

98.

THE NEW YORK TIMES, MONDAY, AUGUST 24, 1964

Be there when the brand-new team of Robert Trout and Roger Mudd swings into action as anchormen for CBS News coverage of the Democratic Convention in Atlantic City. Together with top political analyst Eric Sevareid and a crack CBS News convention team, Robert Trout and Roger Mudd will bring a bright, bold point of view to one of the year's most important television events.

Eric Sevareid keeps you abreast of convention issues with his astute analyses. Harry Reasoner offers sage observations from the convention floor. Martin Agronsky, Charles Kuralt, Mike Wallace blanket the delegations from Alabama to the Virgin Islands. Charles von Fremd, Neil Strawser, Lew Wood, Paul Niven, Dave Dugan report convention news wherever it occurs in Atlantic City. Hughes Rudd patrols the Boardwalk before Convention Hall with walkie-talkie and wireless camera. Stanley Levey is the first news correspondent assigned to cover the labor forces and their influence on the convention. Dan Rather travels with President Johnson wherever he is during the convention. Bill Stout covers fast-breaking events direct from the speaker's platform.

See for yourself
Starting Tonight at 7 on CBS Ⓒ 2

99.

Promoting the news team
During the 1964 presidential nominating conventions,
NBC's Huntley-Brinkley team was running away with the ratings. In an attempt
to win its share of the audience, CBS created a new anchor team, Robert Trout and Roger Mudd.
Dorfsman explored a number of techniques to call attention to the new team
and to CBS coverage of the conventions and election returns.

Cronkite
Sevareid
Moyers
Mudd
Rather
Dean
Schieffer
Wallace
Morton
Kuralt
Rooney
...and more

With a team like this, what more is there to say?

The Republican
National Convention
Gavel-to-Gavel Coverage
Begins Today
11:30am & 7:30pm

The quality of the entire CBS News team
is the most persuasive reason there
is for joining us as the Republicans meet.
It is, after all, the reason that prompted
Americans to spend more time watching
CBS News during the Democratic
Convention than any other television source.

CBS NEWS ◎2

100.

101.

98. The purpose of this ad was to introduce the new anchor team, and to hyphenate the duo in listeners' minds as solidly as Huntley-Brinkley. The ad also played up the amusing combination of names.

99. The whole CBS news team was presented in this ad, with special attention to anchor-men, Trout and Mudd, and veteran analyst Eric Sevareid. The multiple photos, in close-ups and long shots, recreated the visual excitement of the TV screen.

100. Dorfsman never stays married to a single technique; he'll try anything to stir up interest and readership. Here he resorted to the irresistible cartoon approach, parodying the convention as a horse race.

101. An almost all-type ad. The CBS News Team was lined up like an all-star roster of players in a sports event.

"Nothing replaces two feet in motion"

The man who "wrote the book" on convention coverage

...Not even the dazzling technical machinery of electronic journalism. It is an old axiom that no machine can replace the leg-man with a nose for news—the great reporter who can track down, smell out, and come up with the big story... whose contacts cut across politics, business, the arts and sciences...who knows where to go for the inside story.

Or more precisely, Walter Cronkite. When you see him on his evening news broadcast he is sitting at a desk describing, for example, a missile launching or interviewing a political hopeful. But by that time he has already visited every tracking station in the Western Hemisphere or traveled throughout the home state of the man he is interviewing. With the burning curiosity of a natural-born reporter,

he refuses to rely alone on wire service bulletins or the reports of correspondents in the field.

In the three decades he has been a practicing journalist, Walter Cronkite has covered more of the earth's surface than any other newsman in television. As a distinguished critic once wrote of him "Viewers can see and hear every night a face and voice that have guided them through an incredible diversity of experiences, from outer space to underwater, from chats with presidents to exchanges with physicists. It is hard to imagine a cozier mentor than this excellent reporter...with the inexhaustible vitality and the temperamental balance that makes Republicans and Democrats alike find him sympathetic. You don't worry

about what Cronkite thinks. You just sort of trust him."

And there is good reason for such trust. Cronkite brings to his daily reporting a background of research, knowledge and first-hand experience unique in television journalism. It provides the kind of insight and illumination that make his coverage of the Presidential primaries, the national conventions, and the election required viewing.

In short, Walter Cronkite is one of the reasons why the American people are turning more and more to CBS News for the reporting of major events in an election year as they did in the first test of strength in the New Hampshire primary...As for those feet on the desk, don't be misled. He's just recharging his batteries. ⊙ CBS News

Actually, it looks more like an encyclopedia—and Walter Cronkite is still writing it.

It began with the 1952 conventions. For months in advance Cronkite kept filling a notebook with facts and figures on the political situation: shorthand biographies of the candidates, state and regional voting patterns, public comments by key politicians, summaries of major issues that would shape the party platforms.

Some of it came out of books and newspapers (he's a voracious reader). But most of it was the product of old-fashioned leg-work in the great journalistic tradition. During his years as a Washington correspondent he had interviewed most of the leading political figures and built up a vast circle of valuable sources in government and the two-party machinery.

By the time he was anchored down in CBS News' convention studio, most of the notebook's contents were etched in his memory. As he reported the convention's proceedings, and subsequently the election returns, this arsenal of facts enabled him to provide the kind of coverage that, according to The New York Times "...resulted in a landslide victory for the Columbia Broadcasting System."

By 1956 the number of notebooks had tripled. They were now fortified with facts Cronkite gleaned from covering the off-year Congressional and gubernatorial elections. Commenting on television's 1956 convention coverage, Time stated "CBS veteran Walter Cronkite, working his familiar anchor spot, gave the most informed, alert and lucid commentary." At the 1960 conventions The Washington Post asked and answered its own ques-

tion: "What is an anchor man? ...As far as TV goes, one definition could consist of two words—Walter Cronkite."

But perhaps the most significant tribute to his abilities can be found in the comments of his fellow journalists: "Walter's the hardest worker in the business...he's a pro... he does his homework...he cares."

This kind of careful, energetic, creative reporting produces the vital information and understanding Americans need most in an election year to make an intelligent choice among the candidates who seek their votes. It is the kind of information they have been getting not only from Walter Cronkite, but the entire CBS News organization spread out across the nation to cover the unfolding political drama of 1964. In short, it explains why for major news events more and more Americans are turning to ⊙ CBS News

BUY TIME

This ad is presented in the public interest by ⊙ CBS News

As a cub reporter Walter Cronkite was always there with the big story.

He hasn't changed a bit!

It was a routine afternoon in a press-service bureau in Dallas—March 18, 1937. Suddenly a teletype machine began to tap out the fragmentary report of a school explosion in tiny New London, Texas. At the bureau a young reporter noted the bulletin and, without consulting anyone, took off for the scene of the explosion—150 miles away. Three hours later he was picking his way through the rubble of a major disaster: exploding gas had killed 427 children and teachers. He was the first press-service reporter on the scene.

This was Walter Cronkite's first big story. Today, 27 years later, he is involved in covering the biggest stories of an election year: the primaries, the conventions, the campaign, and the Election returns.

In the years between, Cronkite has never stopped going after the big story. He was first among war correspondents to fly on a bombing mission over Germany. He covered the first landing on Normandy beach. He reported the Nuremberg trials. The first television news broadcast to span the U.S. was his report on the Japanese Peace Conference from San Francisco in 1952. He accompanied Presidents Eisenhower and Kennedy on their state visits abroad. His reporting of the first American orbital flight in 1962 was a milestone in television journalism. (After greeting her son, Mrs. Glenn said there was one celebrity she was dying to meet, Walter Cronkite.) As CBS News anchor man, he has been the only television reporter to cover every Presidential and every off-year election since 1952.

In sum, Walter Cronkite combines a rare knack for anticipating fast-breaking news with an authority that inevitably thrusts him into the center of the great events of our times. These qualities stem in part from an incredibly wide range of sources acquired over a generation of leg-work; in part from meticulous research; and in part from an insatiable curiosity about people and places.

This year CBS News will fuse these remarkable resources with the efforts of an Election Unit which for 17 months has been preparing the most comprehensive coverage of primaries, conventions and elections ever undertaken for television. With the support of this unprecedented news-gathering organization, Walter Cronkite will again provide the kind of lucid information and commentary that explains why more and more people are turning to CBS News for the reporting of major events. You can pick up the thread of the big election-year story on his broadcast tonight. ⊙ CBS News

102.-110.

Presenting a national institution
In his time, Walter Cronkite was the #1 CBS newsman and the paragon of a professional news broadcaster. He radiated intelligence, integrity and authority. But to be successful on television also required a warm rapport with the audience. In a series of ads designed to popularize Cronkite, Dorfsman balanced the image of the authoritative figure with that of a down-to-earth, accessible human being.

Number 1

The CBS Evening News with Walter Cronkite is the number one network news broadcast. But it's no one man (or even two-man) operation. Walter's up front. Behind him is broadcasting's most experienced news organization. Beside him is a staff of correspondents without equal. And in front of him are millions of viewers. "That's the way it is," tonight and every weeknight at ⊙CBS NEWS

Based on National Nielsen Television Index average audience for the four weeks ending November 21. Subject to qualifications available on request

1952 "Television's coverage of the election returns... resulted in a landslide victory for the Columbia Broadcasting System." THE NEW YORK TIMES

1954 "CBS, which went into this election much more thoroughly than anyone else, did a superb job." NEW YORK HERALD TRIBUNE

1956 "So again we string along with Walter Cronkite, the CBS-TV anchor man. Cronkite is a calm, un-panicky, reserved type." NEW YORK JOURNAL AMERICAN

1958 "On television it was once again the Columbia Broadcasting System that had the best organized... method of reporting." THE NEW YORK TIMES

1960 "What is an anchor man?...as far as TV goes, one definition could consist of two words — Walter Cronkite." WASHINGTON POST

1962 "When it comes to election coverage, Walter Cronkite is the winner and still champion..." PITTSBURGH POST-GAZETTE

1964 Walter Cronkite extends his record run as the only television reporter to cover every convention and election since 1952. Joined by fellow CBS News Correspondents Eric Sevareid and Harry Reasoner, and backed by television's most experienced news-gathering organization, he's the man to watch at the Republican National Convention in San Francisco beginning tomorrow. ⊙CBS NEWS

How Walter Cronkite got to San Francisco

By driving himself...relentlessly.

He's headed for an unprecedented seventh assignment as a television election year anchorman because he refuses to stay on the sidelines of a big story. He pursues it. Nails it down. Follows through when others might leave well enough alone. It's reflected in a track record unequaled in the annals of broadcast reporting.

Take his coverage, for example, of auto racing's Grand Prix of Endurance at Sebring a few years ago. A noted racing enthusiast, he served in a dual capacity that day—as daredevil driver for a grueling three-and-one-half hours behind the wheel of his own car, and as knowledgeable reporter for the remainder of the 12-hour event. He spent his spare time with the men in the pits.

But it is not unusual for Walter Cronkite to participate in the events he reports. As a war correspondent he flew on one of the first B-17 raids over Germany when he might have covered the story with bombs—feet on the ground. Nor was he known for playing it safe in the North Atlantic, North Africa, on a Normandy beachhead, parachuting into Holland, not in the Battle of the Bulge. More recently, when a swivel chair would have afforded a passable vantage point for a story, he was hoisted by helicopter to a submarine and transferred by breeches-chair to a destroyer. To track down another story he crossed 138 miles of shifting polar ice. For still another he achieved weightlessness in a special airplane maneuver for astronauts.

This is the kind of "driving" which has delivered Walter Cronkite to San Francisco. Teamed with CBS News Correspondents Eric Sevareid and Harry Reasoner, political consultants H. Mende Alcorn, Louis Harris and Theodore H. White, he will present television's most authoritative coverage of the candidates, strategies and rapidly accelerating events at the Republican and Democratic National Conventions, and during the subsequent campaigns and Election.

Walter Cronkite has been in the driver's seat for us at every convention and election since 1952. There's nothing pedestrian about his methods, but we believe he would have walked to San Francisco if it were the only way to get there. ⊙CBS News

Re-elect the Most Trusted Man in America

You'll have three viewing choices on Election Night. You can watch us. You can watch them. Or you can even watch that other one.

A good reason for watching us is because we've got a man on our slate who was recently voted the most trusted American in public life:

Walter Cronkite. *The most trusted American in public life.*

Surprising, but not really that much. Not when you consider that for the last five years more households have been tuned to Walter than any other television newsman? If they didn't trust him so much, they wouldn't turn to him so much.

Consider what *Time* magazine said about him:"...the single most convincing figure in television news."

And what the *Chicago Daily News* said about the way Walter and CBS News covered the Democratic convention?"Once again, as has so often been the case in recent years, CBS' Walter Cronkite did the finest job of convention coverage."

But Walter Cronkite, lest we forget, only heads the ticket.

We've got similar endorsements from the six-man team for Roger Mudd, who'll be covering the South, Mike Wallace, the East, John Hart, the West, Dan Rather, the Midwest. And Eric Sevareid, who'll be doing what he's been doing for us since 1948, to wit, converting everything, and serving up his analyses with his inimitable brand of wry.

On Election Night you have another choice to make. Vote straight CBS News. Re-elect Walter Cronkite.

The man of the people.

In New York, Jim Jensen will anchor tri-state reports with Ralph Penza, Political Editor. Jerome Wilson and Science Editor Earl Ubell, the last ten minutes of each half hour. Remote news units will also report live from the campaign headquarters of Bella Abzug and Priscilla Ryan. A special Election Day poll will allow WCBS-TV to gauge local voting patterns early in the evening.

CBS NEWS: ELECTION '72 STARTING 6:30 PM,⊙2

Children's programming is so important, we're putting our best man on it.

⊙CBS⊙

89

During an interview with CBS News Far Eastern Correspondent Peter Kalischer, Mme. Nhu first used her widely-publicized term "barbecues" in referring to the burning of Buddhist priests. It was broadcast on August 1.

STRONG WORDS

CBS News was the only news organization in broadcasting to provide continuous "live" coverage of the afternoon proceedings of the March on Washington on August 28 and to carry "live" the "I Have A Dream" speech by the Rev. Martin Luther King. In addition to the three consecutive hours of afternoon coverage a special hour-long news summary of the event was broadcast during prime evening time the same night.

STRONG FEELINGS(I)

On September 2 in an exclusive interview with Walter Cronkite, President Kennedy first stated publicly that the anti-Communist war in South Vietnam could not be won unless the Vietnamese government became more responsive to the people's will.

STRONG POSITION

Learning that a French magazine editor had taken clandestine films inside Red China showing the conditions under which the people lived, CBS News' Hong Kong Correspondent Bernard Kalb notified New York headquarters where arrangements were made to broadcast the film on September 11.

STRONG-HOLD

On September 13 in a special half-hour interview with Walter Cronkite, the public received its first rounded political portrait of Senator Barry Goldwater since he became a front-runner for the Presidential nomination.

STRONG POSSIBILITY

On September 18 Teamster leader James Hoffa came out in support of Gov. Nelson Rockefeller's Presidential candidacy in an exclusive interview with Stanley Levey, CBS News business, labor and economic correspondent. It was broadcast on the CBS MORNING NEWS WITH MIKE WALLACE.

STRONG NUDGE

On September 18 CBS REPORTS presented a documentary report on the conflict between Leander Perez, political boss of Plaquemines Parish in Louisiana, and the Roman Catholic Church over the issues of parochial school integration.

STRONG FEELINGS(II)

STRONG ARM

For a total of 9 hours and 42 minutes of which more than 6 hours represented "live" coverage, the CBS Television Network carried the Valachi hearings which started on September 27 before the Senate Investigations Subcommittee in Washington. It was the only network to provide such extended coverage.

STRONG HOPES

CBS News Moscow Correspondent Stuart Novins obtained a rare and exclusive interview in Budapest with Janos Kadar, in which the Hungarian satellite ruler expressed eagerness that full diplomatic relations would be resumed between Hungary and the United States. The interview was broadcast on October 4.

STRONG GIRL

As hurricane Flora ravaged the Haiti mainland, causing destruction and death to more than 4000 people, CBS News Correspondent Bernard Eismann flew into the jungles of Haiti to film the event. It was broadcast that same night (October 6) on the SUNDAY NIGHT NEWS.

STRONG ADVICE

On October 10 CBS News Correspondent Walter Cronkite interviewed former President Dwight D. Eisenhower at his farm in Gettysburg. General Eisenhower stated publicly for the first time that he was in favor of withdrawing the bulk of United States troops from Europe.

STRONG FAITH

In a transatlantic TOWN MEETING OF THE WORLD broadcast via the communications satellite, Telstar II, Protestant and Catholic clergymen in London, Rome, and Princeton, New Jersey met in a face-to-face discussion of the forces working for Christian unity. The broadcast was carried "live" over the CBS Television Network at 8:30 am EST on October 15 and repeated on tape for nighttime audiences the following day at 7:30 pm.

STRONG-MINDED

In the first interview granted to television since hostilities broke out between Algeria and Morocco, President Ahmed Ben Bella in Algiers told CBS News Correspondent Paul Niven that his troops would continue to fight until the Moroccans pulled back to their starting positions. The interview was broadcast on FACE THE NATION on October 27.

STRONG MEDICINE

At 10:30 pm EST Sunday night, November 3, a CBS NEWS EXTRA presented the first films of the insurrection which overturned the South Vietnam government the previous Friday night, showing the occupation of the Presidential Palace and the street fighting. Correspondent Peter Kalischer and CBS News cameraman Juergen Neumann moved into the palace with the troops as they occupied it under fire. The broadcast was acclaimed by the *New York World Telegram & Sun* as "TV journalism at its best."

STRONG TEAM

The real strength of a news organization is its ability to uncover and illuminate the events and forces that shape our lives. As shown above, it may be a struggle for power or a statement of policy; an act of man or of nature. The point is to know where to look for it and be there when it happens; to ask the key question that will yield the news-making answer. This takes a lot of doing. More to the point it takes a world-wide organization of correspondents, cameramen, producers and editors who have established over the years an unequaled reputation for accuracy, enterprise and insight—for being at the right place at the right time with the right information. When all is said and done, this is what produces "TV journalism at its best."

⬤CBS NEWS

111.

Verbal and visual devices

All components work together in this ad designed to promote the CBS News Team.
The provocative two-word captions coupled with familiar faces induce readership. The capsule
news stories demonstrate the broad scope of CBS news coverage. And the repetition
of the word "strong" leads conclusively to "strong team."

112.

Counter-attack

To counter negative criticism of TV as 'mindless' and a 'time-waster,' this ad bombarded readers with a graphic account of all the news and information programs offered by CBS in a single week. Though the ad is merely a listing of the week's schedule, the full page spread, crammed with pictures and summaries of the programs, magnified the effort enormously.

Segregation: Northern-Style
CBS Reports 7:30 Tonight ◉2

CBS Reports:

For an entire generation Germany has been among our closest allies. Now there are signs that the Fatherland may be charting a more independent course. Tonight, CBS Reports explores the unique combination of national characteristics which has helped make the Germans some of our best new friends and their own worst enemies. From gemütlichkeit to hidebound traditionalism, here is a close look at what is happening in Germany today.

10 pm In Color CBS News ◉2

THE GREAT AMERICAN FUNERAL

Tonight's broadcast by CBS Reports is the result of six months' research on the most widely discussed issue of American funeral practices. Numerous participants in the controversy will present their views, including funeral directors, clergymen, and manufacturers of funeral equipment. Among those who will appear is Jessica Mitford, author of the current best-seller, "The American Way of Death." CBS News Correspondent Robert Trout will be the reporter.

CBS REPORTS TONIGHT
7:30 TO 8:30 PM CBS ◉2

The towering figure of Charles de Gaulle whose personal vision of France's destiny has placed him in the forefront of world leadership is the subject of an unprecedented two-part biographical study presented tonight and one week from tonight on CBS REPORTS.

Tonight's broadcast examines in detail, and in his own words, the personality, philosophy, and image of the man who as head of the Free French rallied a defeated and humiliated nation and, after a series of paralyzing postwar governments, finally raised it to a position of major influence in world affairs.

In a series of rare film sequences garnered from French, British, German and American archives, de Gaulle is seen in his early days as a maverick army officer; a gifted specialist in armored warfare; a fugitive from the Vichy Government which condemned him to death; a wartime associate of President Roosevelt and Prime Minister Churchill; and a wildly acclaimed hero returning to his liberated countrymen.

Part II of the report a week from tonight, entitled "De Gaulle: The Challenge," examines the current international policies of the

French leader and their implications for the other nations of the Free World. CBS News Correspondent Charles Collingwood, who has covered General de Gaulle's activities since World War II, is the reporter on both broadcasts.

CBS REPORTS:
De Gaulle: ROOTS OF POWER
(Part I) TONIGHT 7:30-8:30
◉2

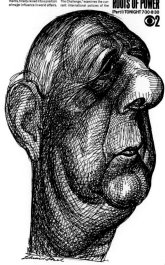

CBS REPORTS TONIGHT 7:30-8:30 CBS ◉9
STORM OVER THE SUPREME COURT

Five distinguished Americans—Archibald MacLeish, Fredric March, Carl Sandburg, Mark Van Doren and Professor Paul Freund of the Harvard Law School—appear tonight in a broadcast that reviews the bitter clashes between the United States Supreme Court and the Executive and Legislative branches since the days of Thomas Jefferson. Reading from some of the Court's key decisions, Messrs. MacLeish, March, Sandburg, and Van Doren reveal the historic role of the Court in the struggle over preserving constitutional guarantees. In an interview with CBS News Correspondent Eric Sevareid, Professor Freund analyzes the changing character of the Supreme Court bench throughout its history. Tonight's broadcast is the first of a two-part series presented by CBS Reports. Part II is scheduled for Wednesday, March 13.

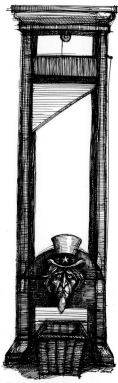

Our Friends, the French

It's difficult to keep a level head about the French... when your oldest ally has become one of your severest critics. Tonight producer-writer Perry Wolff and CBS News Correspondent Eric Sevareid take a provocative look at the differences which have made anti-Americanism the semi-official policy of France. This witty and incisive special broadcast also examines differences Frenchmen are having among themselves. Differences which find the French heart in the eighteenth century and the French mind in the twentieth.

Tonight 10-11 In Color
CBS News ◉2

MURDER AND THE RIGHT TO BEAR ARMS
CBS REPORTS TONIGHT 7:30-8:30 ON ◉2

The Second Amendment to the Constitution, long the subject of conflicting interpretations, has gained increased significance in the wake of last November's tragic events. With pressures mounting for federal regulation of the ownership of firearms, CBS REPORTS tonight examines the law enforcement problems posed by their ready availability. The broadcast includes the views of criminals, police officials, sportsmen and legislators concerning the ownership and use of firearms. It also traces the history of two major crimes in which guns were involved. The reporter is CBS News Correspondent Robert Trout.

CIGARETTES:
A COLLISION OF INTERESTS

The latest developments in the controversy surrounding an $8 billion industry are presented tonight on CBS REPORTS. The viewpoints of tobacco men, advertising and broadcasting officials, and teenagers tempted by the smoking habit will be explored in light of the Surgeon General's recent Report on Smoking and Health. Focusing upon the Federal Trade Commission's proposal to label cigarette packages and advertising with a health warning, the broadcast will present George V. Allen, President of The Tobacco Institute, Governor LeRoy Collins, President of the National Association of Broadcasters, and Surgeon General Luther L. Terry. CBS News Correspondent Harry Reasoner will report.
CBS REPORTS, TONIGHT 7:30-8:30 ◉2

THE GAME OF DIRTY POLITICS

Tonight THE TWENTIETH CENTURY examines the political smear and its effect on American Presidential campaigns, past and present. Smear tactics will be described, and illustrated by photographs, political cartoons and posters dating from the late Eighteenth Century. The reporter is CBS News Correspondent Walter Cronkite.

TONIGHT AT 6:00 CBS NEWS ◉2

In a 90-minute assessment of the year's most explosive world events, twelve CBS News correspondents convene tonight before a distinguished audience in New York City. With Eric Sevareid as moderator, the correspondents will analyze the impact of the year's news developments as viewed from their vantage points around the globe. Primary emphasis will be on the shifts in political and military initiative resulting from the Soviet withdrawal from Cuba and the Chinese invasion of India. The correspondents will also examine such major issues as the Common Market; South Vietnam; the nuclear ambitions of President de Gaulle; the possibility of a separate Soviet-East German peace treaty; and the prospects for disarmament.

YEARS OF CRISIS

Winston Burdett (Rome, Geneva) Richard C. Hottelet (United Nations) Bernard Kalb (Southeast Asia) Marvin Kalb (Moscow) Peter Kalischer (Tokyo, South Vietnam) Alexander Kendrick (London) Robert Kleiman (Paris) Charles Kuralt (Latin America) Blaine Littell (Africa) Daniel Schorr (Bonn, Berlin) and David Schoenbrun (Chief Washington Correspondent)
TONIGHT 7:30-9 CBS ◉2
Broadcast simultaneously on the CBS Radio Network

A sense of scale

Dorfsman has a strong predilection for small space ads. He enjoys the challenge of the limited arena. He believes they are sound economically, and he has mastered the art of designing them. The clue to his success is in the magnification of detail and the scale of photos in relation to text. Regardless of the actual dimensions of his ads, fractions of a page (113-122) or full page (123), he invests them with the impact of a billboard.

Trujillo:
PORTRAIT OF A DICTATOR
10-11 TONIGHT CBS⊙CHANNEL 2

Some call him a public benefactor, one of our strongest anti-Communist allies in the Caribbean. Others call him a murderer, a despot whose rule is on the verge of collapse. After months in the Dominican Republic seeking the full story of the Trujillo regime, CBS News correspondent Bill Leonard succeeded in filming a rare interview with the General, reaching the anti-Trujillo underground, and bringing back this hard-hitting, uncensored report on the controversial strongman who has held his country in an iron grip for 30 years. Don't miss the seventh in the series of notable programs on CBS REPORTS.

123.

Print advertising and on-air promotions are created out of the same basic elements—words and pictures. Though television offers the advantages of motion and sound, it also imposes a formidable challenge: television is an instant medium.

With print ads, a reader can turn back, re-read a passage, linger over a picture, even clip the ad as a reminder to tune in a show. Television offers no such options. In on-air promotions you have less than 30 seconds—sometimes as little as ten seconds—to grab the attention of the audience and deliver a message. To be successful, you must first overcome the built-in resistance to commercials by an audience anxious to get on with the entertainment. Then your "interruption" must be so compelling and memorable that it will prompt listeners to act upon it.

In the early days of television, everyone was a pioneer in the medium. Art directors and writers studied film techniques and mimicked Hollywood in creating on-air promotions. Programs were advertised like coming attractions at the movies, with trailers clipped from the shows themselves. But when Dorfsman took over as Art Director for CBS-TV, he was constitutionally incapable of following the established form. He created special dramatizations for CBS television shows. And he saw absolutely no conflict of interest in using television to promote radio shows like "The Jack Benny Show" (128, 129) and "WCBS Newsradio 88 Traffic Reports" (160). He even took the liberty of using television characters, Edith and Archie Bunker, to advertise CBS Newsradio (159).

A wonderful animated cartoon series for CBS Sports came out of Lou's special ability to recognize opportunities, and his inability to waste anything—time, talent or money. Out of the kindness of his heart, Lou had employed a friend—a gifted cartoonist and animator—who was in need of a job. Exceptional as the man's talents were, there was simply no work for him in the art department. Uncomfortable about paying out a salary for no work, Lou invented a project; he turned the man loose to produce some animated cartoons to promote CBS Sports. The resulting series (143, 144) was delightfully humorous and successful.

Dorfsman enjoyed the challenge of TV's time limitations as much as the extra dimensions of animation and sound. He experimented with a variety of techniques—sometimes with primitive still frames; sometimes he contrived magical animated sequences. His promos for TV and radio shows were small gems; always at least as entertaining as the programs they advertised...and often more so.

124. _DENNIS THE MENACE_

VIDEO:
Footage of wall of building. Close-up of sling shot poised for firing. Pellet is fired; building collapses.

AUDIO:
Voice over: "You'll collapse with laughter with 'Dennis the Menace;' Sunday evening on the CBS Television Network."

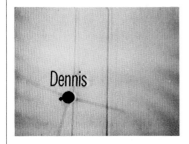

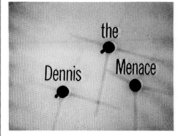

125. _DENNIS THE MENACE_

VIDEO:
Three rubber-tipped darts whizz by and hit wall of building. Fourth dart hits man in the temple.

AUDIO:
(Voice over paced to coincide with dart's landings): "Something… always… happens… on 'Dennis the Menace;' Sunday evening on the CBS Television Network."

126. _GUNSMOKE_

VIDEO:
Close-up of bullets ripping through black shapes. Camera pulls back to reveal word GUNSMOKE, riddled with bullet holes.

AUDIO:
(Sound of gunfire in background.) Voice over: "Saturday night on the CBS Television Network."

127. _GUNSMOKE_

VIDEO:
Still frame of pistol, badge and western hat. Hand reaches in and removes each prop one at a time. When hat is lifted, title GUNSMOKE is revealed.

AUDIO:
(Sound of gunfire in background.) Voice over: "Television's most popular program; Saturday night on the CBS Television Network."

128. _THE JACK BENNY SHOW_

VIDEO:
Close-up of hand on neck of violin. After a few bars of music, another hand reaches in and clamps down on playing hand.

AUDIO:
(Jack Benny's theme, _Love in Bloom_, played in his typical scratchy style.) Voice over: "Join television's greatest vio… (hand interrupts playing)… comedian; Sundays on the CBS Television Network."

129. _THE JACK BENNY SHOW_

VIDEO:
Close-up of glass vase. After a few bars of music the vase shatters.

AUDIO:
(_Love in Bloom_, Jack Benny's theme, played in his typical scratchy style, interrupted by sound of shattered vase.) Voice over: "Well, maybe he won't play,… Sunday night on the CBS Television Network."

130. _THE ED SULLIVAN SHOW_

VIDEO:
A series of frames showing lightning, a volcano erupting, a stampede of elephants, a crowd in an amphitheatre.

AUDIO:
Ed Sullivan's voice: "A really big shoe." Voice over: "Sunday on the CBS Television Network."

131. _THE ED SULLIVAN SHOW_

VIDEO:
Ed Sullivan, as master of ceremonies.

AUDIO:
Ed Sullivan's voice: "From Broadway, Hollywood and Europe — singers, dancers, comedians, circus stars, sports greats — a really big shoe." Voice over: "Sunday night on the CBS Television Network."

133. _I'VE GOT A SECRET_

VIDEO:
Close-up of man in derby hat with generous head of hair. He lifts hat (hair goes with it) to reveal an almost bald head.

AUDIO:
Voice over: "Laughs and surprises on 'I've Got a Secret,' Wednesday on the CBS Television Network."

135. _HENNESSEY_

VIDEO:
Close-up of Navy doctor checking patient's blood pressure. With each pump, his whole body levitates higher and higher off the ground.

AUDIO:
(Sound of air wheezing through pump.) Voice over: "The pressures of life as a Navy doctor lead to lively situations on 'Hennessey,' Monday on the CBS Television Network."

132. _ROUTE 66_

VIDEO:
Headlights of car pick up highway signs flashing by rapidly to indicate speed of car. Final frame holds on sign reading: Route 66.

AUDIO:
(Sounds of screeching tires in background.) Voice over: "Gripping adventure on the highway; Friday night on the CBS Television Network."

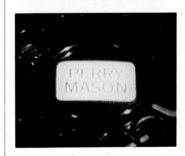

136. _FATHER KNOWS BEST_

VIDEO:
Photos of cast emerge from nest of cubes. Title comes up, nudges father's cube and rotates it to reveal a second photo of father with puzzled expression.

AUDIO:
Voice over: "Meet the Anderson family, where father knows best… usually; Tuesdays on the CBS Television Network."

134. _PERRY MASON_

VIDEO:
Close-up of telephone. Segue to hand disconnecting phone.

AUDIO:
Sound of phone ringing ceases when plug is pulled. Voice over: "Another strange case for 'Perry Mason.' Mondays on the CBS Television Network."

137. *WHAT'S MY LINE?*

VIDEO:
Series of portraits illustrating rich man, poor man, beggarman, thief, doctor, lawyer and Indian chief.

AUDIO:
Voice over: "Rich man, poor man, beggarman, thief…no telling who you'll find on 'What's My Line?' Sunday on the CBS Television Network."

140. *CANDID CAMERA*

VIDEO:
Pair of hands holding newspaper with photo of Allen Funt under headline, WINDOW SHADES DOWN. *Camera pokes through photo from behind.*

AUDIO:
Voice over: "The story behind this headline is comedy…captured by the candid camera; Sunday on the CBS Television Network."

138. *PETE AND GLADYS*

VIDEO:
Camera dollies in on welcome mat outside door. Door opens a crack and mat is yanked inside.

AUDIO:
Sound of footsteps. Voice over: "You'll find Pete and Gladys friendly…(mat yanked inside)…neighbors, Mondays on the CBS Television Network."

142. *I'VE GOT A SECRET*

VIDEO:
Man whispers to another man, "I'VE GOT A SECRET." Words increase in size as voice increases in volume. Second man wiggles finger in injured ear.

AUDIO:
Voice over: "'I've Got a Secret,' Wednesday on the CBS Television Network."

141. *CANDID CAMERA*

VIDEO:
Close-up of Medieval suit of armor. Visor lifts and camera pokes out.

AUDIO:
Voice over: "You never know where you'll find the candid camera, except here, Sundays on the CBS Television Network."

139. *DOBIE GILLIS*

VIDEO:
A huge ice cream sundae is rapidly reduced in size as two spoons alternately whittle away at it and reveal the title, DOBIE GILLIS.

AUDIO:
Voice over: "Dig those teenage appetites…for romance; Tuesdays on the CBS Television Network."

All the preceding 10-second black and white spots signed off with the CBS logo, with no additional typography.

143. *CBS SPORTS*

VIDEO:
Ball bounces into view from top of screen. Words appear in synch with bouncing ball: Keep Your Eye on the Ball. CBS SPORTS

AUDIO:
Marching music.

144. *CBS SPORTS*

One of a series of cartoons, drawn and animated by Len Glasser, offered to all CBS Network stations to promote CBS coverage of basketball, baseball, tennis, golf, and football events. Local station announcers provided live tune-in information specific to their areas.

VIDEO:
Little guy receives football, runs down the field with it. Opponent cuts him off and mimes gorilla approaching from behind. Gorilla pounces on little guy, ball pops out of his hands into arms of opponent who runs off with it.

AUDIO:
Stadium noises and grunts of players.

145. *CBS SPORTS*

VIDEO:
(Drawings and animation by Len Glasser) Man in his living room watching football game on TV. Suddenly football comes bouncing through screen. Man innocently catches it; football team tackles him.

AUDIO:
Grunts of players.

146. *CBS SPORTS*

VIDEO:
Still photos of referee's signals, presented in quick cuts. Words SUPER and BOWL enter screen from opposite sides and converge to read SUPERBOWL.

AUDIO:
Sounds of marching band, whistle blowing, and crowd.

147.   *CBS INSTITUTIONAL*

VIDEO:
(Created by R. O. Blechman) People riding up a store escalator. Little girl in tattered clothing waits in line to see Santa Claus. At her turn, she whispers in his ear. Final frame: she walks away wearing Santa's coat.

AUDIO:
Christmas music.

148.   *CBS INSTITUTIONAL*

VIDEO:
(Designed by R. O. Blechman) Birds singing in tree; snowflakes falling. Woodsman appears with saw. Alarmed, birds stop singing. Woodsman pulls out bow and starts playing on saw. Birds resume singing.

AUDIO:
God Rest Ye Merry Gentleman, *played on violin. Birds chirp along.*

149.   *CBS INSTITUTIONAL*

VIDEO:
(By Ted Andresakes) Close-up of Santa Claus figure skating in circles. Camera pulls back to reveal message cut in ice: Greetings.

AUDIO:
Christmas music.

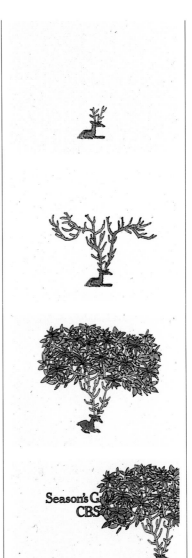

150.   *CBS INSTITUTIONAL*

VIDEO:
(Drawings by Ted Andresakes) Reindeer sitting in snow. Horns start growing larger and larger and evolve into a huge poinsettia. Deer struggles to rise under the weight. Walks away and reveals: Season's Greetings, CBS.

AUDIO:
Christmas music.

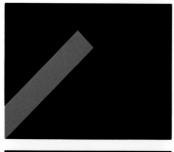

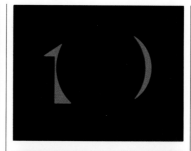

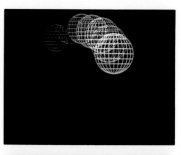

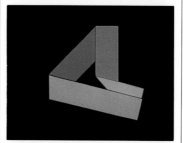

151. *LOGO FOR CHICAGO AFFILIATE*

<u>VIDEO:</u>   <u>NO AUDIO</u>
A blue T, red V and yellow 2, each created out of thin lines of color, overlap each other in successive planes, creating a moiré effect. They move apart to read TV 2 for Chicago affiliate station.

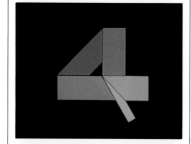

153. *LOGO FOR PHILADELPHIA AFFILIATE*

<u>VIDEO:</u>   <u>NO AUDIO</u>
Starts with black screen. Circular field recedes from center, shrinking in size to reveal the number 10.

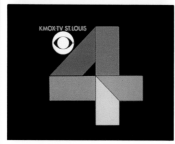

154.   *IN THE NEWS*

<u>VIDEO:</u>   <u>AUDIO:</u>
Globe spins onto screen, changing colors. Globe turns blue; words IN THE NEWS circles globe and then zoom forward to fill screen. Computerized music.

152.   *LOGO FOR ST. LOUIS AFFILIATE*

<u>VIDEO:</u>   <u>NO AUDIO</u>
Animated colored ribbon folds into figure 4 for St. Louis affiliate station. CBS logo emerges from behind.

155. *CBS ELECTION PROMO*

<u>VIDEO:</u>   <u>NO AUDIO</u>
Abstract shapes of black, blue and red merge to form the 1970 election logo; 70 wipes on; stars and stripes wipe over 70.

⊕CBS NEWS CAMPAIGN '72
THE ELECTION YEAR

156. *CBS ELECTION PROMO*

<u>VIDEO:</u>   <u>NO AUDIO</u>
A series of angular lines enter screen from upper right and lower left. They converge at center screen to form the number 72.

157. *CBS NEWS*

<u>VIDEO:</u>   <u>NO AUDIO</u>
Starting with early 1970s, numerals click by as on an odometer until last frame freezes on 21ST CENTURY, a CBS Television News Special, narrated by Walter Cronkite.

ELECTRONIC VIDEO RECORDING

ELECTRONIC VIDEO RECORDING

ELECTRONIC VIDEO RECORDING

ELECTRONIC VIDEO RECORDING

158. *CBS LABS*

<u>VIDEO:</u>   <u>NO AUDIO</u>
Animated line assumes configuration of letters EVR — Electronic Video Recording — followed by a series of rainbow-colored lines that emanate and grow in size to full height of the insignia for CBS Labs.

162.   *CBS NEWSRADIO 88*

In this series of spots, two identical radios are seen side-by-side. One is identified as WCBS NEWSRADIO 88. In each spot, a disaster befalls the "other" radio.

VIDEO:
Knobs pop off.

AUDIO:
Voice over: "Nothing is as good as CBS Newsradio 88."

VIDEO:
Antenna collapses.

AUDIO:
Voice over: "Nothing is as good as CBS Newsradio 88."

159.   *CBS NEWSRADIO*

One of a series featuring Edith and Archie Bunker. In each promo, Archie reads an item aloud from the newspaper. Edith offers a comical innocuous interpretation. Archie responds with typical disgust, "Aw Edith..."

VIDEO:
Edith and Archie in their living room from "All in the Family" series.

AUDIO:
Voice over: "Don't be a dingbat. Get the news and get it right..." (Final frame freezes on local radio call letters.)

160. *CBS NEWSRADIO 88 — HELICOPTER TRAFFIC REPORTS*

VIDEO:
Close-up of nuns seated in station wagon, stuck in traffic. Nun in driver's seat taps resignedly on steering wheel; others gaze heavenward as if for help, then smile at the sight of CBS traffic helicopter.

AUDIO:
Traffic noises mingle with traffic report from car radio announcing tie-ups, followed by sound of helicopter. (Voice Over): "Anyone planning to drive in this town during rush hour...better look for a little help from above. Newsradio 88 has its own traffic helicopter, and we'll give you at least 18 traffic reports during rush hours. Now we're not promising miracles; we're just going to help you get where you're going. Newsradio 88."

161.   *CBS NEWSRADIO 88*

VIDEO:
Close-up of newsdealer. Camera slowly dollies back to reveal he is in his stand surrounded by newspapers and magazines.

AUDIO:
Radio news report in background. Voice over: "There's good news. There's bad news. Sometimes you like what you hear. Sometimes you don't.

No matter. You should know what goes on in the world.

When Sid Garfield wants all the news...the latest news...he turns to someone he knows:

Newsradio 88. Have we got news for you." Background radio sign off: "This is Lou Adler, Newsradio 88."

VIDEO:
Explosion and puff of smoke.

AUDIO:
Voice over: "Nothing is as good as CBS Newsradio 88."

VIDEO:
Line-up of portable radios goes down, domino-fashion.

AUDIO:
Voice over: "Nothing is as good as CBS Newsradio 88."

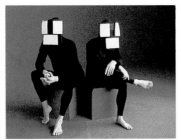

165.   *CBS SPECIAL*

VIDEO:
Title appears on screen. The letter "A" is rocketed out of position in word PRESENTA-TION by a small star which expands into a large one.

AUDIO:
Jazz trumpet.

166.   *CBS CHILDREN'S SPECIAL*

VIDEO:
Title appears on screen. The letter "T" in "PRESENTA-TION" grows into a tree with an owl roosting in it, signifying an educational program.

AUDIO:
Background music.

163.   *CBS CHILDREN'S HOUR*

VIDEO:
(Directed by Dick Loew) Close-up of children putting on theatrical makeup. Final frame: little girl in comedy mask; little boy in tragic mask. Title appears over images.

AUDIO:
Sound of orchestra tuning up. Sound of baton tapping calls orchestra to attention. Orchestra goes silent; children's faces freeze for final frame.

164.   *CBS AFTERNOON PLAYHOUSE*

VIDEO:
(Directed by Dick Loew) Two Mummenschanz mimes wearing cage-like frames over their heads, with pads affixed covering their features, draw a series of facial expressions to represent a range of emotions.

AUDIO:
Light chamber music.

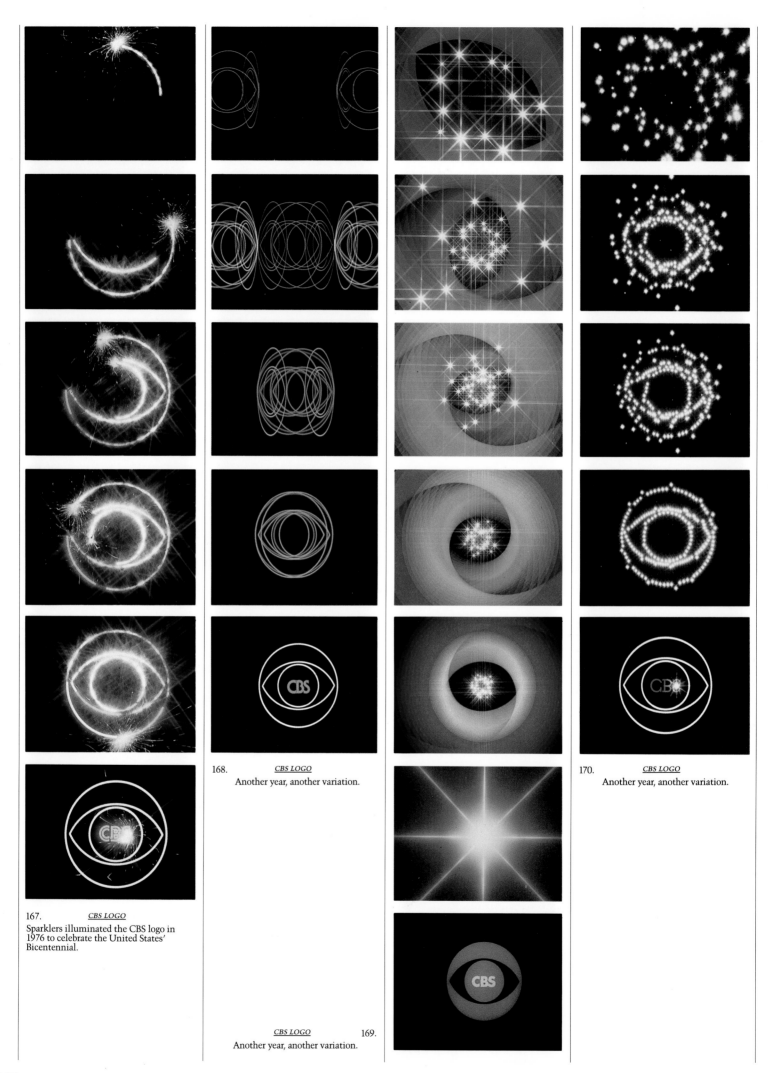

167. *CBS LOGO*
Sparklers illuminated the CBS logo in 1976 to celebrate the United States' Bicentennial.

168. *CBS LOGO*
Another year, another variation.

CBS LOGO 169.
Another year, another variation.

170. *CBS LOGO*
Another year, another variation.

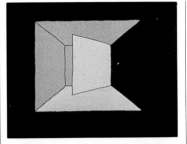

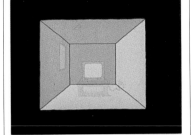

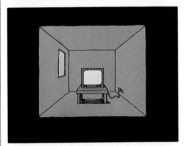

171.   *THE LATE SHOW*

VIDEO:
(Animated cartoon designed by Milton Glaser.) Room unfolds: details of room fade in. A few stars emanate from TV screen, then increase in number, frequency and size until they flood the frame.

AUDIO:
Background music.

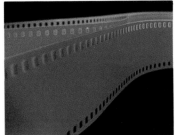

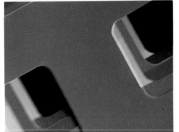

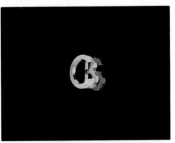

172.   *THE CBS MOVIES*

VIDEO:
From close-up of film strip, camera zooms in on sprockets... through sprocket hole to close-up of spinning film reel which turns into spinning 3-dimensional CBS letters. Title appears on black screen.

AUDIO:
Background music.

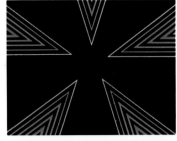

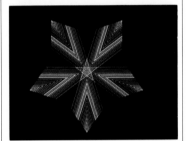

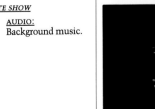

173.   *CBS LATE MOVIE*

VIDEO:
Animated star formation expands, recedes and expands again. Final frame: THE CBS LATE MOVIE, *with colored lines of star rotating behind title.*

AUDIO:
Background music.

174.   *CBS INSTITUTIONAL*

One of a series in which world-record feats were dramatized and compared with CBS's 17-year record as America's number-one network. Other promos in this series included the record-setting chicken-plucker, brick-splitter, face-slappers and one-handed lady chinner.

VIDEO:
Man walking on hands. Background changes to illustrate a variety of terrains.

AUDIO:
(Background of Viennese music.) Voice over: "In 1900, Johann Hurlinger walked on his hands from Vienna to Paris in 55 days. That's an actual world record. But how about this for a record: For 17 years in a row, CBS is America's number-one network!" Handstand Walker (groans): "17 years?"

175.   *CBS TELEVISION*

One of a series created around the theme of a travelling troubadour who tours the United States singing the praises of CBS and its 18-year record as the number-one TV network.

Among the locations visited by the troubadour in this series were a Maine fishing village, a New Orleans Jazz festival, the Midwest wheat belt, a California beach, and a Western rodeo.

VIDEO:
Close-up and panoramic shots of rodeo.

AUDIO:
(Troubadour plays guitar and sings throughout:) For 18 years we're the best, CBS. Who's the best? CBS! We're the best, CBS...."

176.   *CBS NEWS*

<u>VIDEO:</u>
In a series of frames, a pair of hands manipulates a miniature globe and performs a series of sleight-of-hand tricks, i.e. takes interlocking pieces apart, reassembles them, bounces globe, reveals globe within globes, plays the old shell game, and finally spins it.

<u>AUDIO:</u>
Voice over in sync with action:
"Here it is. The world. A nice place. You think people would leave it alone. But somebody's always taking it apart and putting it together …almost. It sure gets bounced around. But it bounces back, so far. On top of that, it's getting smaller, and smaller, and smaller. And it can get away from you if you're not careful. But what are you going to do? CBS News has professional worldwatchers who'll watch the world for you. You watch CBS News."

From sign on to sign off during the past 12 months the programs that came before our cameras attracted the biggest audiences in all television...as they have consistently done over the past five years...and as they show every promise of doing throughout this season.

CBS
TELEVISION
NETWORK

L ike every other business enterprise, a broadcasting network has something to sell. Its products are airtime, talent, and most important, programs.

To sell itself and its products effectively to a sponsor, a network has to talk numbers. It has to talk about ratings…about listeners…about potential customers per advertising dollar. It must also demonstrate that it is better equipped to deliver such benefits than any other network media.

But numbers, percentages, charts, and graphs make highly resistible reading matter, even to the people who are supposed to care about them. So selling the sellers is the ultimate challenge for a network's advertising department.

The sampling of CBS ads addressed to the trade, in this section and elsewhere in the book, demonstrate Dorfsman's grasp of both the network's and the clients' business problems, his perceptiveness about human motivations and his graphic inventiveness. In all of the fact-filled ads, statistics are not dragged in like an afterthought; they are presented in a straightforward way, but imaginatively dressed up for the occasion. You'll see photographs that are really bar charts, typography turned into pictures, logos that do more than tell who paid for the ad, and an ingenious ad that evolved from a telephone number.

The range of work, which started in the early '50s, also documents how—in the face of television's enormous threat—Dorfsman fought a convincing battle for radio as an advertising medium. For historic interest, there are also several early ads that Dorfsman deplores as "sexist" in the face of the contemporary Women's Movement; but they were on target in their time.

Though directed at CBS clients and their advertising agencies, Dorfsman's work was studied avidly by copywriters, art directors, type directors, account executives, and corporate managers. He possibly holds the record as the most interviewed and most reviewed art director of the century. Hardly a year has gone by, since 1954, without attention being paid to his work and his commentaries on visual communication in such publications as Communication Arts, Graphis, Industrial Design, Print Magazine, Art & Industry, Advertising Age and Marketing Communications.

The breadth of Dorfsman's influence has won him the unofficial accolade of "the advertiser's advertiser."

177. (Overleaf)
Just a camera, a logo and a few succinct lines of copy here, but the grand scale and elegant restraint of this trade ad communicated CBS's secure and commanding position in the field.

178. An early trade ad depicted the market for daytime TV sponsors. The ad was a daring departure from most found in trade magazines. No headline. No spurious motivation. The human interest photo and the logo told the whole story.

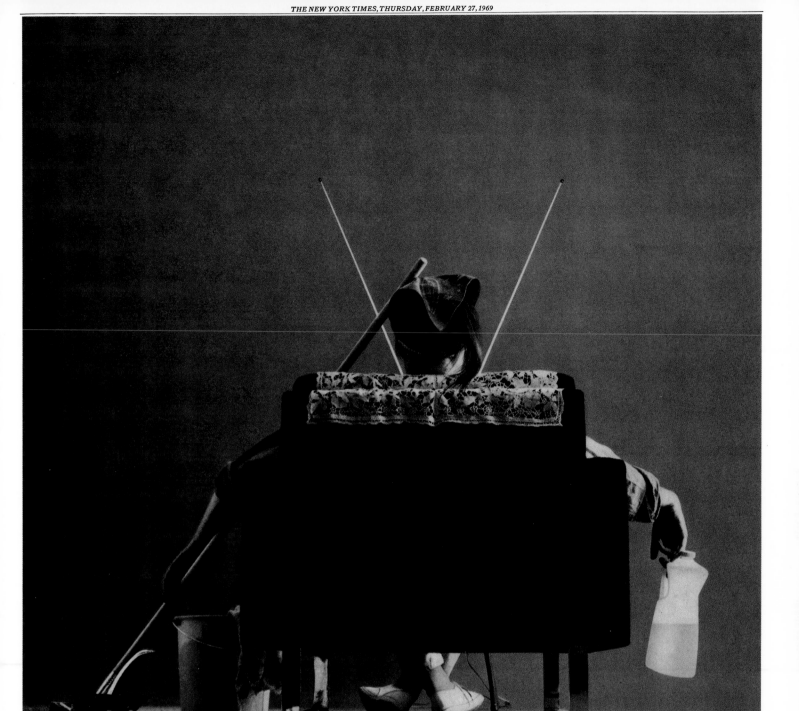

How come we keep millions of women from scrubbing, cleaning, waxing, polishing, washing, ironing, cooking and baking...

Yet at the same time we keep selling them cleansers, polishers, detergents, waxes, bleaches, soap, soup and mixes?

Simple. The more ladies watch television, the more they're sold on today's time-saving products. And time saved is time spent watching more daytime television than ever before.
Especially the CBS Television Network. For the 15th straight year attracting the biggest average daytime audiences. Now 34% bigger than the second network. So that's how come.

The daytime leader for 15 straight years.

Source: Audience estimates based on NTI AA household data, Monday-Friday 10:00 a.m.-5:00 p.m. Homes using television January-December 1968 vs. prior years.
Competitive data January-1 February 1969 and January-December of prior years. Subject to qualifications available on request.

She turns us on.

She may have curlers on her head and sneakers on her feet but we've got a great mutual attraction.

We've got something she wants. Diversion. 41 million women like her spend 10 hours a week watching daytime TV. We know because they spend more of this time watching CBS (29% more than one network, 53% more than the other).

And she's got something we want. Buying power. When she's not using soaps, detergents, powders and polishes, she watches TV to learn about soaps, detergents, powders and polishes she's going to buy.

And just in case you think our infatuation is a fleeting one, the CBS Television Network has been Number One with daytime audiences for 15 years.

CBS◉

Audience estimates are for Monday-Friday 10:00 am—5:00 pm and are based on Nielsen Audience Composition reports, October—II November 1969 and Nielsen's People Using Television, November 1969 (latest available, projected to 1969 women population base). Historical data are Nielsen Television Index AA home estimates for January-December 1955-1968 and January—II November 1969. Subject to qualifications available on request.

179.

Ancient marketing history

Dorfsman vehemently disapproves of the archaic sexism of this ad, and the one on the previous page, but they are included for their historical context. In the 1960s, before the revolution in women's economic and social status, the ads were not considered offensive or deprecating to women. They conveyed two facts quickly: homemakers turned on daytime TV and CBS loved homemakers — curlers, aprons and all — for their purchasing power.

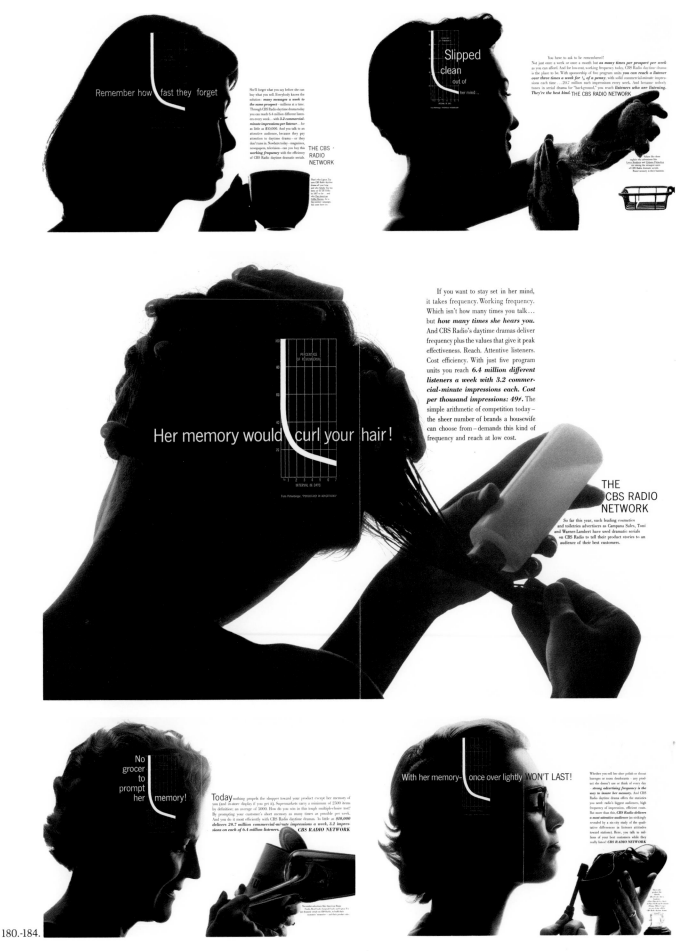

180.-184.

Statistics without yawns
Numbers, graphs and charts are never seductive reading matter, even for
advertisers who care about them. These ads conveyed statistical information dramatically.
They illustrated the natural rapid loss of memory for product names heard only once, the necessity for frequent repetition of brand names and the economy of radio advertising for that purpose.
The low key photos gave equal focus to consumer, product and statistical data.

EASY AS
PL1-2345

It's easy because it's radio. One phone call from you and radio's in selling action for you tomorrow. It's easier still because it's WCBS Radio you're calling. No other radio station reaches so many different New York families (over 1.6 million*) every day. And selling comes easiest of all when you use famous, established personalities for the job... the kind that listeners have told us they believe in most**... and the kind that WCBS Radio has nothing but. Jack Sterling, for example, and Lanny Ross, Jim Lowe, Martha Wright. Performers like these give new conviction to a sales story. And this moves products. So just give Sales Manager Tom Swafford a ring (handiest phone number in town) and **WCBS RADIO** you're in business. Lots of business.

REPRESENTED BY CBS RADIO SPOT SALES

*Most recent Cumulative Pulse Analysis **Motivation Analysis, Inc. Study of Listener Attitudes

185.-186.
In these ads, the microphone and the unique WCBS phone number were coupled to demonstrate the simplicity with which advertiser's could reach the station and their markets.

EASY AS
PL1-2345

Just like that, you're right next to your customers! No other advertising medium moves faster. Call us today, and tomorrow New York's most persuasive radio salesmen deliver your message. Star personalities like Jack Sterling, Lanny Ross, Jim Lowe, Galen Drake, Stan Freeman and Martha Wright give a product story very special delivery. Welcome as old friends all over New York, they're believed in the way only old friends are (as a major study of listener attitudes revealed). And they do your selling on the station with the widest circle of friends in New York (over 1.6 million different families a day*). Want to move your products fast? Just pick up the phone. We expedite! **WCBS RADIO**

Represented by CBS Radio Spot Sales

*Most recent Cumulative Pulse Analysis   185.-186.

The mike as a device
In the 1950s when radio was in danger of being effaced by television, Dorfsman took a frontal attack. He created a series of trade ads which shoved the radio microphone right up front in the customer's view. Each ad was a visual reminder of radio's continued existence and success as an entertainment and advertising medium.

"Be Sociable..."

"Be sociable, have a Pepsi." That theme earmarks one of the important advertising campaigns of broadcast history: Pepsi-Cola's current 14-week drive on all four radio networks *at once.* Pepsi tapped network radio for this promotion to reach and register with a total population. (Campaign magnitude: an estimated half-*billion* impressions.) As the company said, "...no other medium offers the speed, penetration, saturation and continuity; nor can any other medium reach so many people at a comparable cost per thousand impressions." So whether you need all four networks or one (we know one)—have network radio, and be sociable. Mix with people.... *Circulate* more!

CBS Radio Network

87. This ad symbolized Pepsi Cola's endorsement of radio as an advertising medium. (See story on page 27.)

88.- Television offered
91. pictures, but the mike was the definitive symbol of radio. These ads reported CBS Radio success stories.

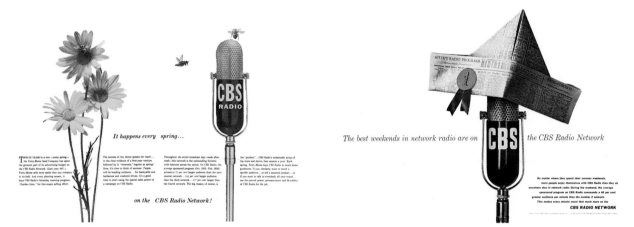

It happens every spring...

on the *CBS Radio Network!*

The best weekends in network radio are on CBS   the CBS Radio Network

the Girl

the Place

the Time

the CBS
Radio
Network

The Importance of Good Connections...

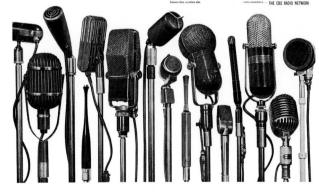

THE CBS RADIO NETWORK

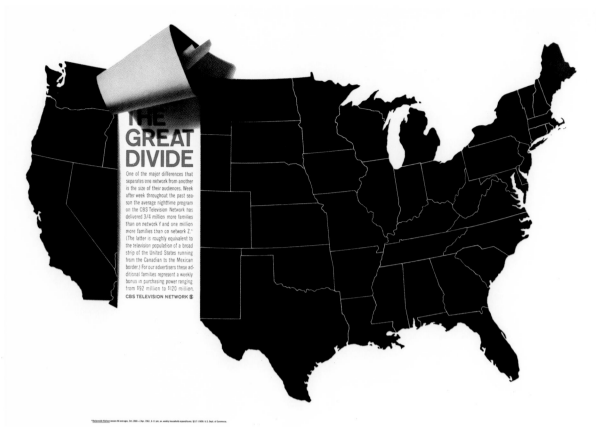

<u>Palatable statistics</u>
Pictures, graphic devices and word play reinforced numbers, turned the abstract into the
concrete and made heavy statistical data more readable.

THE WAY NETWORK TELEVISION LOOKS

Here is a clear, complete and concise picture of the performance of the three television networks during the 1959-1960 season. If you are investing your advertising dollars in nighttime television (or plan to) you might find it particularly significant that by every measure of leadership the CBS Television Network remains far ahead of its two rivals.

Source: All data are national Nielsen Television Index average audience figures for Oct. 1959—May 1960, for the evening hours (6—11 pm), covering all sponsored programs.

TOP PROGRAMS The following table shows how the three networks compare in terms of high-rated programs. In the average Nielsen report the CBS Television Network won more than half the places in the top 10, 20, 30, and 40 programs.

PROGRAMS	CBS	NET. X	NET. Y
Top 10	6	2	2
Top 20	11	4	5
Top 30	17	6	7
Top 40	21	9	10

HALF-HOUR WINS This season an average of 54 half-hour time periods per week were commercially programmed by at least one network. All three networks were in direct competition during an unprecedented number of these time periods—a total of 44, or 81%. The CBS Television Network had the top-rated program in more than half of these most competitive 44 time periods. It also had the top-rated program in more than half of all evening time periods.

AVERAGE RATINGS This season, for the first time, Network Y has edged out Network X in terms of average rating. While the difference between the "second" and the "third" network has been narrowed, the CBS Television Network has maintained the same advantage over the "second" network (now Network Y) that it had a year ago.

	AVERAGE RATING	CBS ADVANTAGE
CBS	21.1	
Net. Y	18.8	+12%
Net. X	18.4	+15%

NIGHTS OF THE WEEK The CBS Television Network earns the highest average-audience rating on four nights of the week, Network X captures two, and Network Y leads on only one.

AVERAGE RATING	CBS	NET. X	NET. Y
Monday	22.4*	17.5	18.6
Tuesday	21.2*	17.8	18.8
Wednesday	17.0	25.9*	17.0
Thursday	17.1	19.9*	16.9
Friday	19.5	16.1	21.7*
Saturday	28.6*	15.8	15.7
Sunday	22.0*	13.4	19.6

AVERAGE HOMES REACHED At present each Nielsen television rating is expressed as a per cent of all television homes able to view the program in question.

HOMES REACHED	CBS ADVANTAGE
CBS	9,091,000	
Net. X	7,818,000	+16%
Net. Y	7,757,000	+17%

THE CBS TELEVISION NETWORK

The early returns on the CBS Late Movie.

In its first five weeks...
The CBS Late Movie averages 7% more homes than Johnny Carson in time periods when they are in direct competition.
The CBS Late Movie reaches more than twice as many homes as Dick Cavett.
The CBS Late Movie nearly doubles the audience formerly reached by CBS.

And, in the one week when Nielsen measured audience composition, The CBS Late Movie outperformed both Johnny Carson and Dick Cavett with young adults...total adults... women 18 to 49...and large families.
In other words, many happy returns. Especially for the late movie's early advertisers.

Based on National Nielsen Television Index AA household estimates February 14-March 17, 1972. Comparisons are for all competitive time periods within the Monday-Friday 11:30 pm-1:00 am time segment. Data for "audience formerly reached" January 3-February 13, 1972. Audience composition data February 14-20, 1972. Qualifications available on request.

192. The number of homes in the peeled-away section of the map was equal to the extra number of homes advertisers could reach through the CBS Television Network.

193. The IN and OUT basket provided a literal translation of CBS's standing in 133 Nielsen reports: IN first place 131 times; OUT only twice.

194. The TV camera was chosen to illustrate this ad because it interpreted the headline literally; it also enlivened the statistics-laden page.

195. A light touch with the headline leads directly into the statistical data.

Tonight the CBS Television Network will bring you the swiftest, clearest report and analysis of the Election returns by the nationwide team of CBS News correspondents, the news gathering organization which first reported the winners in 1952, 1954, 1956 and in 1958

Tonight the most experienced news-gathering team in broadcasting and an exclusive new IBM computer will join forces to report the decisions of what promises to be the biggest electorate in the nation's history. CBS News assignments find...WALTER CRONKITE at the "anchor desk"; EDWARD R. MURROW, ERIC SEVAREID and DAVID SCHOENBRUN providing expert analysis and review; HOWARD K. SMITH manning the computer that will produce predictions from very early returns; DOUGLAS EDWARDS keeping track of the six key states; CHARLES COLLINGWOOD, STUART NOVINS, GRANT HOLCOMB, CHARLES KURALT and GEORGE HERMAN covering the East, Midwest, Far West, South and Congressional races; and a network of 300 reporters in every state and population center phoning in last-minute returns direct to the CBS News Central Switchboard in New York. You will also see CHARLES VON FREMD with Senator Kennedy, PAUL NIVEN with Vice President Nixon, NANCY HANSCHMAN with Senator Johnson, RICHARD C. HOTTELET with Ambassador Lodge, WELLS CHURCH at Republican Headquarters and RON COCHRAN at Democratic Headquarters.

STARTING AT 7:30 PM CHANNEL 2

A special IBM computer will immediately process the earliest returns and forecast the winner of the Presidential contest. Be sure to tune in CBS News right from the start.

HOW SHARP IS YOUR TELEVISION?

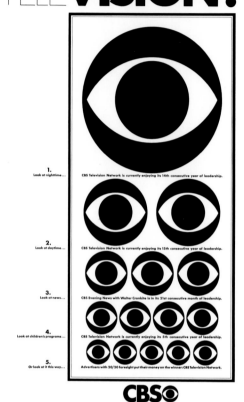

1. Look at nighttime... CBS Television Network is currently enjoying its 14th consecutive year of leadership.

2. Look at daytime... CBS Television Network is currently enjoying its 15th consecutive year of leadership.

3. Look at news... CBS Evening News with Walter Cronkite is in its 21st consecutive month of leadership.

4. Look at children's programs... CBS Television Network is currently enjoying its 5th consecutive year of leadership.

5. Or look at it this way... Advertisers with 20/20 foresight put their money on the winner: CBS Television Network.

CBS

RIGHT ON

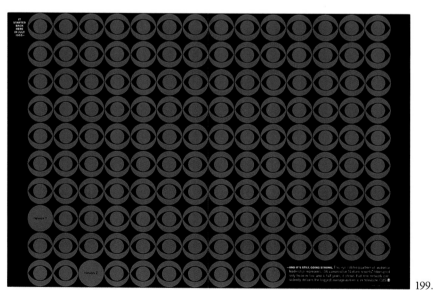

Your birthday means a lot to us—we grew up together! CBS

Focus on the logo

The CBS eye is a remarkable symbol. It was derived from a primitive pictograph, yet it defines precisely one of the century's most sophisticated inventions. Designed by Dorfsman's predecessor, Bill Golden, for a one-time promotion, it was miraculously saved from the trash basket by the wise intervention of Frank Stanton. The creative department was thrashing around for a new visual symbol for another campaign, Stanton cut short the discussion, held up the CBS eye and decreed that it would remain their logo forever.

96. The three instantly recognizable symbols identified CBS with election returns.

97. The eye chart and CBS logo were a perfectly natural device for this trade ad dealing with audience viewing habits. The ad presented statistics to prove CBS Network Television scored highest of all the networks in daytime, nighttime, news and children's programs.

98. A gracious ad congratulated NBC on its 50th anniversary and shrewdly gave CBS equal attention.

99. This double-page spread dramatized the overwhelming popularity of CBS Television. In 136 consecutive Nielsen Reports, CBS was declared the #1 network 134 times, indicated by 134 logos. The two non-CBS winners, listed as Network X and Network Y, are lost in the crowd.

200. The logo in an ad for daytime television.

201. 202. The CBS eye is a natural substitute for the letter O in these ads: the ideal integration of word, image and message.

200.

We have
an eye for
the ladies

and they
have an eye
for us

It is always pleasant to learn that you are more appealing to women than the next man —and if you are a broadcaster or an advertiser it has its practical advantages.

During the average minute of the day, for example, 3,932,000 women have their eye on the CBS Television Network—some 514,000 *more* than are watching our closest competitor and 2,529,000 more than the third network. (Among *young* women our plurality is respectively 461,000 and 957,000.)*

This ability to catch a woman's eye can be attributed in large measure to the variety and dramatic quality of the Network's daytime schedule. It presents the three most popular daytime programs in television, including AS THE WORLD TURNS and THE EDGE OF NIGHT, both of which recently celebrated their 1000th broadcast on the same day. Equally, such courtroom dramas as THE VERDICT IS YOURS and such special documentary programs as WOMAN! seem to be uniquely responsive to the needs and interests of most women. The first has been widely acclaimed by bar associations for illuminating the processes of the law, while the second has provided clear insights into the complexities of raising children and the recent tendencies toward early marriage.

In the hours when television presents programs primarily designed to entertain and inform America's housewives (10 am to 5 pm) the CBS Television Network now attracts 3 per cent more of them than it did a year ago. And it reaches them at an 11 per cent lower cost per thousand than any other network.†

This is why the nation's advertisers are currently spending 2.1 million more dollars a month sponsoring programs on the CBS Television Network than on any other.

CBS Television Network

201.

Annual reprt!

For the eighth
consecutive year the
CBS Television Network
is attracting
the biggest audiences
in television.

202.

1960 SUMMER OLYMPICS IN ROME...EXCLUSIVE ON THE CBS TELEVISION NETWORK

You will be more than a good sport if you take your customers to the Summer Olympic Games in Rome, via the exclusive broadcasts of the CBS Television Network. You will be the farsighted sponsor of an exceptional advertising vehicle. All signs point to the gathering of an unprecedented television audience—vast, excited, and attentive, coming back day after day.

People are still talking about this network's coverage of the Winter Olympics at Squaw Valley: viewers still marveling at the thrills of Olympic competition; advertisers still marveling at the size and quality of the television audience. *Five out of every six upper and middle income families,* and three out of every four lower income families, watched the Winter Games. If you make cars or stoves or other "high-ticket" items you will be interested to note that upper income families watched most, as Nielsen average-minute ratings show:

The broadcasts from Squaw Valley also attracted more *adult* viewers per family than any other Winter program—with the result that a leading cigarette maker was the first advertiser to sponsor a part of the Summer series. (Because of the number of viewers of *all* ages, a famous cereal maker soon followed.) Altogether, more than 100 million Americans tuned in.

Yet the Winter Games were scarcely more than a warm-up exercise for the Summer Olympics —the world's greatest sports spectacle—to be held this year in the ancient thoroughfares and modern arenas of the Eternal City. Television tourists will follow the Marathon from the Capitoline Hill along the Appian Way, past the Coliseum to the Arch of Constantine. Sports enthusiasts will see Herb Elliott run the 3:54 mile, the seven-foot high-jumping John Thomas, the fabulous Konrads swimmers—the foremost men and women athletes of our time—drawn from every quarter of the globe.

To bring the Summer Olympics to the American people within a few hours of each event,

jet planes will shuttle tapes daily from Rome and Paris to New York. From August 26 to September 12, the CBS Television Network will present a total of 32 broadcasts, averaging more than one hour of coverage a day. Advertisers who want to get a running start on the new Fall selling season will be interested to know that two-thirds of these broadcasts will occur on or after Labor Day Weekend. Thus far P. Lorillard Co. has purchased one-quarter of the series and General Mills, Inc., one-eighth.

In a truly unique combination of advertising values, sponsors of the Summer Olympics will gain the *continuity* and *frequency* of impact found in a regular series, together with all the *excitement* and *prestige* generated by a newsworthy "special" of major dimensions. Not to mention a huge circle of new friends brought to you exclusively on the CBS TELEVISION NETWORK.

GO!

23 out of 40
The CBS Television Network presents *more than half* of Nielsen's *top-rated shows—including six of the eight hits* of the new season (pictures numbered 5, 11, 25, 29, 39, 40).

17 out of 30
Including top-rated shows of all kinds: comedies, westerns, variety programs, suspense shows, drama.

11 out of 20
Including five top-rated comedy programs (5, 10, 11, 14, 18)—more than the other two networks combined.

6 out of 10
Including television's top-rated show for more than four years (1); television's most popular new show (5); the show with the longest record of popularity in television (9).

This remarkable record, based on the latest nationwide Nielsen report,* is actually an old story: Throughout the past 134 Nielsen reports issued since July 1955 the CBS Television Network has averaged 22 of the 40 top-rated programs.† In 100 of these reports it has presented more of the Top Ten than the other two networks combined. In sum, if you are an advertiser, producer, performer or viewer, the place to be is The CBS Television Network.

CBS◉

*2nd January report. †Evening programs; average audience rating basis.

Photographs of CBS stars, grouped and bracketed, converted Nielsen ratings into meaningful information for the advertiser. This ad demonstrated CBS' superiority in four categories of programming.

Inventive use of typography to dramatize the fact that CBS had the best three comedy shows. Each "ha ha ha" is actually a comparative bar chart.

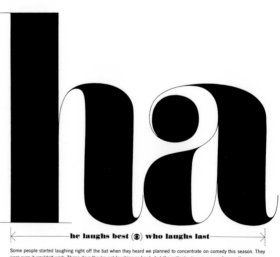

he laughs best ◉ who laughs last

Some people started laughing right off the bat when they heard we planned to concentrate on comedy this season. They were sure it wouldn't work. These days they're not laughing so hard—but the nation's viewers are, and so are the sponsors of our comedy programs. The audiences attracted by the average comedy program on the three networks this season tell the story: Network Y—7.3 million homes...Network Z—8.9 million homes...CBS Television Network, 9.5 million homes.* Moreover, in the latest Nielsen report three of our funniest shows are in the Top 10—and two of them are brand new this season. But the thing that keeps all our advertisers smiling is that the CBS Television Network attracts the biggest average audiences in every category of entertainment, laughs or no laughs. *Nationwide Nielsen, 6-11 pm, AA, I Oct. 1960—I Mar. 1961 † I Mar. 080, AA (CBS: 7 of Top 10)

CBS Television Network

204.

Design devices
Cold statistics were warmed up and humanized with pictures and graphic elements; the messages came through quickly, clearly and with impact.

205. A pictorial bar chart compared the CBS Gemini Booster audience with that of other networks.

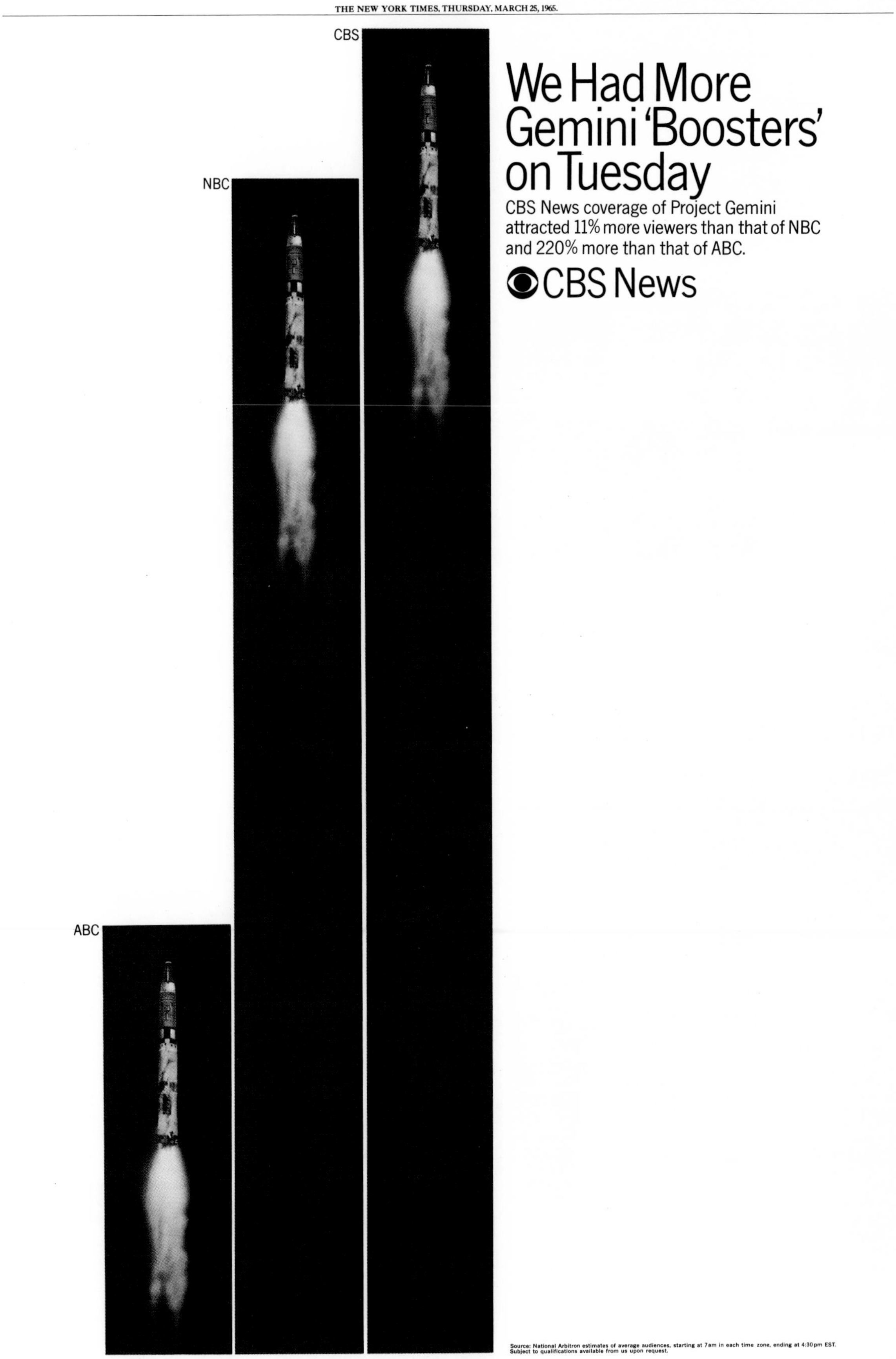

THE NEW YORK TIMES, THURSDAY, MARCH 25, 1965.
CBS
NBC
ABC
We Had More Gemini 'Boosters' on Tuesday
CBS News coverage of Project Gemini attracted 11% more viewers than that of NBC and 220% more than that of ABC.
CBS News
Source: National Arbitron estimates of average audiences, starting at 7am in each time zone, ending at 4:30pm EST.
Subject to qualifications available from us upon request.

205.

MIS ING
S$OMETHING?

Yes–
you are missing
from $92,000,000 to
$120,000,000 in family
purchasing power
<u>each week</u> if your
television advertising
is not on the CBS
Television Network.
You're missing it
because week after
week this season
the average nighttime
show on our network
is delivering 3/4 million
<u>more</u> families than
on Network Y – one
million <u>more</u> families
than on Network Z.*
CBS Television Network

*Nationwide Nielsen season AA averages. Oct. 1960—Mar. 1961, 6-11 pm: av. weekly household expenditures: $117 (1959) U.S. Dept. of Commerce.

VARIETY   Wednesday, March 27, 1957   Wednesday, March 27, 1957   VARIETY

TELEVISION: A sponsor using today's most popular advertising medium reaches an average of 7.9 MILLION families in the average nighttime minute.* And, depending on the program buy, the sponsor's commercial message allowance generally ranges from two to six minutes.

RADIO: A sponsor using the CBS Radio Network IMPACT plan complements and insures television's effectiveness. He reaches a net of 8.3 MILLION families and he delivers over three minutes of commercial messages per family— at the most efficient costs in all advertising.

*He does far better than that across the street, on CBS Television.

IMPACT

ON THE
CBS RADIO
NETWORK

Typographical games

In recent years the love affair with typography has become contagious; art directors and designers have universally discovered the design potential inherent in typography. But these efforts (206-210) go back more than 30 years and represent the mutual influence of Lou Dorfsman and Herb Lubalin on each other.

SOUND

is still the most attractive way to do real selling...to achieve continuous exposure, economically. After spending a big season (and small fortune) elsewhere, Hazel Bishop will now be selling on the CBS Radio Network, where they'll be making commercial minute impressions for less than 50¢ a thousand...and they'll have ten different occasions every week to tell the customers what to ask for when they're

BUYING

Beginning this summer, Hazel Bishop will sell cosmetics on Woody Herman and the News, and the new midafternoon Fred Robbins Show on CBS Radio. Other major purchases recently made on CBS Radio: McKesson & Robbins, now sponsoring The Godfrey Digest Friday evenings; F.W. Woolworth Company, sponsoring the hour-long Sunday afternoon musical program, The Woolworth Hour; Amoco, also on Sunday afternoons with Rhythm on the Road.

NICE

thing about network radio... it's always there to do the heavyweight selling. Of all the ways to advertise, the Campana Sales Company chose the CBS Radio Network exclusively to sell Ayds Reducing Candy during their slimmest selling season. Result: a 59.7% increase in sales. And no matter how you measure media, what counts most is a healthy sales

FIGURE

Morning segments of CBS Radio's Arthur Godfrey Time tipped the scales for Ayds. And of the resultant sales gain Campana wrote, "All in all, we feel that you have paved the way to give us our biggest year for Ayds through 1955." To assure this end, Campana has wisely elected to continue on the CBS Radio Network through the heat of summer competition.

EVERY

medium grows some each year, but some grow faster than others. And while the average radio family has 2.2 sets, it seems that's not enough. People are now buying nearly a million new radios a month—a gain of 40% over radio sales last year. From our viewpoint at CBS Radio, it's a unique endorsement: the U.S. finds radio so entertaining that every shopping day a new radio set is bought every

SECND

With people buying as many new sets, radio today is all over the house—and as big as all outdoors. While television has moved into the parlor, radio has moved everywhere else...into 97 million places where it does not compete with television. Less than a fourth of all radios are now in living rooms. Some 16 per cent are in dining rooms and kitchens, 26 per cent are in bedrooms and "other rooms," 24 per cent are on the go in the family car, 9 per cent are in public places.....And wherever people are, whatever they are doing, they listen most to the CBS RADIO NETWORK.

E␣HILARATE! ◉

This Fall, the CBS Television Network will again chalk up the biggest attendance record in football. The same go-go-go spirit that first brought professional football home to a nationwide audience (the late National Football League Commissioner Bert Bell attributed the game's phenomenal rise to this network's pioneering coverage) is also responsible for many other CBS Television Network sports firsts. First to give the nation a front row seat at international competitions through exclusive coverage of the 1960 Winter and Summer Olympics. First to use video tape in sports, making it possible to rerun thoroughbred races, crucial golf rounds and scoring football plays as soon as

they are over. First to televise the whole incredible range of sporting events from rugby to auto racing, from sky diving to figure skating—through the introduction of the weekly Sports Spectacular series. And throughout the year, this network continues to bring a hundred million television fans such major events of every season as the college bowl games, the Triple Crown, the UN Handicap, the PGA and Masters golf tournaments, and baseball's Major League Games of the Week. Sports play an exhilarating, exciting part in the powerful CBS Television Network line-up, which again this season has the balance, depth and quality to **DOMINATE**

iNNO

When a network program schedule keeps ▬▬ winning the largest nationwide ces for six years, the natural instinct is to leave well enough alone. But the tw only to give fresh twists to old favorites but to break out with exciting new prog do it with a unique courtroom series dramatizing the terrifying moral choices (like "The Defenders" whose premiere outrated the other two networks combi with programs that satisfy the city dweller's yearning for the simple life (like and Me" and "Window on Main Street")...or with captivating fantasies of talki

Captivate! ◉

Women are watching more daytime television than ever before—and watching more of it on the CBS Television Network than on any other. And with good reason. Day after day they can anticipate exciting new chapter in their favorite daytime dramas—among the longest running programs in television. In fact, back in 1950, this network was the one to innovate the whole idea of daytime television, opening up to housewives a wonderful world of entertainment and information throughout the day: A world that could titillate them with inventive games. A

world where they could watch CBS News' distinguished correspondents elucidate the crucial issues of our time. A world in which a Captain Kangaroo could fascinate not only children but mothers as well. In short, a world of daytime programming that would captivate the biggest audiences in network television, as it has for the past three consecutive years. There's no question about it: when it comes to having a way with women, **Dominate**
advertisers can always depend on the CBS Television Network to

To date CBS has 15% bigger daytime audiences than Network B...80% bigger than Network C. Also 4 of the top 5...7 of the top 10 ...10 of the top 15 programs. Source: Nielsen, year to date, 7 am to 6 pm, Mon.-Fri., AA basis.

titi

Here's the funniest line in television: Andy Griffith, Candid Camera, Jack Benny the Menace, Danny Thomas, Red Skelton, Dobie Gillis, Pete & Gladys, Hennesey Knows Best, Bob Cummings, Dick Van Dyke, Father of the Bride, Ichabod and Me Goes to College, Mr. Ed and The Alvin Show. It adds up to 25% of the CBS Te Network nighttime schedule—more top-rated comedy, more new comedy, and a

211.-216.

The type is the picture
All type ads must generally work very hard to gain the kind of reader attention that dramatic or pretty pictures guarantee. According to Dorfsman, however, "provocative words beat dull pictures any time!" In these ads (211-216) he demonstrates how typography can provoke curiosity, create a sense of urgency and excitement, and illustrate an idea.

VATE!

...ng chipmunks...You add the element of adventure to the comedy of Bob ... , or create a team of smooth investigators who track down their quarry with ... u refresh the air with the comic spirit of Dick Van Dyke, the hilarity of a best- ...ther of the Bride"), the adventures of a pioneer circus, the heart-warming humor ...y" Berg as a college freshman...This kind of innovation carries the rich ...hat in the intense competition for viewers, the **dominate** ...ision Network and its advertisers will once again

FASCINATE!

Sir Laurence Olivier Frank Conroy
Cyril Cusack Mildred Dunnock Martin Gabel
Thomas Gomez Julie Harris Roddy McDowall
George C Scott Fritz Weaver Keenan Wynn
Dick Wasserman David Susskind Ralph Bellamy
...

What may well turn out to be a landmark in television drama will take place on Sunday night, October 29, on the CBS Television Network. Sir Laurence Olivier and Julie Harris, supported by one of the finest casts ever assembled, will appear in a magnificent two-hour production of "The Power and the Glory." They are part of the unprecedented array of performers, producers, directors and playwrights whose talents will be on display during the coming weeks. In the course of this notable dramatic season the network will present six original Westinghouse specials (sample: "The Dispossessed" with Ralph Bellamy, Dina Merrill, and Earl Holliman), four adaptations of famous classics on The Golden Showcase (sample: "The Picture of Dorian Grey" by Oscar Wilde); and Leland Hayward's "The Good Years" a brilliant evocation of the century's early years. And beyond these glittering highlights viewers will be enthralled week in and week out by The U. S. Steel Hour, Armstrong Circle Theatre, The Twilight Zone, The Defenders and G. E. Theater. A kaleidoscopic world of drama unmatched in television and offering still further evidence that **DOMINATE** the CBS Television Network has the flair, balance and quality to

ate!

...ze of comedy than can be found on any other network. And that's not counting ...ating "special" programs as last Wednesday night's romp with Borge and Benny ...pcoming Danny Kaye Show. Happy viewers make happy customers make happy ...—a pretty sure indication that during this season **dominate** ... Television Network and its advertisers will again

ELUCIDATE!

ACCORDING TO WEBSTER: To make lucid, explain, enlighten; as demonstrated each week by 13 hours and 10 minutes of news and public affairs programs produced by the 475-man CBS News staff: SEE: CBS Reports, Eyewitness, The Twentieth Century, Washington Conversation, At The Source, Joint Appearance, College of the Air, Calendar, Accent, The Great Challenge, Camera Three, Look Up and Live, Lamp Unto My Feet, Douglas Edwards with the News (Monday through Friday), Charles Collingwood with the News (Monday through Friday), Harry Reasoner with the News (Monday through Friday), The Saturday News with Robert Trout, Ned Calmer with the News, The Sunday News Special. SEE ALSO: CBS News correspondents Howard K. Smith, Walter Cronkite, ...

Deadlock on disarmament, blockade in Berlin, conflict in the Congo, tornado in Texas—wherever and whenever it happens, the nation's viewers will know and understand it better when exposed to the crisp reporting and clarifying insights of CBS News' distinguished staff of correspondents and cameramen stationed throughout the world. Measured by whatever yardstick you may choose—enterprise, experience, reliability or acclaim, they add up to what The New York Times has called "the ablest news staff in broadcasting"—a reputation for responsibility that goes back over a quarter of a century to the days when CBS News pioneered such broadcasting techniques as the foreign news round-up and the documentary in depth. These qualities were never in more demand than they are today, as the events and issues of our time grow increasingly urgent and complex. It is these qualities that continue to inspire the respect and confidence of the public in CBS News—and offer still further evidence that in the coming season the program schedule of the CBS Television Network will continue to **DOMINATE**

20th-Fox's CBS Radio Network Buy May Innovate a Pattern
Variety, January 18, 1956

SCHLITZ RETURNS TO RADIO, BUYS IN MORNING GODFREY
Broadcasting-Telecasting, February 20

R. J. Reynolds Buys Sat. Night Show As Four Sign for CBS Radio
Broadcasting-Telecasting, March 19

MORE CBS RADIO BIZ; SIMONIZ BUYS GODFREY
Variety, March 28

Quaker Oats' Brace of CBS Radio Buys
Variety, April 4

COLUMBIA PICTURES TO USE EIGHT CBS RADIO SHOWS
Radio Daily, May 2

CBS RADIO REPORTS $1,000,000 WOOLWORTH RENEWAL
Radio Daily, May 8

Seven New Sponsors Sign for Arthur Godfrey Time
Radio Daily, May 18

HAPPY DAYS FOR CBS RADIO; COLGATE SIPHONS TV COIN FOR AM
Variety, May 23

SLEEP-EZE BUYS 3 CBS RADIO DAYTIME SHOWS FOR $10,500 WEEKLY
Radio Daily, May 24

CBS Radio Shouts 'Eureka' As $10,000,000 Pours Into Daytime
Variety, June 6

BRISTOL-MYERS BUYS CBS RADIO DRAMA
Radio Daily, June 8

Corn Products Purchases CBS Radio Sponsorship
Radio Daily, June 14

FOUR CBS RADIO PROGRAMS BOUGHT BY GENERAL FOODS
Broadcasting-Telecasting, June 18

Gulf's Summer Ride on CBS Radio
Variety, June 20

BING SING SOLD AGAIN
Variety, June 20

Wrigley Chewing Off a Big Chunk of CBS Daytime Radio
Variety, June 27

CBS Radio Sells News to P.&G.
Advertising Age, July 16

CBS Radio Signs Ex-Lax to Year's $400,000 Contract
Broadcasting-Telecasting, July 23

STANDARD BRANDS BUYS $1,500,000 CBS-AM SOAPS
Variety, August 1

CBS RADIO DAYTIME NEAR 'SRO' STATUS
Broadcasting-Telecasting, August 6

Colgate Mad About Those Soaps; Inks $1,500,000 More
Variety, August 8

Slenderella International Fattens Its CBS Radio Budget
Broadcasting-Telecasting, August 13

"What's New?"

And that's part of what's new.
Those are some of the trade paper headlines about CBS Radio's sales upswing this year. Increasingly, advertisers have been discovering that the CBS Radio Network offers the most exciting buying opportunities today. Because of the top-ranking stature and popularity of the programs. And because of the community dominance of the stations that broadcast them, city by city, across the land.

VARIETY   Wednesday, October 3, 1956

...an impressive documentary-in-sound — so impressive, in fact, that CBS rushed to rebroadcast this week the suspenseful full-hour reconstruction of how Columbia Lecturer Jesus de Galindez, a Basque, was kidnaped from Manhattan...

...a fascinat at times, terr documentary journalism o uncommon n

EXCITING AS AN ALFRED HITCHCOCK MOVIE... RADIO AT ITS BEST...

An expertly assembled radio documentary... an intriguing hour of radio...

!

...a remark documenta

...a tightly knit program chock full of information with the overall impact of a sledgehammer...the network deserves immense credit for laying out the entire story in all its details and with all its "it can happen here" impact.

...excellent CBS Radio documentary...

CBS RADIO REPEATS "THE GALINDEZ-MURPHY CASE" ... IN RESPONSE TO NUMEROUS REQUESTS FROM LISTENERS ...

THE GALINDEZ-MURPHY BROADCAST ...A RADIO EVENT THAT SHOULD TAKE VIEWERS AWAY FROM TV SETS...

...admirable de

217.

Typographic devices
By freeing himself of the traditional picture-headline-copy format
and limiting himself to typographic devices, Dorfsman provided himself with a
whole new set of design ideas. In these ads, the same old media
story looks new and invites readership.

218.

Worth Repeating

The Columbia Broadcasting System turned in a superb journalistic beat last night, running away with the major honors in reporting President Johnson's election victory. In clarity of presentation the network led all the way... In a medium where time is of the essence the performance of CBS was of landslide proportions. The difference...lay in the CBS sampling process called Vote Profile Analysis...the CBS staff called the outcome in state after state before its rivals. JACK GOULD, The New York Times (11/4)

◉ **CBS News**

219.

217. The ad is a listing of news and success stories about CBS Radio and CBS Radio advertisers in vaudeville poster format.

218. Excerpts from favorable critical reviews of CBS Radio programs are presented in cartoon-style balloons — a highly readable device.

219. A favorable review of a CBS News broadcast was sandwiched between quotation marks; the compressed copy block compels attention and the quotation marks are authoritative. The device was repeated in an election promotional brochure. (254.)

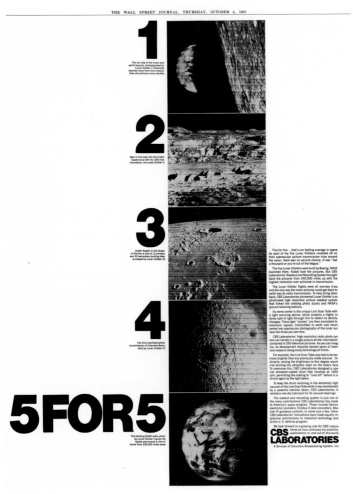

1

The far side of the moon and earth beyond, photographed by Lunar Orbiter I. Scientists learned more from this mission than all previous moon studies.

2

Man's first look into the Crater Copernicus with its 1000 foot mountains, via Lunar Orbiter II.

3

Crater Kepler in the Ocean of Storms is one of 12 primary and 32 secondary landing sites surveyed by Lunar Orbiter III.

4

The first overhead photo transmission of Orientale Basin, shot by Lunar Orbiter IV.

5FOR5

This striking NASA radio photo by Lunar Orbiter V gives the Apollo astronauts a view of home from 240,000 miles away.

Five for five...that's our batting average in space. As each of the five Lunar Orbiters rocketed off on their spectacular picture transmission trips around the moon, there was no second chance. It was "bet a thousand or you're out of the league."

The five Lunar Orbiters were built by Boeing, NASA launched them. Kodak took the pictures. But CBS Laboratories' Readout and Recording System brought back the pictures from 240,000 miles up with the highest resolution ever achieved in transmission.

The Lunar Orbiter flights were all one-way trips, and the only way the moon pictures could get back to earth was by radio transmission. To help bring them back, CBS Laboratories pioneered Lunar Orbiter's sophisticated high resolution picture readout system that linked the orbiting photo studio and NASA's ground receiving stations.

Its nerve center is the unique Line Scan Tube with a light scanning device, which projects a highly intense spot of light through film to detect its density changes. These light "pulses" are then translated to electronic signals, transmitted to earth and reconverted into spectacular photographs of the lunar surface like those you see here.

CBS Laboratories' high resolution radio photo system can handle in a single picture all the information contained in 250 television pictures. As you can imagine, its development required several years of intensive research along many technological fronts.

For example, the Line Scan Tube rays had to be ten times brighter than any previously made scanner. Ordinarily, raising the brightness to this degree would risk burning the phosphor layer on the tube's face. To overcome this, CBS Laboratories designed a special phosphor-coated drum that revolves at 1200 rpm, permitting the coating to "cool off" before it is struck again by the light beam.

To keep the drum revolving in the extremely high vacuum of the Line Scan Tube while it was bombarded by a powerful electron beam, CBS Laboratories invented a new dry lubricant for its vacuum bearings.

The readout and recording system is just one of the many contributions CBS Laboratories has made to America's space program. These include Gemini electronic recorders, Nimbus II data converters, Mariner IV guidance controls, to name just a few. Other CBS Laboratories' innovations have made equally impressive contributions to industrial technology and to the U.S. defense program.

We look forward to a growing role for CBS Laboratories as man continues his scientific explorations in, and out of, this world.

CBS LABORATORIES

A Division of Columbia Broadcasting System, Inc.

220.

Last Sunday Night Our Entertainment Made News.

In Los Angeles, the CBS Television Network's 1972-73 entertainment programming walked off with top honors at the 25th annual Emmy presentation ceremonies. Winning a total of 25 awards for outstanding achievement. More than any of the competing networks.

Two days later, in New York, CBS News swept the field at the first separate Emmy presentation ceremonies ever held to honor News and Documentaries exclusively. Winning 11 awards for outstanding achievement. More than any of the competing news organizations.

Last Tuesday Night Our News Made News.

CBS

Winning 36 Emmys helped make Sunday and Tuesday newsworthy for us. And for the many talented people who help make us newsworthy to viewers. Sunday, Tuesday, and every day.

221.

OFFICE OF THE CHAIRMAN

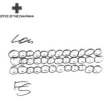

222.

<u>Speed reading</u>
There are times when a quick one-two punch communicates better than
a detailed sales pitch. In these ads the repetition of words and pictures intrigued the eye
and delivered the messages quickly and succinctly.

We interrupted January again and again for something special

and February's getting to be pretty special, too.

JAN20 — Special Broadcast: The Inauguration of Richard Nixon (10:30am-4pm).

JAN20 — Special Broadcast: The Inaugural Balls, the Nixon victory celebrations (11:30pm-12:30am).

JAN21 — Exclusive Interview with Tran Van Lam revealing ceasefire terms (Sunday News/Radio).

JAN22 — First Report on death of Lyndon Johnson, from LBJ press aide (Evening News).

JAN22 — Special Broadcast: "LBJ: 1908-1973," a tribute to the late President (10-11pm).

JAN23 — Bulletin: White House requests television time for ceasefire announcement (1:19pm).

JAN23 — Special Series on the energy crisis begins. First of a five-parter on CBS Evening News.

JAN23 — Special Report: President Nixon's address on Vietnam peace agreement (10:10-10:19pm).

JAN24 — Special Report: Henry Kissinger conference analyzing ceasefire terms (11am-12:24pm).

JAN24 — Special Report: President Johnson's funeral procession through Washington (1-4:43pm).

JAN24 — Special Report: "Vietnam: Peace in Perspective," a full-hour news analysis (10-11pm).

JAN24 — Special Broadcast: "Some Friends of President Johnson" (11:30pm-12:30am).

JAN25 — Special Report: President Johnson's funeral services in Washington (9:30-11am).

JAN25 — Special Report: President Johnson's internment services in Texas (3-22-4:59pm).

JAN27 — Special Report: Vietnam peace treaty signing ceremonies from Paris (9:30-10:12am).

JAN27 — Special Report: Ceasefire takes effect. Reports from Saigon, Key Biscayne (6:59-7:30pm).

JAN28 — First Satellite Film Reports on the first hours of the ceasefire (On "60 Minutes").

JAN7 — Special Broadcast: "Meet the New Senators," a first look at the legislation (12n-1:30pm).

JAN8 — First Report: Live from New Orleans on the rooftop sniper shoot-out (2:43-3:16pm).

JAN8 — Special Broadcast:"Nixon:The Next Four Years-The Correspondents' Report" (10-11pm).

JAN10 — First Television Interview with mother of New Orleans sniper (Evening News).

JAN15 — First Report that agreement on ceasefire terms had been reached (Morning News/Radio).

JAN15 — First Report confirming Vietnam ceasefire agreement reports (Bulletin—11:49pm).

JAN16 — First Report on the timing and terms of the Vietnam ceasefire (Morning News/Radio).

JAN19 — First Report on Vice President Spiro Agnew's Southeast Asia trip (Morning News/Radio).

FEB1 — Exclusive: "A Conversation with Henry Kissinger," with Marvin Kalb (9-10pm).

FEB1 — Exclusive: "LBJ: The Last Interview," filmed 10 days prior to LBJ's death (10-11pm).

FEB1 — Exclusive: "An Interview with President Thieu," with Bernard Kalb (11:30pm-12:30am).

FEB12 — Live satellite coverage of first POW arrivals in Manila (3:13-4:59am, 10-10:33am.)

FEB14 — Special Report: Return of POWs to U.S. Live from Travis Air Force Base, Calif.

January 1973. It was an extraordinary month.
America buried a President. Inaugurated a President.
We went through the last phases of an agonizing war.
We crossed our fingers in hope at a peace table in Paris.
Held our breath in horror at a rooftop shoot-out in New Orleans.
CBS News was there, bringing it to you on radio and television.
Telling you what was happening. (Often, before anyone else told you.)
Analyzing why it happened, and what might happen next.
This never-failing ability to keep on top of what's going on in the world,
the nation, the neighborhood is one of the things
that make CBS News something very special throughout the year:
the number one source for news in the free world today.

CBS NEWS

ELECTION NIGHT

CBS	24.1
NBC	23.2
ABC	9.5

NIGHT AFTER NIGHT

CBS	15.8
NBC	14.9
ABC	6.3

223.

224.

220. The ad for CBS Laboratories indicated their involvement in space explorations.

221. The line-up of Emmy Awards and the parallel wording of the headline delivered the CBS success story in entertainment and news programming.

222. A note from Frank Stanton congratulating Lou on Emmy awards ad (221).

223. By listing the actual dates of CBS news specials, the ad made an impressive statement about the frequency of such programming.

224. This abbreviated ad made an instant comparison of TV networks and their percentage of listeners.

How to stand a city on its ear.

Rarely does a radio station win so many different awards for so many different endeavors.

Rarely does a news radio station win so many listeners. WCBS Newsradio 88 has been receiving both kinds of applause - awards and audiences - and in fact they belong together. Because the listeners respond to what the award giving judges respond to: our continuing day-in-day-out effort. In 1975-1976, these honors:

New York State AP Broadcasters Association Three First Places and Three Special Mentions (a unique showing in NY radio) for Best One-Day News Effort, Best Spot News Coverage, Best Enterprise Reporting, Individual Reporting, Local Documentary, Regular Local News.

Newswomen's Club of New York Front Page Award for Best Radio Reporting.

Ohio State Special Award for Advancement of the Art of Broadcasting for "A Life to Share" - community seminars designed by WCBS to help parents with problems.

American Bar Association Silver Gavel Award for 20-part WCBS Report on "Rape, the Law and You."

Radio/Television News Directors Association (RTNDA) Three Northeast Regional Awards (a unique showing in NY radio or television) for Spot News Reporting, Editorial Excellence, Edward R. Murrow Award (for reporting on community problems).

Society of the Silurians The only award given to a radio or television station this year for 15-part WCBS Report on "Teenagers and Birth Control: A Modern Dilemma."

San Francisco State Broadcast Media Award for "Teenagers and Birth Control."

New York Press Club Byline Award for Spot News.

George Foster Peabody Public Service Award for "A Life to Share."

In view of recognition like this, perhaps it isn't surprising that Newsradio 88 achieves high honors with listeners as well.

We're the most listened-to news station in the New York market - and being first here means being first nationally.

Perhaps even more impressive, against all the different stations and program formats in this tough, competitive area, we've made news and information so compelling for listeners that out of 43 audience-measured stations, we rank in the top three.

It means we can thank you, for all the awards. Above all, for the one of your time and attention.

WCBS NEWSRADIO 88
News, All Day. All Night.

225.

THE BIGGEST NUMBER FOR NEWS IN NEW YORK

That's not just a claim. It's a fact.

Newsradio 88 is the most-listened-to all-news station in the New York area. More adults listen to us. Mornings. During the day. In the evening. At night. On weekends.

What brings the crowds?

What we do and how we do it twenty-four hours a day.

We cover this local market like a blanket. We look at, and into, every aspect of our listeners' lives. We dig deep into the rising school budgets, into arson in the inner city, into the commuter rail headache. We tell you who's on strike, what's happening at

City Hall, what it all means to your family's health, happiness and pocketbook. We bring you sports, weather, traffic, medicine, Wall Street, Broadway, and the world.

And we do it all with authority. With specialists, with analysts, with reporters in the street and a helicopter in the skies. When we head out across the world, we bring you the country's leading news organization, CBS News, with special insights from the likes of Walter Cronkite, Dan Rather, Harry Reasoner, Mike Wallace.

We bring you a smile sometimes, a lump in the throat sometimes. And New York's most-honored news all the time. For the fact is,

WCBS Newsradio 88 has won more awards than any other radio station in town. Awards, among others, for local news reporting, spot news reporting, enterprise reporting. For feature reporting, documentaries, editorials, public service and series reporting.

Which, as we see it, leads to an obvious conclusion.

Obviously, we're not just the biggest number for news. We're also the best.

WCBS NEWSRADIO 88

226.

Announcing

At WCBS/Newsradio 88, we keep regular hours. Our special features and reports are carefully scheduled between news segments.

No doubt you've already discovered that parts of your day dovetail with parts of our day. Like clockwork.

You might, for example, get up at Gordon Barnes Weather-time; dress by Helicopter Traffic-time; gulp coffee by Ed Ingles Sports-time; race out by Ray Brady Business-time; get in by Hughes Rudd CBS News-time.

Of course, the flow of news on a given day can alter feature times slightly. But this weekday program schedule is a very good guide to Newsradio 88.

We thought you'd like to keep it handy. That way, our time can be your time.

AM

ANCHORMEN:
LOU ADLER &
JIM DONNELLY

6:00 CBS NEWS/ DALLAS TOWNSEND
6:06 WEATHER/ GORDON BARNES NEWS
6:12 SPORTS/ED INGLES NEWS
6:23 FIRST LINE REPORT/ DAN RATHER & MARVIN KALB
6:29 WEATHER/ GORDON BARNES NEWS
6:38 SPORTS WORLD ROUNDUP/WIN ELLIOT
6:45 WCBS RADIO EDITORIAL OR REPLY NEWS
6:50 BUSINESS NEWS/ RAY BRADY NEWS
6:55 TRAFFIC REPORT— HELICOPTER & MASS TRANSIT
6:57 WEATHER/ GORDON BARNES
7:00 CBS NEWS/ CHARLES OSGOOD

7:06 WEATHER/ GORDON BARNES NEWS
7:10 TRAFFIC REPORT— HELICOPTER & MASS TRANSIT
7:12 SPORTS/ED INGLES NEWS
7:18 NEWSRADIO UNIT REPORT
7:25 TRAFFIC REPORT— HELICOPTER & MASS TRANSIT
7:27 WEATHER/ GORDON BARNES NEWS
7:36 TRAFFIC REPORT— HELICOPTER & MASS TRANSIT
7:42 SPORTS/ED INGLES AND PAT SUMMERALL NEWS
7:51 BUSINESS NEWS/ RAY BRADY NEWS
7:56 TRAFFIC REPORT— HELICOPTER & MASS TRANSIT
7:57 WEATHER/ GORDON BARNES

8:00 WORLD NEWS ROUNDUP/DALLAS TOWNSEND
8:14 TRAFFIC REPORT— HELICOPTER & MASS TRANSIT
8:17 SPORTS/ED INGLES NEWS
8:24 TRAFFIC REPORT— HELICOPTER & MASS TRANSIT
8:28 WEATHER/ GORDON BARNES NEWS
8:36 TRAFFIC REPORT— HELICOPTER & MASS TRANSIT
8:37 NEWSBREAK/ CHARLES OSGOOD NEWS
8:47 SPORTS/ED INGLES NEWS
8:52 TRAFFIC REPORT— HELICOPTER & MASS TRANSIT
8:55 BUSINESS NEWS/ RAY BRADY

8:58 WEATHER/ GORDON BARNES

ANCHORMAN: JIM DONNELLY

9:00 CBS NEWS/HUGHES RUDD NEWS
9:09 TRAFFIC REPORT
9:12 SPORTS/ED INGLES NEWS
9:20 REPORT ON LAW ENFORCEMENT/ JERRY NACHMAN
9:26 TRAFFIC REPORT
9:37 BUSINESS NEWS/ RAY BRADY NEWS
9:45 WCBS RADIO EDITORIAL OR REPLY
9:53 REPORT ON MEDICINE/ LOU ADLER NEWS

ANCHORMAN: GARY MAURER ANCHORWOMAN: RITA SANDS

10:00 CBS NEWS/ DALLAS TOWNSEND NEWS
10:12 SPORTS NEWS
10:21 MIKE ROY'S COOKING THING NEWS
10:36 WEATHER/ GORDON BARNES
10:37 DEAR ABBY
10:42 BUSINESS NEWS/ RAY BRADY NEWS
10:50 SPECTRUM NEWS
10:54 THE ENERGY CRISIS/ JIM DONNELLY NEWS

11:00 CBS NEWS/ CHARLES OSGOOD NEWS
11:13 SPORTS NEWS
11:18 LET'S TALK LAW/ DEAN ROBERT McKAY (MON-WED) LET'S TALK PSYCHOLOGY/ DR. LAWRENCE BALTER (THURS. FRI) NEWS
11:25 NEWSRADIO UNIT REPORT

11:26 BUSINESS NEWS/ RAY BRADY NEWS
11:36 WEATHER/ GORDON BARNES
11:37 WILLIAM WOOD ON ON THE PRESS
11:42 STENDAHL REPORT
11:45 WCBS RADIO EDITORIAL OR REPLY
11:53 REPORTER'S JOURNAL/ STEVE FLANDERS NEWS

PM

12:00 CBS NEWS/ RICHARD C. HOTTELET NEWS
12:13 SPORTS NEWS
12:21 ACCESS/ CHARLES BAILEY NEWS
12:26 BUSINESS NEWS/ RAY BRADY
12:27 STOCK MARKET REPORT NEWS
12:36 WEATHER/ GORDON BARNES NEWS
12:42 FUTURE FILE/ JONATHAN WARD
12:56 PETS AND WILDLIFE/ ROGER CARAS

ANCHORMAN: HARVEY HAUPTMAN

1:00 CBS NEWS/ DOUGLAS EDWARDS NEWS
1:13 SPORTS NEWS
1:26 BUSINESS NEWS/ RAY BRADY
1:27 STOCK MARKET REPORT NEWS
1:42 TRACK CALL
1:48 REPORT ON LAW ENFORCEMENT/ JERRY NACHMAN NEWS

ANCHORMAN: BOB GLENN

227.

<u>Seizing the initiative</u>
In the 1960s, radio stations gave up the battle with television for
general audience appeal and went into specialized programming — all music,
all talk and all news. When CBS's New York station, WCBS, followed the Westinghouse
station, WINS, into the all-news format, Dorfsman seized the initiative and
produced some bold ads to assert WCBS's domination of the area.

The light that didn't fail.

228.

229.

225. A portable radio looms over the New York City skyline with the Empire State Building's spire pointing to 88 on the radio dial, suggesting the omnipresence of WCBS reporters and listeners. The ad was adapted from a TV commercial.

226. A series of ads focused attention on the number 88, the WCBS AM/Radio dial setting.

227. An ad detailing the daily WCBS schedule. The addition of photos, symbols and minute-by-minute programming enlivened the page and gave the appearance of an expansive schedule.

228. Dorfsman capitalized on the historic New York City blackout to score points for WCBS Radio. When TV couldn't function because of the electrical failure, car and battery-operated portable radios kept people informed of developments. CBS News Radio was the prime clearing house for reports from listeners, and official news bulletins to listeners, during the crisis.

229. All's fair in love and competition for business. In this ad Dorfsman took a friendly gibe at the competing all-news radio station, WINS, and used their call letters to proclaim WCBS leadership in the ratings.

Homes—Washington

LINCOLN mod 3 fam brk, oil, gar garden, subway, vacancy $28,500 Weeks Realty 44-14 30th Ave RA 1-1233

LINCOLN 2-fam brk; poss 3 lg mod rms; carpetg; extras; inc $1080; $5000 n: $22,750. Agt. AS 8-1880

LINCOLN GOING, GOING !! NEW 2 FAMILY—BRICK 23rd Ave & 42nd St. Heights Realty

BAYSIDE $20,50 Neatness & condition reflect the care & maintenance this tidy 2 story detached frame has received from its owner. Located on a quiet tree lined street in the lovely Bellcourt area (212 & 36th Ave). Living room, full dining room, huge eat-in kitchen, large pantry 3 bedrooms, bath upstairs, 2-car garage, 45x100 (60 at rear). Open to offers.

BAYSIDE "TALL OAKS" $35,000 3 bedrms "THRU CENTER HALL RANCH," 60x100 1 car gar, fin bsmt. 1½ bath. BLAKE, 196-20 No. Blvd. FL 7-8300.

BAYSIDE—Country club section. Split-level, 3 years old, 8½ rms, 2½ baths, finished basement, fully air-cond, carpeting, storms, screens, all applncs,many extras, $40,000. FA 1-3184

BAYSIDE—Dutch Colonial, Bell Court 6½ rms, firepl, gar, 40x100. Value at $22,990. Agent—IN 3-0200

BAYSIDE, 11 room house, $37,000 Principals only. Perfect location for doctor. BA 9-1823.

BAYSIDE 2 fam brick full possession 3½ & 4 rm apt. 12 yrs old, near everything $23,750. Howe BA 5 9600

BAYSIDE. Cape Cod styling, brk bngl. 7½ yrs. gar, 50x100. Nr yacht basin. $26,500. Make offer. Agt. FL 9-2580.

BAYSIDE. NEW 2 FAMILIES-BRICK 43rd Av & 215th St. Heights Realty

BAYSIDE — Luxury plus! Solidly built 4 bedroom house on a well-groomed 40x100 lot. 1st Fl: living rm separate family TV rm, huge new ultra mod kit, "right out of the magazine" with lots of space in it for family dining! 2nd Fl: 4 bedrms, and new colored tile bth, bright and shiny "like new" condition from top to bottom! New oil hot water heating. Extras include: refrig, washer, dryer wall-to-wall carpeting, etc. etc! Located in one of the best parts of town and super-convenient to LIRR, stores etc! Owner bought another. Asking absolute giveaway. $22,490. THOMAS VAN RIPER, 219-02 North BAyside 4-1000

BAYSIDE—ultra mod 9 yr old brick 2 house unit on 103x113 lot. House No. 1—Cape Cod: 7 lge rms (3 bdrms, 2 baths) finishd bsemnt. House No. 2—ranch: 6 rms, 3 bdrms, 2 baths, 2 heating units garage. Sold as a 2 fam house—extras! $58,500. Tortora. 201-25 No. Blvd. BA 5-8500

BAYSIDE HILLS. $32,500 6 rms, 2 baths, brick Ranch. Detached garage finished bsmt. Deluxe features. Wkdys after 3—all day Sun. BA 9-9377.

Homes—Oregon

CLACKAMAS "Waterfrnt" Whiteston
LUXURY & ECONOMY
big solidly built "THRU CENTER HALL COLONIAL" on ¼ acre overlooking L. I. Sound. Huge outdoor summer dining rm. w/big brick barbeque pit & dance floor. 8 massive rms. 1st floor—living-dining rms. w/rugged stone firepl. that'll be the winter "cook-in center" mod equipped "convenience" kitch. w/breakfast rm. Large cor. bedrm, color tile "necessitarium." 2d floor—4 corner, sunny bedrms; 2 w/ picture windows overlooking the Sound, 2 rich color tile baths. Topping this 14 yr old mahogany stone & brick mansion is a "never needs repair" slate roof. 2 car cadillac gar. Boating. Yacht clubs, etc. 40 min. to Asking $65,000. Brochure available. BLAKE, 196-20 No Blvd. FLushing 7-8300

CLACKAMAS DELUXE CENTER HALL
CUSTOM BUILT RANCH-ALL STONE
Holy'wd baths; bath in master bedrm, huge eat-in kitch, expensively equipped with wall oven, dishwasher & many other extras; 2 car gar; rear patio; attractively fenced with costly hedges; Pr $36,500. Situated in one of the North Shore's most desired sections.
DU RITE REALTY
25-93 Francis Lew Blvd. BA 5-5800

BELCHHURST-WHITESTON
New 3 bdrm custm rnch, gar, 1½ bths, semi-fin bsmt. $25,000. 154-63 13th Ave, cor 157 St. IN 1-9269; FL 9-3441.

MULTNOMAH $22,990 Large 8 room frame house on 8,000 sq ft plot, good location. Trilsch 14-51 150 St. Whstn. HI 5-0701.

BELLE HARBOR—2 fam brick
5 & 5 rms; 2 bths each. Finished bsmt. Ocean block. Buehler NE 4 5544.

BELLE HARBOR, Mod 2 fam, 5 rm upper & lower, 3 baths, choice cor 60x100, 2 gar gar, $35,000 NE 4-8406; GR 4-7215

BELLE HARBOR, ocean block, 60x100, 1 fam brick & asbestos shingle 7 rms, 2 baths, fin bsmt, oil heat. $39,500. Call NE 4-7882 or WH 3-7177

BELLE HARBOR BEACH BLOCK
NEW 1 FAMILY
With Rentable Apartment
MODEL—177 BEACH 120TH ST.

BELLE HARBOR, 1 family, 7 rooms, 2 baths, $27,500. Walter H. Blum & Sons, 237 Beach 116 St. NE 4-7400.

BELLE HRBR—Ocean blk, brk, 7 rms, 2 bths, $32,000. Also summer rentals. E. Rae Robbins, 145-13 Neponsit Ave.

BERGENFIELD
Now accepting applications
for Garden apt vacancies
3-3½-4-4½ ROOMS
Apply 51-L Liberty Road
DUmont 4-4727 DUmont 4-1565

MULTNOMAH
3 bedroom apt, immediate occupancy
Near schools, buses, stores
Apply 51-L Liberty Road
DUmont 4-4727 DUmont 4-1565

BERGENFIELD
2 BEDROOM APTS, $160
Garden type; air cond; FREE parking. Near school & shopping. Ample play room for children DUmont 5-5957.

BREWST. Modern exclusive 1½, 2½, 3, 4 rm apts. Scenic estate, some studios $58-$98 inc util. Fein, Brewster 9-3763.

MULTNOMAH, 1 VINCENT RD
3½-5½ large attractive rooms. Close to everything! Moderate rentals

Homes—California

SAN BENITO EXCLUS GARDEN APT Spacious 3½ rms, beautifully furn Gar on prem. Mr. Hummel, DE 7-2405

SAN BENITO —755 RIVER RD
3½ ROOMS $110
Mod elev bldg Supt or BE 7-5711

SAN BENITO Vic. Bryn Mawr Ridg 2½, $89—3½, $109. Central Ave., 1 mi no. Cross County Cntr. SP 9-5678.

SAN BENITO Sublet 4-rm apt (2 bed rooms) bright; modern building Available April 1. $175. WO 1-5925.

SAN BENITO, 3½, $130, elevator near RR Sta., Truxton Apts. 100 Parkway Rd., DE 7-0240.

SAN BENITO 5 rms, 2-fam 2d flr mod kitch, 1 block to Bronxville station; $125. DE 7-0507.

MONTEREY see vic Chauncey St & Evergreen Av. 2-story, 2-family frame, coal heat, approx 19x100; erected prior to 1916; partially vacant. Asking $12,-900. Owner will take back mtge for $7,000. Broker. X3650 Times

BUSHWICK, 2 family brick with store. Oil, 5 & 5 rm apts. Excel cond. $16,000. Owner, MI 7-1848.

70'S Between River Drive & West End Av. 15 furnished rms. Inc $12,200 Net profit $5,200, cash reqd, $20,000. Alfred Kohn & Co. SW 7-3300.

70's E. Spectacular new studio, plus

Homes—Idaho

Cedarhurs—$23,500. Mdrnzd
4 bedroom Colonial. Needs nothing but a family to live in it Living room fireplace, dining room, country kitchen, laundry & ½ bath on first floor. All spacious. Full basement, attic. Low taxes Principals only.
CE 9-8777

BOUNDARY 1-family Colonial, 3 bedrms, maid's rm, 2½ baths Completely modern. Nr schl, shopg, transit. Reduced to $25,000. Leaving state. Lillian L. Mitchell: FA 1-6799; FR 1-2884

BOUNDARY 2-family. Choice location. 5-rm apts available Good income. Ask'g $21,990. Lillian L. Mitchell FA 7-6799 FR 1-2884

Cedarhurs CharmingColonial
8 rm, 3 bath; rec modernized; $35,000. See 1-3: Sun. Brenner, 415 W. Bway.

BOUNDARY Beaut 3 bdrm, 3 com- plete baths, 2 car gar, attic & bsmnt. Well landscaped. Principals only. CE 9-7546

BOUNDARY 5 rm Cape, brick & asbestos dead end street, full bsmt & attic. Many extras. $15,800. MO 7-8112

BOUNDARY 7 rm split, w/wo furn, garage. Carpet. Appliances, Storms. Screens, Fences. MO 7-2869.

BOUNDARY Charming cottage in wooded area, completely furnished, Fireplace, 2 bedrooms Plot 160x100, ¼ mile swimming, boating, fishing. Price $12,000. Call Mon-Fri 9-5, NYC, EL 5-3416

Homes—Wyoming

COMMACK—Beaut. 1½ yr old Colonial ¼ acre, 7 lge modn rms, 1½ bths, refrig, washer, dryer, storms, screens, power mower, etc Hi GI mtge $128 mo $18,990 Forest 8-1532

COPIAGUE. New 3-bedrm Cape, built for Executive but unused. Fieldstone trim, beautifully landscaped. Adjacent to schools, sta & shopping. $17,200. Must see to appreciate. Owner. AMityville 4-4374 (9-5 Mon to Fri)

DARIE COUNTRYWARDS' QUESTS

1956 COLONIAL—2 STORY—with 5 bedrooms, 3 baths. Delightful with nice flow of rooms. Big, light and airy. Acre plus.
$65,000

1951 HOSPITABLE COLONIAL—Spacious in and out. 4 double bedroom and one single—4 baths. Beautiful playroom 1st floor. Over an acre with Sound view.
$65,000

1960 1-FLOOR COUNTRY HOME on an acre plus. Unusual details for gracious living and entertaining. 3 bedrooms, 2½ elaborate tile baths 2 living rooms—2 fireplaces. Tailor made kitchen modernly equipped Much to admire—a gem to own.
$65,000

45 Corbin Drive opp P. O. OL 5-1497

DARIE Friendliest Yg Exec Area Few min: excel schl, church, shop cntr train. Charm newly painted colonial. 3 bdrms, 1½ bth, w/w crpt, cust drapes 1 bsement & attic, lg lndscpe yd. Being Transferred. Low 30's Owner OL 5-3735

DARIE 6-yr old Cape, 4 lge bdrms. 2 baths, walk beach; $39,000. Kelsey Brown Sherwood OL 5-2546

DARIE —BEAUTIFUL COLONIAL ON ACRE IN 2 ACRE ZONE, $42,000 SOUND REALTY, OL 5-4412.

DARIE Calif Ranch. 3 bedrms, 2½ bths. acre, 2-car gar........ $47,500 ROSS P. WILKINS OL 5-9759

574 Post Rd. Darie OLiver 5-1443
Established Over 30 Years
MEMBER DARIE BOARD REALTORS

Homes—Nevada

LOUDON JUST LISTED
custom-built-one year old Colonial. Panoramic view of L. I. Sound. 4 bedrms, 2½ baths, deluxe kitchen. Dry basement-potential playroom, 2 car gar. Attractive plantings. Transferred owner. $42,500.
Sun by appt. Mrs. Lawrence OL 5-2152

LOUDON Commuting. Colonial split over ½ ac 3 bdrms, 2 tiled baths, liv rm, fpl. Dining ell, scr. porch. A-1 kit Panelled family rm. On dead end circle 34,900.
Complete descriptions by mail
Shown only by

DOUGLASTON 60x125 Up a quiet country road to an elegant Southrn Colonial integrating generous proportions & excellent construction. Large entrance foyer, living rm, firepl, separate dining rm, extra special kitchen w/built-ins, breakfast area & laundry; family rm w/sliding glass doors to patio, den, 4 bedrms, 2½ baths, basement, garages. On level 1½ acres with community swimming lake. $48,900.

DEER PARK. 5 rm Cape, brick & asbestos dead end street, full bsmt & attic. Many extras. $15,800. MO 7-8112.

DEER PARK 7 rm split, w/wo furn, garage. Carpet. Appliances, Storms. Screens, Fences. MO 7-2869.

EAST HAMPT — Charming cottage in wooded area, completely furnished Fireplace, 2 bedrooms Plot 160x100, ¼ mile swimming, boating, fishing. Price $12,000. Call Mon-Fri 9-5, NYC, EL 5-3416

EAST MARION. Architectural gem, 5 spacious rms, liv rm 32x16, oil heat. Sound view. Beach rights. ¾ acre. $19,000. TR 3-2448.

E. MEADOW. $16,000. All brk Cape, overszd grnds, 4 bdrm, bsmt, gar, front & rear terr, extras, convent.
BELLMORE. $19,000. 6 yr old split, att gar, 7 lg rm, cov patio, extras, $16,800 exist mtg. Save fees.
E. HEMPSTEAD. $17,500 overszd Cape, 8 yr old, 4 bdrm, sep din rm bsmt, det gar, patio, newly decor.
HEMPSTEAD. E. $16,000 brk & shngl Cape, 2 bdrm + fam rm, expansion, bsmt, gar, extras, city sewers.
1196 Fulton Ave. Hempstd. IV 6-2600
2090 Front St. E. Meadow. IV 9-8000

EAST MEADOW $19,990
ALL-BRICK RANCH
¼ Acre — 2-car Gar — 2 Bths
THE BUY OF A LIFETIME! No exaggeration—a 10-yr-old All-Brick Ranch worth many thousands more! On ¼-acre nursery grounds, features 6 enormous rms, incl large din rm, eat-in kitchen, 25' liv rm, 3 twin-sized bedrms, 2 full baths. Custom features incl plaster walls + exp attic for 2 more bedrms. Near public & parochial schools.
REDUCED FROM $23,500!
812 Fulton Ave. Hemp IV 9-3935

EAST MEADOW PROPER—LOW TAX
FULL SESSION SCHOOL AREA
See the NEW 1961
Colonial & Hi Ranch
4 bedrm, 3 baths, 2-car garage & featuring the ALL NEW VISTORAMIC KITCHEN
at the low, low preview price of
$22,990 to $24,990
Meadow Pkway to Hempst Tpke, right (east) 1 mile to Bellmore Rd. Right (So) 8 blks to model. PE 1-9606

EAST MEADOW, Immaculate 7 rm Lakeville split level on 65x155 professionally landscaped plot offers 3 large bedrms, full dining rm, large living rm with firepl, 2 full baths, full bsmt+ playrm, fully air cond throughout, gar, screened patio, extras galore. Top Location. $27,500.
1802 Hempst Tpke, East Meadow

EAST MEADOW. All brick 3-bedroom center-hall Ranch, newly decorated, new wall-to-wall carpeting, all utilities, many extras. 60x100. Beautifully landscaped. Large patio, enclosed porch. Walk to school, shops & bus. Price

Homes—Montana

FLOYD-FOUNTAIN $22,990 High Rise Ranch with 4 bedrms, 1½ bths, formal din rm, 16x24 panld fun rm gar. Model at 6th St & Newbridge Rd or call:
DUFFY PE 1-7520

E. BARBOUR Lakeville Estates Ranch, $21,500. 3 bdrms, 2 bth, full bsmt, att. screened in breezeway & gar. Attic fan, all applncs, many extras incl. 2nd cr. Take over 4% GI mtge. Wonderful neighbors. IV 9-9243.

EAST BARBOUR 6½ room, center hall Ranch, finished basement, 2-zone heating, w/w carpeting, air-conditioner, attached garage, patio, large shade trees & many extras. Principals only. $23,500. IV 1-0643.

E. BARBOUR. Lakeville Ranch, 3 bed- rms, garage, covered patio, fin bsmt, w-w carpet, strms & scrns, dishwasher, washer & drver, 4½% GI mtge. $22,500. Principals only IV 3-2603.

EASTBARBOUR EXPRESS—Large Split Level, playrm+fin basemt, garage. Brick & Cedar. Terrific neighborhood! $18,990. EXPRESS REALTY, 1790 Hempstead Tpke. East Meadow. IV 3-9581

EAST BARBOUR $19,990
ALL-BRICK RANCH
¼ Acre — 2-car Gar — 2 Bths
THE BUY OF A LIFETIME! No exaggeration—a 10-yr-old All-Brick Ranch worth many thousands more! On ¼-acre nursery grounds, features 6 enormous rms, incl large din rm, eat-in kitchen, 25' liv rm, 3 twin-sized bedrms, 2 full baths. Custom features incl plaster walls + exp attic for 2 more bedrms. Near public & parochial schools.
REDUCED FROM $23,500!

EAST BARBOUR brick, 3 bdrm, ctr hall ranch, newly dec, new carpeting, many extras, 60x100 landscaped, encl porch, schl, shop. $16,500. SU 1-2086

EAST BARBOUR Cape Cod, 8 yrs, 3 bedrooms family rm, patio, lrg shade trees, storms, screens, 20' dormer, asking $19,000. IV 1-0238

EAST BARBOUR, Suburban Greens. Top location. 7-rm Split. 1½ bths. huge playrm, bsmt, gar, covered brk patio. 4½% mtge. Extras. PE 1-6135

EAST BARBOUR—J. Martin Del Rio. 7 room ranch, den, furnished basement, extras. $29,900. IV 6-6879.

E. MARLCOPA bedrm ranch, 2 bths, 2-car gar 2-zone ht, finished basmt. air-cond., refrig, a fortune in extras, 4% mtg. $20,990. PY 6-7822.

EAST MEADO Joseph Martin Del Rio spacious ranch, centrally air cond fin basemt, 2 patios, w/w carpeting many extras. $31,000. IV 3-1434.

E MEADO Lkvlle. Rch, Real Swmmg Pool, living rm w/fpl, 2 Mstr Bdrms Plus 2 Bed Pine Panld Den, 2 Bths, Fin Bsmt, Gar. $25,500. IV 9-9444.

E MEADO , solid brk 7 rms, 2½ baths. St level. 2-car gar, storms, screens appliances, beaut ww carptg, landscaping. $28,000 IV 1-6244.

EAST MEADO -4 bedrm all Brick Cape, 1½ baths full bsmt, many extras, immaculate, $17,500 IV 9-0612

E MEADO Lge, modern brk, 7 rms, ctr hall, din rm, bsmt att gar, prch. ¼ ac. Extras. $20,700 IV 1-2280.

E. NORTHPORT—Transferred Assume 4½% GI mtge Cape Cod, 7 rms, 2 complete bths, glassed-in tubs. Modn kitchen din rm liv rm with mahogany paneling, mural paper, built-in cabinets, fireplace, jalousied breezeway, att gar Alum storms/screens Full bsmt, built-in storage space 20x15 patio. Fenced in area, acre, FHA value $21,000 Owner selling at $21,000. Principals only FOrest 8-0382.

E. NORTHPORT—8-rm Cape, ½ acre, 1½ baths, gar, full bsmt, air-conditioner, decorator shades, patio, walk to RR, schools, churches. Asking $18,500. FO 8-1853

E MEADO Lge, modern brk, 7 rms, ctr hall, din rm, bsmt att gar, prch. ¼ ac. Extras. $20,700 IV 1-2280.

E. NORTHPORT—Transferred Assume 4½% GI mtge Cape Cod, 7 rms, 2 complete bths, glassed-in tubs. Modn kitchen din rm, liv rm with mahogany paneling, mural paper, built-in cabinets, fireplace, jalousied breezeway, att gar Alum storms/screens Full bsmt, built-in storage space 20x15 patio. Fenced in area, acre, FHA value $21,000 Owner selling at $21,000. Principals only FOrest 8-0382.

E. NORTHPORT—8-rm Cape, ½ acre, 1½ baths, gar, full bsmt, air-conditioner, decorator shades, patio, walk to RR, schools, churches. Asking $18,500. FO 8-1853

EAST NORWIC North Shore
SENSATIONAL BUY
for person with discriminating taste. Contemporary All Brick Split Level. 5 bedrms 3 baths. Thermostatically air-conditioned thruout. 2 zone heating system. Fully paneled den. Brick fireplace. 8 ft wet bar. All utilities, fully carpeted. Immediate occupancy. Principals Only WA 2-4165.

Homes—Utah

EAST SALT LAKE SACRIFICE!! SPLIT LEVEL on 80x100—Three bedrooms and 1½ baths, 22 foot recreation room—Eat in Kitchen. Take over 4½% G.I. Mortgage—No commission. No Closing Costs—ASKING $14,500. Principals only—CALL ALL DAY SUNDAY OR AFTER ? P. M. ALL WEEK. AT 3-9306.

E PATCHOG (South Country Shores) Ranch—5 lge rms, fireplace, bsmt playroom, garage 1/3 acre. $17,500. GR 5-8391.

SALT LAKE $26,000
5 YEAR OLD TWO FAMILY
5 over 6 rms. Deep plot, garage, 1½ blocks to public & Parochial schls & RR station.
TRI TOWN AGENCY
at E Rockaway RR sta Ly 9-3324

EAST SALT LAKE Custom-built 2- family 4 yrs. Fieldstone & cedar shingle, 6 & 6 rms, 4¾% GI. Corner plot 85x85. LY 9-7688

EAST WILLISTON
FULLY AIR-CONDITIONED
4 BEDROOM HOME
Sitting high above this lovely village with a gorgeous view & attractive surroundings, this house offers the ultimate in modern comfort, 2½ baths, fireplaced living rm, large kitchen, family rm, 2 car garage. On over 1/3 acre. $36,800

LOOKING FOR IMPROVEMENT?
A family with imagination and a little creative spirit will love this home and can turn a small investment into a valuable asset. It is well-built, has a modern heating system, and many unusual features such as its basement den with woodburning fireplace, 3 bedrms, 1½ baths, full dining rm, fireplaced living rm, ¼ acre. Well worth a look.
LOW-LOW $22,500
86 HILLSIDE AV Williston Pk PI 7-7600
148 Mineola Blvd, Mineola PI 6-7200
Nights PI 6-7436
EXCLUSIVE WITH DECCA MA 1-630

Homes—Arizona

EAST WILLISTON—Split Level, 4 bed rms, 2 baths, 2 car gar, recreation rm. Princ only: $30,000. PI 2-4935.

E. WILLISTON Mineola, Westbury New ranches, capes & colonials, from $19,500. Childs-Kramer, PI 6-3075.

E WILLISTON C/H Split, 1½ bth gar, patio, $28,490. Hillside. PI 6-3715

MARICOPA ARGO VILLAGE

Homes—North Dakota

GREENE Solid brick ranch, $23,000. 3 bdrms, full bsmt, gar, attic fan, plaster, storms & screens. LO 1-7676

GREENE 7 rm 3 bedrm all brick ranch, fin bsmt, 2 bths, plenty extras. $23,990. FL 2-4576.

GREENE Colonial, 7 rms, $24,000 3 bedrms, den, full basmt, many extras included. FL 2-8903

FARMINGDALE, split, brick, cedar like new. See to appreciate. 3 bdrm, 1½ bth, full bsmt, extras. $19,990. Pvt. CH 9-3688.

FARMINGDALE. BRICK SPLIT
7 rooms, 1½ baths, 1/3 acre. On court Extras. $19,990. CHapel 9-8957.

FARMINGDALE, Lge split, 3 bedrms, 2 baths, rec rm, shaded lot. $21,500. Principals only CHapel 9-3651.

FARMINGDALE 7 yr brick, ranch, 6 rm, 3 bdrm, fin bsmt, gar, 2 patios, extras, gd loc $18,000 CHapel 9-1917.

GREENE PARK $28,990
ENGLISH TUDOR
BRICK-SLATE-STUCCO
5 big bedrms (4 on one flr) room for total of 7 bedrms. Magnificent Architecture & construction. 28 ft livgrm, fieldstone fireplace, banquet dingrm, lge modern eat-in kitchen, den on 1st flr, fin basement 2 baths, 2-car garage. Close to all conveniences.
Fieldstone 3-1100
251-10 HILLSIDE AVE

GREENE PARK—3 bdrms, 9 yrs, over- size gar, aluminum strms-scrns, w to w carpeting. Many extras. $23,500. PR 5-1699

FRANKLIN SQUARE
Spacious 6 rm Morton House in Pool area. Landscaped oversized lot. Garage, many extras; immed occupancy. 4% GI mortgage. Principals only. HU 7-0084.

Homes—South Dakota

FRANKLIN Morton Ranch, 7 rms, den, 2 bths, garage, pool area, extras. Immediate occupancy. $21,500. Owner IV 9-4108.

FRANKLIN large Morton ranch, 7 rms, center hall, 2 baths, patio, garage Asking $26,000. IV 6-7668.

FRANKLIN lge Ranch, trms, cnter hall, 2 bths, patio, gar, finished bsmt, extras. Ask $26,000. IV 6-7668.

FREEPORT. Exclusive N/W $29,900
Slate Roof-Brick Colonial
4 Bedrooms—2½ Baths
Club-Like Finished Basement
THRU hall to exceptionally large eat-in kitchen. Log-burning fireplace in spacious living room. Real family size dining room opening onto rear screened terrace overlooking wide open parklike treed grounds. Come See The Rest. At Your Service Every Day of the Week.
ALSO—VACANT 4 bedroom Ranch, 2 baths, 7 yrs old, completely redecorated. Move In At Once—$27,000.
"HOMES OF DISTINCTION"
29 W Sunrise Hway, FR 9-3203

FREEPORT, immaculate custom built split level. Situated in one of Freeport's prime residential sections. Center hall, 3 master bedrooms plus maid's room, 25 ft den, formal dining room, large eat in kitchen 1½ baths, full basement, oversized garage, all appliances included. Must be seen to be appreciated. Asking $22,990.
Exclusive with: DOW REALTY
109 W. Sunrise Hway Freeport, FR 8-5685

FREEPORT, Beautiful custom Georgian type home center hall 4 bedrms 3 full baths den fin basmnt. Plenty closets Large porch, patio, Attached 2 car garage, All rooms king size. Home in superb condition. Must be seen to be appreciated. Suitable for professional or executive. FR 9-2660.

FREEPORT—Beautifully decorated & landscaped 7 rm custom blt Ranch. plaster walls, superior const. 4 lge bedrms, 3 full bths, all appliances, porch, bsmt attic, sewers, $29,990—private FR 8-0383

FREEPORT N/W. $33,990 New gorgeous 4 bdrm Colonial in choice loca. Dir: Sunrise Hwy to Brookside Av, north ½ mi to California Av east 1 blk to model, Greenbrier Homes

FREEPORT S/W—Fieldstone & brick Col. lge livingrm frpl, den, diningrm bths, 2-car gar, beat. Lndscpd. $22,500.
RADTKE
249 W Sunrise Hwy FR 8-6066

FREEPORT Waterfront, 4 yr, 3 bdrm, 2 bths 20x20 livrm, 15x25 playrm carpet, sundeck, patio-dock, extras. GI 4½% $23,990. FR 9-1128.

FRPT NW. $29,900 col, side thru hall. 7 rm, 3 bdrm, 2½ bth, den, fin bsmt, scrnd porch, att gar, Agt BA 3-4440.

FREEPORT N W. Stearns Park, (Bald- win schools). Georgian brick, 4 master bedrms 3 baths, maid's room & bath. $47,500. Owner FR 8-7479 or FR 8-7685

FREEPORT. Beaut 8 rm split, fin porch & basement, W W carpet, New alum storms, Sacrifice at $20,990. MA 3-0154.

FREEPORT on Randall's Bay—modern ranch owned by builder, beautifully located, full bulkheading & boat slip. Ideal for boat lover swimming in bay, 100 ft terrace along waterfront. 3 bedrms, huge living and dining room plus extra large den overlooking garden. 2 fireplaces. Ideally laid out kitchen, dinette and laundry room, fully equipped. 2 full bathrooms, 2 car garage with large storage space, and additional bathroom for summer use. Very low taxes. Priced at $52,500 for quick sale. Phone for appointment FR 9-1885

FREEPORT N/W $29,900
4 Bdrms 2½ Bths
Living rm with firepl, full din rm, nice kitch, screen terr, attached garage, top location. You pay taxes on 100'
"PRE-SELECTED HOMES"
48 So Bergen Pl FReeport 8-8050

GARDEN $85,000
CUSTOM BUILT HOME—PRIVACY
BORDERING GOLF COURSE
1¼ professionally landscaped acres, completely fenced in, complete privacy. Underground sprinkler system. Close to finest shopping center of NYC leading branch stores. Wood frame & cedar exterior artistically built. 5 yrs old. Pnld liv rm w/fpl, also lge formal liv rm, Sun porch, Pwdr rm, Formal din rm. Modern up-to-date electric kitch & bkfst area. Mstr bedrm, tiled bath. 2nd fl: 2 bedrms, bath. Driveway gate electrically controlled (also doors of 2-car gar). Ask for Brochure 1239.
AMERICAN LISTINGS, INC.
745 Fifth 22, MU 8-3824
or Hubbell & Klapper, Rltrs, PI 7-2900

GARDEN ASKING $35,000
A Taylor Warner Exclusive
Just listed. This beautiful white brk Colonial home with slate roof in desirable Mott sect. spacious living rm with frplce full dining rm, lrg mod ktchn with breakfast bay, pwdr rm, circular staircase, up to 3 lge bdrms & bth. Truly an exquisite home, oversized gar on extra lrg plt.
MAY ONLY BE SEEN WITH
TAYLOR WARNER
We are not affiliated with any other office. See our many exclusive listings. 101-7th Street Est 1919 PI 2-7100

GARDEN
This distinctive home is nicely placed on very large plot. Built to exacting standards of owner who is in the business. Narrow clapboards, pine wainscoting, irregular width pine plank floors upstairs, etc. From the outside you won't believe there are 3 nice bedrooms plus a den—guest room with room to

Homes—Minnesota

DAKOTA-DODGE NEW COLONIALS
SEE WHAT WE OFFER
IN LARGE NEW HOMES
FOR THOUSANDS LESS
Center hall, liv rm, fireplc, bookcases, full din rm, kitch, breakfast rm, den, laundry space, patio.
8 rms, 2½ baths $31,750
9 rms, 2½ baths $3?,500
RALPH RICCARDO CORP
Inspect model at 162 Willow St.
Weekdays PR 5-3400 Sun PI 1-6911

DAKOTA-DODGE
NEW BRICK SHINGLE COLONIALS
2-story, 4 bdrm, center foyer, den, 2½ baths, 1st floor laundry, 2-car.
3 Euston Rd. Plot 78x100 ...... $45,000
224 Kensington Rd. Plot 80x100 $43,500
179 Oxford Blvd, large plot .. $57,500
NW Cor Sackville-Stwart, 80x110 $54,500
OTHER PLOTS AVAILABLE
Will Build to suit From $31,250
F & G CONSTRUCTION CO
PI 6-5127

GARDEN CITY
Colonial. One of its kind, 1st flr features—large living rm, fireplace, family dining rm, eat-in kitchen, bedrm & bath; 3 bedrms, 2 baths 2d; 2-car garage. $42,500.
THOMAS J. MOLLOY JR.
662 Franklin Ave PI 7-2010

DAKOTA-DODGE
6 BEDROOMS, 4 BATHS
Large colonial in Estates section, 1st flr includes sunporch, den, powder rm, 3 fireplaces & roofed terrace. 2 car garage. Asking $49,950
"Garden City's Oldest Realtors"
Hilton Av & 7th St. PI 7-2900
(Diagonally opposite Gard City Hotel)

DAKOTA-DODGE
SPLIT-LEVELS
We have several splits, all with 3 bedrms & 2 baths, priced from $29,500 to $32,500. Call us and we'll be happy to show them to you.
SUBURBIA BANK BLDG
1000 Franklin Ave. est 1885. PI 1-7100

DAKOTA-DODGE
McCLELLAND HOUSE OF THE WEEK
Small country estate in heart of this beautiful vill over ½ acre of secluded property, 7 bedrms, 3½ bths; wonderful home for lge fam; nr sta. $47,500.
"SEE OUR PHOTO FILES"
73 Nassau Blvd PI 2-8888

Garden City Asking $42,500
STRATFORD SCHOOL
Ranch cape, 120x110, 4 bedrms, 2 bth, living rm w/fplc, dining room, eat-in kitchen, space for extra bedroom and storage. Bsmt playrm. Att 2 car garage
736 Franklin Ave cor Stewart PI 1-8860

GARDEN CITY
Colonial ranch, lrg landscaped plt, 2 car att gar, living rm, fireplace, dining rm, den, master bedrm & bath 1st 3 bdrms, bth 2nd, terr, awn $43,500.
Nassau Blvd Station PI 6-7077
(Same Location For 35 Years)

DAKOTA-DODGESpacious Col, brck & clapboard, lrg living rm, fireplace, full size dining rm, kitchen, den, pwdr rm, 3 bdrms & bth on 2nd, jalousied terrace, oversized gar $32,950.

DAKOTA-DODGE $49,000 6 bedrm 4½ bth English Tudor. Exclus loc on lrg plot, formal din rm & all necessities for gracious living.
Bordini Real Estate IV 3-2500
541 Hempstead Tpke. West Hempstead

Homes—Colorado

HUERFANO CITY — $38 500
4 B.R. 2 BATHS—Playroom
Patio — MANY EXTRAS
Owner PI 6-8529

HUERFANO brick Cape Cod ex- pansion attic, 2 years old, fireplace, alum scrns, strms. Prncpls PI 1-8450.

HUERFANO Cape Cod 67x100 4 lrg bdrms, 2 bths, eat-in kitchen many extras 4½% mtg asking $32,500 PI 2-1591

HUERFANO CITY—4 BIG BEDROOM
Cape Ranch—Big House—
Big Plot—$32,000. PI 7-5292.

HUERFANO 139 STRATFORD AVE
CORNER OF OXFORD BLVD
Beautiful slate roof Colonial completely modernized. Plot 120x150, 4 bedrms, 3 bths, 2d flr, 2 bdrms, 1 bth 3d flr, immense living rm, den, exquisite new kitchen adjacent to laundry rm finished basement with built-in bar. 2-car gar with maid's qtrs above.
ANDOVER AT GARDEN CITY CORP.
RO 6-4930

HUERFANO SOUTH $24,500 Ranch, less than 2 yrs old, 3 bdrms, mdn kitch, full basmt, garage.
Bordini Real Estate IV 3-2500
541 Hempstead Tpke, West Hempstead

HUERFANO
Gurgling Brook...
Redwood Contemporary...
Over an acre—with a brook running to a nearby pond—proper features for a modernistic ranch! Cathedral ceilinged fireplace living room—paneled; glass wall dining wing opening onto patio. Paneled den 19x20! Open ceiling kitchen with breakfast balcony! Three chambers, two swank tiled baths. Double garage. Phone jax throughout. Excellent condition.
AT $31,500 . . . EUREKA!
SHOWN BY MARY FORD
GENERAL EASTERN CO.
Northern Blvd at Glen Cove Road
Greenvale, N. Y. MAyfair 1-5230

FREMONT MORGAN ISLAND Waterview Split, wonderfully landscaped ½ acre, cathedral living rm, 4

Homes—New Mexico

BERNALILLO-Victorian house with old fashioned space & privacy, all modern conveniences. 1 acre, beautiful trees, landscaped terrace, new custom kitchen, solid cherry paneled library, large shuttered living rm, basement playroom, 7 bedrms, 3½ baths, $35,000 OR 6-2118

BERNALILLO 30 yr 4½% GI mtge, $29,000 Artist designer's 4 yr old home, 3 bdrms, 2½ bths, 2 zone heating playrm, firepl almost ½ acre-lovely old trees. Charming-must be seen to be appreciated. OR 6-1387.

BERNALILLO Sound. Custom blt ranch, 10 rms, 4 bdrms, 3 baths, closed porch wd burn firepl 2½ acres, beaut indscpd, fruit orchard, pvt beach rights, pvt road many extras $45,000 OR 1-3706

BERNALILLO 1/3 acre, 7 rooms, 3 bed- rms, 2 baths, 5½ yr old split, fireplace, 2 car garage den, beach. Near schools & churches. All appliances, carpet. Princ only. $29,500. OR 6-3106

BERNALILLOEstate area, beaut ranch on 1/3 ac wooded plot, 4 bedrms, mod ktch, 1½ baths, den, nr schls, $23,000.
SILAS GOLDBERG & SON, INC.
25 Glen St. OR 6-2700

BERNALILLO Famed "Roxbury" area, 4 bedrms, ¼ acre zone, tall trees, gar, frpl, low cash, only $22,500.
RANGER Rlty 77 School St. OR 6-9000

BERNALILLO Rambling Homestead nr acre, tall trees, fpl in liv rm, 4 bd 3 baths, new kit, 2 car Red $36,800.
GENERAL EASTERN CO MA 1-5260.

BERNALILLO-5 rm bungalow on hill, nicely landscaped and fenced, near private beach. $11,000. OR 6-9069 3-7 PM.

GLEN HEAD, SEA CLIFF & NEARBY For Real state See John MacCrate

QUALITY, OWNER-BUILDER Frplc, full dining rm, Lrg kit, 4 bdrms, nr schools $18,500

Homes—Wisconsin

GLEN HEAD. Must sell fast, 4 bedrms, 2 baths, choice area, big lot, gar, $23,800. Ranger Realty, OR 6-9000

GLEN HEAD, 9 yr cent hall ranch, 3 bedrms, 2 bths, dry bsmnt, porches, patio, $29,500, lo w tax, OR 6-5473.

GLEN HD. Sturdy, 3-bdrm, small Col. Exclnt, gar, fruit trees. Ask $25,000. Ursula Johnstone OR 6-5380; 4620

GLEN HEAD Just Move In $37,900 LUXURY 4 BDRM, 2 BTH RANCH J. J Duffy, Inc. OR 6-2600

Great Neck-Kings Point Rnch
4 yr old custom built by one of finest builders, centrally air-conditioned by Carrier, 7 very large rooms, 2 baths, magnificent 14'x22' paneled den. Finished basement with large extra rooms and room for additional rooms. Most beautiful full acre loaded with trees. 20'x66' reinforced concrete patio with barbecue. Private road adjacent to school. Pool area and dock privileges. Principals only. $54,500. HU 7-2134.

TREMPEALEAU WISC. $49,500 MAGNIF CUSTOM BRK/STONE. SLATE OF 4 BDRM, 2½ BTH DEN TOP POOL, DOCK AREA. PRICED FOR QUICK SALE!
1st OFFERING EXCPTNL $26,900 YOUNG BRK/SHNGL, ¼ ACRE LANDSCPD GRNDS, 4 BDRM, 2 BTHS MANY EXTRAS. MOVE RIGHT IN CONDITION!
GUTTERMAN
544 Middle Neck Rd. HU 7-1177

TREMPEALEAU $37,500
BRAND NEW
LISTING
5 BEDRMS, 2 BATHS SMALL DEN LARGE PANELED LIVING RM DINING RM AREA WITH FIREPLACE. ULTRA MODERN KITCHEN WALK TO SCHOOL, HOUSES OF WORSHIP, SHOPS, TRANSPORTATION.
WM. ERSKINE HU 2-7460

TREMPEALEAU SACRIFICE—$23,500
BRICK & STONE RANCH
spac livrm w/fireplace dining rm modrn kit 2 bedrms ceramic bath expansion area for additional 2 rms full basmt gar terraced grnds 60x100
Douglaston Associates, BA 9-8966

PIERCE NECK $24,990
NEW COLONIAL
Custom built home on tree-lined street at City line Subway-bus. Quick occupancy. 6 rooms, Hollywood kitchen, 1½ baths, garage. 28 NASSAU RD. (½ block Northern Blvd). Inspect 10-5

PIERCE NECK. POOL AREA. English Tudor; magnificent gardens for complete privacy, 4 master bdrms + maid rm, 3½ bths, mahog library, oak den large modern kitchen, paneled rec rm w/fireplc & bar Low 50's. HU 7-2222

TREMPEALEAU $29,900 Fieldstone brick & frame colonial.

Homes—Nebraska

NEB. Pool area! Distinctive 2-stor English res. Perfect cond. Slate roof all rms king size. Den, new kitch, pwd rm on 1st fl, 4 bdrms, 2½ bths on 2nd 125 ft plot. Low taxes! 4½% mtge Asking $29,500. Simon. HU 2-7575.

RICHARDSON Spic and span 2 story, 3 bdrm, mod kitch & bath, det 1 car gar. Priced for quick sale $21,750.
FRANK M. McCURDY CO. INC
154 Montague St TR 5-2266

RICHARDSON Colonial center hall 6 large rooms, 1½ baths, modern kitchen, garage screened porch, corner plot low taxes Askg low 30's HU 2-3186.

GRT NK Kings Immac 2 story white Col. ctr hal, walnut den. ? bdrms 3 new bths very low taxes asking $39,500. Simon. HU 2-7575

RICHARDSON-UNIVERSITY GRDNS Beautiful English Tudor home on 80x120 plot. Must be seen to be appreciated. $47,500. Phone HU 7-1059.

RICHARDSON Custom built (5 years). spacious, 3 bedrooms, 2 up, one down 2 baths, glass porch, extras, $31,900 HU 7-8414.

RICHARDSON Designer's home. Lg contemp ranch. Ctr hall, 5 bdrms, 3½ bths, huge den pan, bsmt, pool dock camp tennis. In 50's. HU 2-8067.

GT. NK. Thomaston, Make offer. Own- er HU 2-7845. Engl Tudor, A-1 cnd. Lo tax, Pool. Mny xtrs, 21 Terrace Dr

RICHARDSON KINGS POINT Ranch 3 bdrm, 2 bths, many extras ideal acreage. $47,000. HU 7-5072.

GT NK, Lake Ranch, 3 bedrms, 2 baths, 18x24 den, air-conditioned, 2-car. $49,900. Owners Agt. IN 1-6860.

RICHARDSON-AAA location, Builders pkge, 5 bedrms, 3 baths, pool. $56,500. HU 7-2591.

RICHARDSON Kings Point, Bob Rose Ranch, pool, dock, fully air cond. spklrd. $58,500. HU 2-3238, owner.

RICHARDSON KINGS POINT
ONLY TEN GRAND CASH...
and you have hit the jackpot of the Season! Owner will take second mortgage from any sound buyer! His over-an-acre estate is gorgeously landscaped. His slate-roofed Colonial is simply charming:—center hall, bay-windowed fireplace living room, powder room, square dining room, glass-block den with fireplace, flagstone terrace, stainless steel kitchen (wall oven, dishwasher et al) Breakfast room. Four family chambers, two tiled baths. Maid's room, third bath. Three car attached garage. The grand style of living—on low cash down!
Never before advertised ......$64,500!
Exclusively shown by
GENERAL EASTERN CO.
510 No Blvd, Lake Success, HU 2-8772

COLFAX-CUMING POINT
ONE OF THE WORLD'S BEAUTIFUL HOMES ON A DREAM WATERFRONT SETTING. TWO STORY PRESTIGE CONTEMPORARY OF THE FINEST MATERIALS & CONSTRUCTION, INCLUDING STONE, MARBLE, GLASS & PEGGED WOOD. 3 HUGE FAMILY BEDRMS PLUS MASTER SUITE. MAID'S SUITE AND TREMENDOUS DEN. GORGEOUS WHITE SAND BEACH AND NEW YORK SKY-LINE VIEW. THIS IS THE EPITOME OF BEAUTY & LUXURY. OFFERED AT $175,000 AND BY APPOINTMENT ONLY.
WE ALSO HAVE ESTATES AVAILABLE IN THIS AND OTHER AREAS.
RELIABILITY—INTEGRITY
31 North Station Plaza HU 7-7777

GREAT NECI $37,500
Center hall, spotless brick Colonial, slate roof. In addition to the usual there are 4 bdrms, 3½ Hollywood baths, huge screened porch One of our most beautiful "Tree-lined Streets" close to ransportation.

FREE POOL & PARK.. $49,500
All brick Center Hall Colonial, slate roof, centrally air-cond, huge livg rm, dining rm, flagstone floored paneled

Homes—Texas

DEAF SMITH Pool/Dock Area 5-yr-old corner, 1 fam duplex semi-det 6 rms, FULL BASE, gas heat, storm & screen windows & doors, Venetian blinds, washing mach, refrig, added rear porch with aluminum awning & garden tool house, beaut shrubbery NEW AREA. 2 blks from school, shopping & trans. Existing mtge approx $11,400. OR FHA mtge approx $2,500 down payment to qualified buyer. RARE

RUSSELL GARDENS Both young, spacious Colonials with 4 bedrms, den, many luxurious extras, High $40's.
123 Middle Neck Rd. HU 2-8220

DEAF SMITH
OPPORTUNITY!
WAS $26,500—NOW $24,900

Homes—Illinois

GREENLAWN. All brick ran home, 1 yr new, 6 rms, 2 bth club bsmt, scrns, storms, wall carpeting, gas heat, ½ acre, being transfd. Askg $31,500. P only Weekdays EV 6-7988; FOrest 8-4852.

HENDER BAYS Ranch 1/3 terfront 5 rm 2 car gar Beaut liv rm $22,000 Murphy Rampas Hampton Bays 2-0726 or HAnov

Hempstea West $4
Defies comparison at price, & location. Tremendous center dor home on prefessionally la 130x130 plot on Garden City master size bedrms, 2½ baths quarters & bath). 28 ft carpet nut paneled living rm (fireplc Arthur's dining rm, modern k breakfast rm, huge paneled fa rm, warm sun-filled sun pch, bsmt. laun rm. 2 car. Loads o
Exclusive. Eldorado PI 7-3705

HENDERSON 6 rm ranch, 4 plaster walls, all elec kit oven, oil HW heat, dishwater & doors, broadloom, partially basement, fenced yard, fron 19,990 after 5 PM Mon-Fri, Sat, Sunday. IV 6-6748.

HEMPSTEAL
"A" residential area, nr bus & living rm, dining rm, eat-in k bedrms down; 3 bedrms up; basemt, 1½ baths, oil heat, gar 60x100, low taxes. IV 1-1010 patio, double garage, many Principals $33,990 IV 9-0884

Homes—Iowa

HUMBOLDT WEST Brk., slate rf., Col., att. gar frpl., lge. din. rm., w/w c eat-in kitch., scrn patio, 1½ bdrms., pine bsmt. w/bar, ex IV 6-4260.

HUMBOLDT W. Custom built 6 yrs, 7 rms, 3 bedrms, de sized kitchen, walk-in closets, f cond, sprinkler system, fire ala tem, 2-car garage, walk to shopping, transprtn, $37,900 IV

HUMBOLDT West—Buxton R bdrm, 2 bath. Firepl in wood den, porch, pool area, all ap Garage. Extras. $27,000. IV 6-8

HUMBOLDT W. Compare & 4 bedrm Cape, 2 up, 2 dn, fin. bsmt, frpl, bar, porch, w schools, extras. IV 3-7593.

HUMBOLDT Custom 3 yr Cor Ranch 3 bedrms 1½ bath garage, full bsmt, patio, co location $21,000—IV 3-0841

HUMBOLDT W. legal 2-family lent condition 4&3 large rms. rent free $20 000 IV 1-

HUMBOLDT $18,000 attrac tree shaded plot, 8 rm, 2 bt 2-car garage. Vigilant. IV 6-2

HUMBOLDT W. LUXURY Large wooded plot, Walk Schools, shopping, $37,800. I

HEMPSBURG WEST. 8 yr old rms 1/3 acre, gar, patio, cen widow must sell $21,900 RO

Homes—Kansas

HEMP W—Cape Cod 7 rm, Nr schls & shopg, 57x100 p $18,750. Call owner—IV 1-8019;

MARSHALL. ¼ acre +, 5 baths, 3-car gar. Choice locat taxes $27,500. J. M. Serenci: I

MARSHALL HARBOR
FIRST OFFERING
A first class uncrowded com pool park & boating area; t schools; beautiful landscaped view overlooking bay.
HERE IT IS
outstanding 10 rm ranch, 4 lge liv rm w/marble fireplc; rm, paneled den; playrm, maid ters, lge screened terrace, grill; oversized garage low nance. $59,500 HU 7-2411 HU

MARSHALL SCH
BUY OF THE YEAR!
CHARMING 3 BEDROOM HO
CAR GARAGE, FIREPLACE,
SCREENED PATIO, WALK
EVERYTHING ....
richard j. block, inc
station plaza, hewlett FR

HEWLETT PARK
g luxurious home on 1 1/3 acre od: ideal for mother & daugh doctors home & off; excl buy F

MARSHALL EAST ROC 2½ year Colonial front split 3 2½ baths, den + finished Waverly Park school district. ing + many extras $35,500. LY

BAUNSEE SCHOOL DISTRICT Custom built center hall Col, 3 baths, charming paneled Convenient stat, shopping, all Extras, $29,000. FR 4-4317.

FLOYD-FOUNTAIN Extreme able 4 bdrm, 2½ bath home nificently landscaped 2/3 ac course area. Anita F. Stante FR 4-4204

Homes—Oklahom

HEWLETT. Beautiful new 2 s onial, 4 bedrms, 3 baths. Hu off East Rockaway Rd. 1 blo Union Ave TW 1-3600.

GRADY-GRANT PARK-gracio gant 10 room home, has eve Tremendous buy now. FR 4-3

GRADY-GRAN—COLD SPRING Cape Cod Beauty—Lg. Econom Din. Rm.—Fam. Kit.—4 Bdrms, —Playrm, with bar—Bsmt. & acre—Walk to R. R.
YOUNGS AND GARNER, REA
35 East Main St., Hunt, HA
1911 N. Y. Ave., Hunt. Sta. H

GRADY-GRANT Executive Professional spot w/country phere adj village, $26,500 $22,0 Beautiful home. Avail now! 8 rm, 1½ bths, All schools & c SEE IS BELIEVING! Call R KEEN Rlty Co. HA 1-1865

HUNTINGTON—Wincoma
MAGNIF WATERFRONT CO
Spacious thruout, 5 bedrms, 3 sep maid's quarters, 165' o beach & mooring.
HARVEY OF HUNTINGT
25A, E. of Glynn's Inn HAmilto

GRADY-GRANT ASKING
PLANNING LARGE FA
MOVE UP—NOT OUT—AS IT
See this 3 bdrm expandable Ran
J. J. REALTY 85 N WO
HA 3-2201 Just

GRADY-GRANT—LLOYD HAR 7-yr custom ranch, 3 1/3 ac... New farm ranch 2½ ac, view Brick Col. 5-ac estate..... as
OAKWOOD REALTY MYrt
25A & Goosehill Rd, Cold Spr

GRADY-GRANT (Dix Hills). F 3 bedrms, 2 baths, 2-car gar fenced acre, playrm, hi mtge,
ANNE BYRNE
3047 E Jericho FOre
Closed Sunday Home H

GRADY-GRANT Crab Meadow Rental June thru Labor Day, bedrm-modern-In Pvt Assn on your private bath house & 1¼ hrs commuting. ANdrew 1-5

GRADY-GRANT Village mo house 3B, finished attic, dir kitch, dinette 2 bath basem playrm, low tax, perf loc. 21,800. HAmilton 3-2996

GRADY-GRANT (Cold Sprin Ranch, 5 bdrms, 3 bths, sw 1/5 ac wded. $36,000. Loesel M

HUNT. Hilltop setting, prest 4 bdrm, 2 bth col fam rm, ac transfd rare value

Traditionally, major business organizations with sizable budgets departmentalize their advertising and design projects. Consumer advertising is generally turned over to an ad agency. Packaging, displays, logos, stationery and annual reports are farmed out to design studios. Public relations, trade advertising, promotional and marketing projects are sometimes handled in-house, sometimes turned over to specialists in each of those areas.

Until recently, every one of the above functions was handled in-house at CBS. In his capacity as creative director, Lou was responsible for some 900 consumer, trade and institutional ads a year. But that was only the tip of the proverbial iceberg compared with the mass of promotional materials directed at sponsors, prospective sponsors, CBS-owned stations, affiliates, and advertising agencies. In addition, there were the mandatory press kits to help promote CBS shows.

On the surface, press kits and promotional brochures do not sound like glamorous design problems, and it's a fact that most top flight art directors turn a cold shoulder on such projects and assign them to subordinates. But to Dorfsman, every problem is embraceable, and large or small, it's treated with loving care. His experience in the exhibit business and his fascination with three-dimensional design resulted in some ingeniously packaged CBS promotions. His instinct for spotting a promotional opportunity, and developing it on a grand scale, were evident in two image-enhancing publications for CBS that have become classics: the Football Book and the Moon Book.

As initiator of many of these projects, and art director of most, Dorfsman was scrupulous about every aspect. Press kits had to provide useful information in functional attractive holders. Brochures had to be provocative and look so valuable they would not be swept into wastebaskets along with the stacks of commonplace promotional materials accumulating on executives' desks. To that end he paid special attention to paper, printing, typography and packaging. Almost every project was invested with some dazzling detail—an elegant embossed cover or an inventive die-cut. The object of all the nurturing and polishing was to make those at the receiving end think: "What a superior operation this CBS network is!"

230. (Overleaf)
The grand gesture

How can you justify the purchase of a double-page spread in a newspaper just to run a 1/3 column ad? In a period when American families were on a home-buying spree, this facsimile of a real estate spread in a newspaper was a stopper. The ad was another graphic interpretation of the statistics reported in (192), indicating the extra homes CBS Television delivered to advertisers. Although Dorfsman fabricated the entire real estate spread with fictional homes for sale in all states of the union, the ad was so convincing, prospective buyers called to bid on the properties.

231. Cover for booklet containing Frank Stanton's address at the annual Public Service Award Dinner, December 1969. The sepia line drawing, set in a blind embossed center panel on heavy, antique stock, simulated a costly etching.

"...the only way we can
keep the right to know alive
is by expanding it —
making sure that our citizens
know more about our government
and its actions, not less."

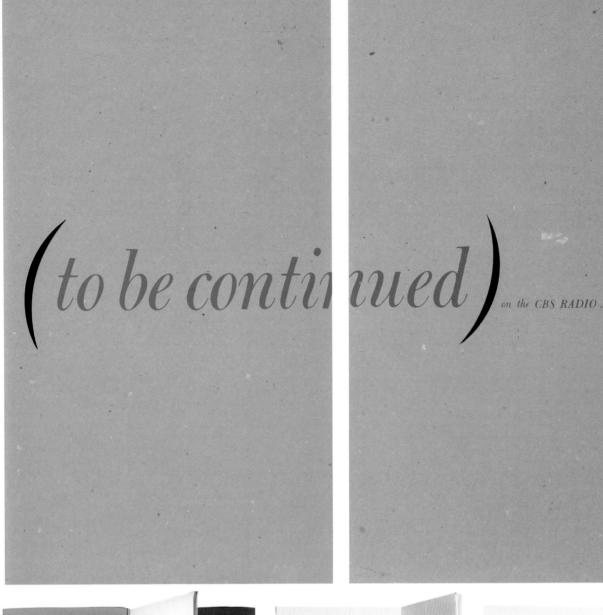

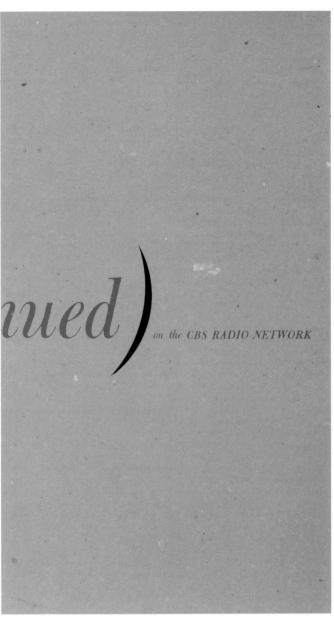

(to be continued) on the CBS RADIO NETWORK

The case for daytime radio

With the advent of television as a communications medium, radio in the '50s
was in danger of becoming the neglected stepchild of the broadcasting industry. In his position
as Art Director of CBS Network Radio, Dorfsman pulled out all the stops to prove that it
was still a dynamic selling force. He projected the vitality of radio in thoughtfully
researched, imaginative and costly-looking promotional brochures.

232. A book of case histories
of CBS Network Radio
soap operas, proved
their enduring popular-
ity. To emphasize the
theme of continuity —
of programs and audi-
ence loyalty — the
words "to be contin-
ued" started on the
front cover, continued
across the front and
back endpapers and
over to the back cover.
They were also the
words with which
radio soaps signed off
in those days.

233.

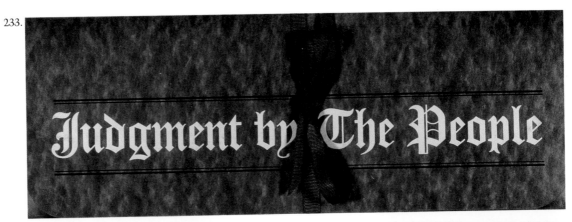

234.

233. Based on the premise
that listeners are the
ultimate judges, this
piece presented statisti-
cal evidence of the
popularity of CBS
Radio's daytime serials.
The cover, printed on
mottled brown and
black heavy oak tag,
folded down to resem-
ble a legal document,
with the words "Judge-
ment of the People"
gold stamped on
the front flap.

234. Brochure open to title
page with message
to broadcasters and
advertisers.

235. Inside pages, in accor-
dian fold format, sup-
ported theme of the
mailing with testimo-
nials affirming the
popularity of CBS
programs.

235.

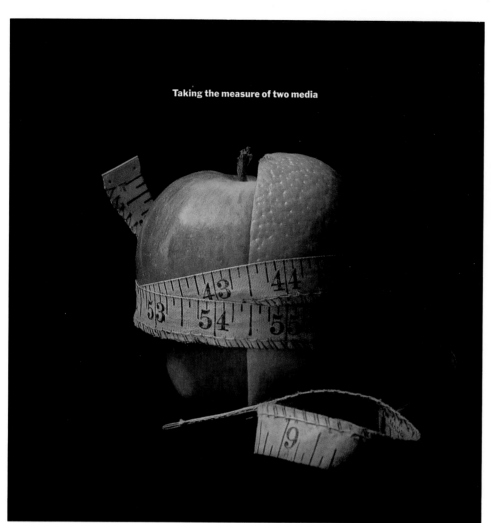

Taking the measure of two media

**Taking the Measure of
Two Media**

**A Comparison of the
Advertising Effectiveness
of Television and Magazines
Based on a
New Research Technique
Designed by the
CBS Television Network**

December 1962

(We did it!)

Efforts to equate the proverbial apples and oranges of the advertising world have
finally borne fruit. For the first time a major research undertaking compares the
efficiency of two different advertising media on an even footing—in this case magazines and network television. The CBS Television Network, which developed this
precedent-setting research, has revealed its findings in an equally advanced animated
film and in a detailed book. To attend a viewing of the film, where you will receive a
copy of the book, contact your advertising agency or the CBS Television **CBS**
Network Research Department, 485 Madison Avenue, New York 22, N.Y.

<u>Opportunities everywhere</u>
It is a Dorfsman axiom that you don't have to dig in remote places for promotional
opportunities. Many of his pet projects were triggered by something he saw, read, discovered
accidentally, or by giving an old idea a new twist.

236. A new research technique developed at CBS demonstrated that, contrary to conventional advertising dogma, you *could* compare the effectiveness of two different media — magazines and television, to be exact. Dorfsman visualized the findings as a rebuttal of the old bromide, "You can't compare apples and oranges." This brochure provided a scientific explanation of the complex research technique. With a superb still-life photo on the cover, he elevated a commonplace cliché into a persuasive promotional theme.

237. Even the disc fastener on the envelope carried through the apple and orange theme; one disc was red, the other, orange.

238. Title page of the brochure.

239. Using the same apple and orange theme, this trade paper ad invited advertisers and agency executives to come see the promotional film demonstrating the new CBS research.

240. An article in *Advertising Age* set this brochure in motion. The story dealt with the complex problem of building a market for luxury items, such as wine. Dorfsman extrapolated the problem to include other slow-selling merchandise such as gourmet delicacies, imported foods, seasonal items, and ethnic specialties outside the mainstream of popular diets. The brochure presented the case for advertising such eccentric products on radio, where frequent affordable messages could translate into more frequent sales.

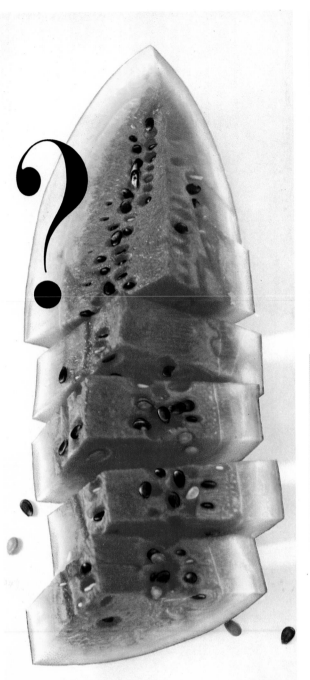

The question of how to sell a product that isn't a daily necessity — one that people just don't think of buying very often — was given cogent analysis in *Advertising Age*. It is reprinted here because it has much broader significance — as basic selling strategy — for almost every advertiser.

For example, on CBS Radio today an advertiser buying one strip of daytime drama units reaches 6.4 million different listeners, more than three times each, in a single week.

And that's 20.7 million commercial minute listener impressions, at 49¢ a thousand, delivered to a housewife audience—on shopping days.

These are the peak values that attract so many of the nation's most value-conscious advertisers to CBS Radio daytime drama. It merits your fullest appraisal.

240.

LAST NIGHT, for the first and only time in months, our dessert at dinner was watermelon. It was red, ripe, juicy, and delicious. "Why," I asked my wife, "don't we have watermelon oftener?" She thought for a moment, a puzzled look on her face. "I really don't know," she said. "I suppose I just don't think of it very often."

Certain kinds of food products—meat, bread, butter, sugar, salt, milk, etc.— are daily necessities, or nearly so, and are such habitual purchases that shoppers think of them almost automatically. But there are many other kinds of products that rarely enter the housewife's mind as she plans her daily menus. These infrequently-bought products are not necessarily costly luxuries or unenjoyable to the family; they are bought infrequently for the simple reason that the housewife seldom thinks of them.

Elmo Roper has reported to the Wine Advisory Board that vast numbers of Americans fail to buy wine oftener because they think of it only rarely. The Roper survey disclosed that many millions of people have a high regard for wine, enjoy its taste, consider it moderate, think it is healthful, and believe it to be relatively inexpensive. Despite this very favorable attitude, they consume wine infrequently. Mr. Roper says that the major reason, in the interviewee's own words, is that "I don't think of it very often."

This problem is by no means confined to watermelons and wine; any product that is not a "habit purchase" has to contend with it. It is possible that tea, for example, would be enjoyed with greater frequency in the home if more people

For frequency you need and can afford... The CBS Radio Network!

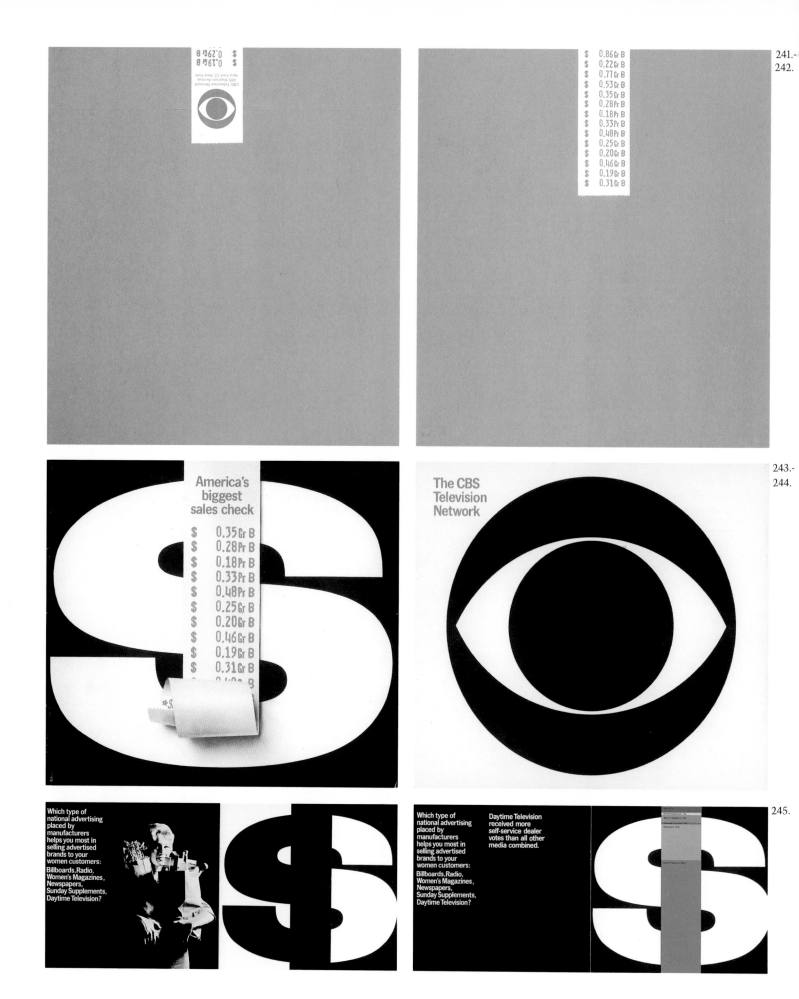

241.-
242.

243.-
244.

245.

Communication through symbols
Bombarded as advertisers are with promotional material, it takes imagination and flair to keep customers seated for yet another sales pitch. In a number of promotional brochures, familiar symbols were used in unfamiliar ways to engage attention and deliver facts succinctly.

241.- A cash register tape, a
245. dollar sign and the CBS
eye telegraphed the
point of this brochure
which reported that
merchants voted day-
time television the best
selling medium for
their advertised brands.

241.- The mailing envelope
242. was sealed with a
facsimile of a cash
register tape.

243. Front cover of booklet.

244. Back cover of booklet.

245. Inside spread demon-
strating the effective
use of a short page for
the question-and-an-
swer format.

246. In the early '50s, when
television began to
impinge on radio as an
advertising medium,
Lou found some inspir-
ing statements by
Alfred North White-
head regarding the
effectiveness of words
and sounds. The infor-
mation became the
basis for this promo-
tional brochure for CBS
Radio. The embossed
ear on the front cover
and the microphone on
the back were intrigu-
ing design details that
commanded attention
and summed up the
message.

247. An inside spread.

246.

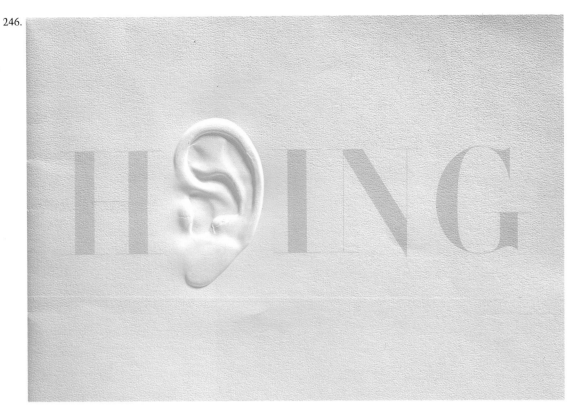

247.

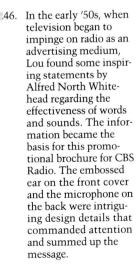

it. We can hear it wherever it comes from. (We see, by way of contrast, into just the wedge of space before our eyes. And to watch or to read what we see, we sit down.) But we *hear* up, down, and all around us—we hear globally. So radio never ties anyone down. We hear while we're on the go, as everyone knows who drives. Demanding so little in return for all the pleasure it gives, radio's fun to live with. It gives the listener the company of thousands of friends he otherwise might never have. It serves up a combo to keep time when he brushes his teeth, or a symphony at the end of his day. It keeps coming up with information...instruction ...inspiration he's glad to have. And it tells him a lot about the products he needs—which is why *people who sell things like radio.* Radio tells the sponsor's story by moving one step at a time. The second the entertainment comes

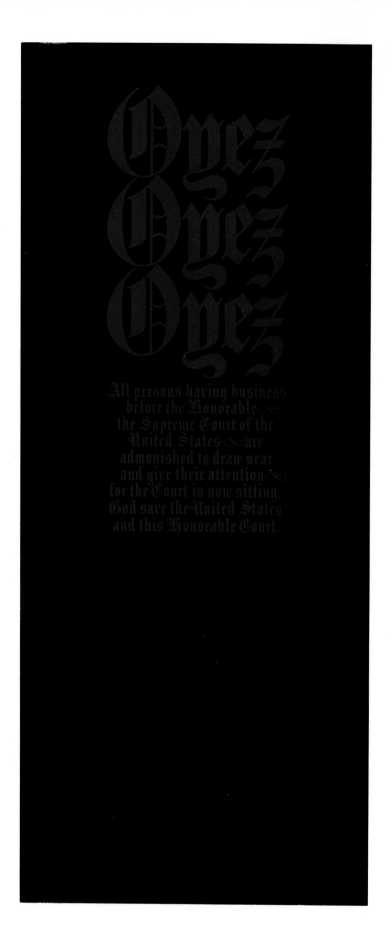

Storm Over the Supreme Court

A CBS News Broadcast
as presented over the
CBS TELEVISION NETWORK
Wednesday, March 13, 1963
7:30-8:30 pm, EST

Reporter
ERIC SEVAREID

Producer
WILLIAM PETERS

Executive Producer
FRED W. FRIENDLY

Part Two

"THE SCHOOL PRAYER CASE"

248.

Intimations of CBS leadership

A CBS news special about the Supreme Court examined the ramifications and interpretations of "freedom of the press." Under discussion were questions of the news media's responsibility in reporting news, the right to protect sources of information and similar relevant problems. This follow-up brochure to advertisers and affiliates recapitulated the broadcast, and affirmed CBS leadership and responsibility as a disseminator of public information.

Black – 1937; Stanley Reed – 1938; Felix Frankfurter – 1939; William O. Douglas – 1939; Frank Murphy – 1940.

The debate over the role of the Court continued into the forties, but now much of the controversy existed within the Court itself.

Two learned men sat side by side on the bench for nearly a quarter of a century, and engaged in a constitutional duel rivaling that of Marshall vs. Jefferson. Justice Hugo Black, born in Clay County, Alabama, a Birmingham lawyer and United States Senator before assuming his place on the Court, and Justice Felix Frankfurter, Vienna-born, educated at City College, New York, and for 25 years a distinguished professor at Harvard Law School. They filled the new Supreme Court Chamber with eloquence worthy of Holmes and Brandeis, as they argued over the interpretation of constitutional guarantees and whether the Court was attempting to engage in law making. When the Court upheld basic laws directed against the Communist party, such as the Smith Act, which made it illegal to advocate the overthrow of the government by force or violence, Justice Frankfurter sided with the majority:

Felix Frankfurter: *(Archibald MacLeish)* Congress has determined that the danger created by the advocacy of overthrow justifies the ensuing restriction on freedom of speech.... Can we establish a constitutional doctrine which forbids the elected repre-

sentatives of the people to make this choice? Can we hold that the First Amendment [of the Constitution] deprives Congress of what it deemed necessary for the government's protection?[26]

Eric Sevareid: Justice Black disagreed.

Hugo Black: *(Mark Van Doren)* Undoubtedly, a governmental policy of unfettered communication of ideas does entail dangers. To the Founders of this nation, however, the benefits derived from free expression were worth the risk.... I cannot agree that the First Amendment permits us to sustain laws suppressing freedom of speech and press on the basis of Congress's or our own notions of mere "reasonableness".... The First Amendment, as so construed, is not likely to protect any but those "safe" or "orthodox" views which rarely need its protection.[25]

Eric Sevareid: Justice Black's single-minded dedication to the Bill of Rights was such that he refused to let the First Amendment be breached even at the cost of protecting hate-mongers. In a 1952 dissent, he warned the Court that protection of the good name of any race or minority group, at the price of freedom of expression, was a hollow victory indeed.

Hugo Black: *(Mark Van Doren)* My own belief is that no Legislature is charged with the duty, or vested with the power to decide what public issues Americans can discuss. In a free country, that is the individual's

was recited until June 25, 1962, when a 6 to 1 decision of the United States Supreme Court declared the practice unconstitutional, and a new storm broke over the Supreme Court. Both Houses of Congress exploded.

Senator James O. Eastland: *(Democrat, Mississippi)* You know, it's a terrible thing to say that you can't have prayer in the schools of this country. Why, the state is founded upon religion, and I ask you, sir, to think—isn't the number one—one of the number one objectives of atheistic communism the destruction of the religious and spiritual life of this country?

William J. Butler: I didn't go there to strike God down, or to make an attack on religion. I didn't go there on behalf of a bunch of atheists. I went there on behalf of people that believe deeply in God, and who wanted to worship God their way, and I wanted to make this very clear to the Court, that I came there in the spirit of Jefferson and Madison, in the conviction that if the civil magistrate is kept out of this area, that the religious freedom of us all is that much more secure.

Announcer: CBS REPORTS: "The School Prayer Case." Here, now, is CBS News Correspondent Eric Sevareid.

Eric Sevareid: Good evening. In "Storm Over the Supreme Court" Part One, we examined the history of the High Court from John Marshall's day to Earl Warren's. Tonight—the biography of a single decision: The Regents' Prayer Case. Before the case was over,

it filled these four massive volumes, more than 1800 pages. But it all began with this single page issued in 1951 by the New York

Board of Regents, the state's highest educational body. This statement recommended that a 22-word prayer be offered at the beginning of each day of school. Some school districts ignored the recommendation. Others, including the Herricks school district, on Long Island, complied. Mrs. Mary A. Harte, a member of the Herricks school board for the past nine years, explains:

Mary A. Harte: I picked the Regents' Prayer myself. When I made the motion in 1956, in July, it was seconded by Mr. Vitale and—but it didn't pass. There was a 3 to 2 vote, so we didn't—nothing happened that year. The next year, in July, I brought it up again, and there was no second, so there was no prayer in the school. The third year, in '58, I brought it up again, and at that time it

249.

248. On the cover, "Oyez, Oyez, Oyez," the traditional words used in opening a court session, were printed in glossy red on black cloth reminiscent of judges' robes.

249. The full transcript of the broadcast, plus pivotal scenes, were reproduced on inside pages.

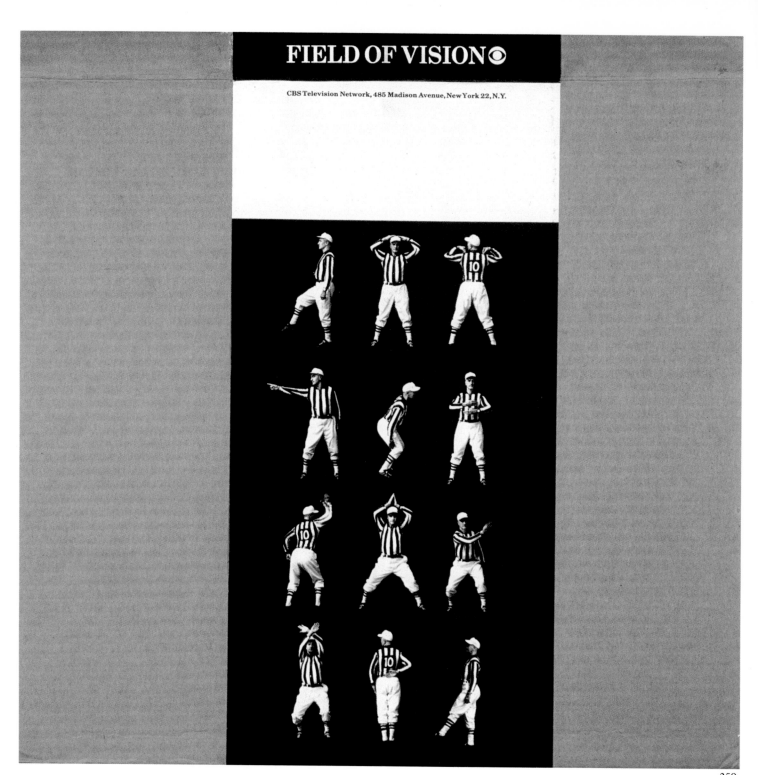

FIELD OF VISION ◉

CBS Television Network, 485 Madison Avenue, New York 22, N.Y.

250.

The Football Book
While casually shooting photos of the New York Giants in action for his
newspaper ads, Dorfsman conceived of producing this ultimate across-the-board
promotional book. (See story on page 28.) His prime purpose was to impress the National
Football League's management with CBS's technological capacity, its initiative and superb
showmanship, and thus help win renewal of the NFL broadcast franchise. In addition to NFL
executives and players, the book was also distributed to sponsors, prospective clients, CBS
stations and affiliates, and advertising agency personnel. The integrity and quality
of this book put the network in an auspicious light at a critical time.

144

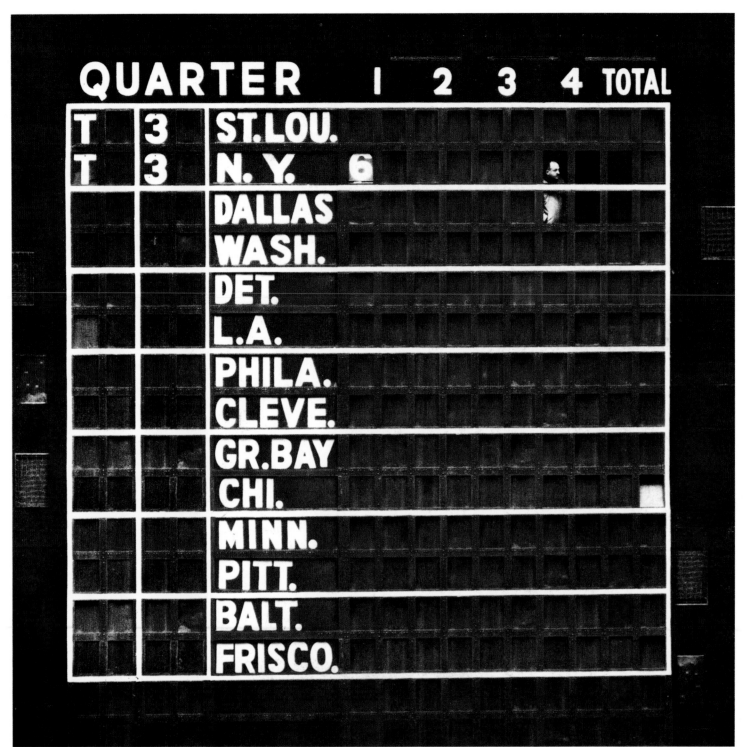

251.

250. The book was mailed in a plain brown corrugated box with a provocative wraparound label of referee signals. True to form, Dorfsman took special pleasure in using photos from a previous ad (14).

251. The cover, a photo of an actual size scoreboard, listed the 14 teams and seven games played almost simultaneously on the designated Sunday, all of which were reported in the book.

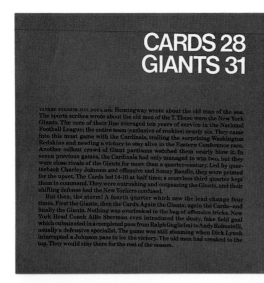

CARDS 28
GIANTS 31

YANKEE STADIUM, SUN., NOV. 4, 1962. Hemingway wrote about the old man of the sea. The sports scribes wrote about the old men of the T. These were the New York Giants. The core of their line averaged ten years of service in the National Football League; the entire team (exclusive of rookies) nearly six. They came into this must game with the Cardinals, trailing the surprising Washington Redskins and needing a victory to stay alive in the Eastern Conference race. Another sellout crowd of Giant partisans watched them nearly blow it. In seven previous games, the Cardinals had only managed to win two, but they were close rivals of the Giants for more than a quarter-century. Led by quarterback Charley Johnson and offensive end Sonny Randle, they were primed for the upset. The Cards led 14-10 at half time; a scoreless third quarter kept them in command. They were outrushing and outpassing the Giants, and their shifting defense had the New Yorkers confused.

But then, the storm! A fourth quarter which saw the lead change four times. First the Giants; then the Cards. Again the Giants; again the Cards--and finally the Giants. Nothing was overlooked in the bag of offensive tricks. New York Head Coach Allie Sherman even introduced the dusty, fake field goal which culminated in a completed pass from Ralph Guglielmi to Andy Robustelli, usually a defensive specialist. The game was still steaming when Dick Lynch intercepted a Johnson pass to ice the victory. The old men had creaked to the top. They would stay there for the rest of the season.

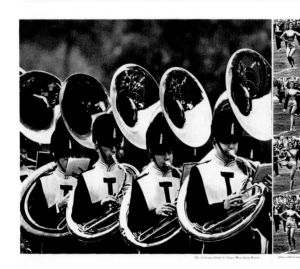

252.

252. The inside pages of the Football Book were crammed with action photos and stadium sidelights. Local newspaper photographers were commissioned to shoot the pictures; the final photos were edited from their nega-

Two reasons why the Giants won the Eastern Conference Crown, in a moment they became a one-man wall, defiant, often, impenetrable.

You've won, and it's a refreshing new feeling....

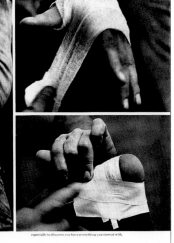

especially to discover you have everything you started with.

All the officials were doubly busy in this high-scoring free-for-all: 8 touchdowns, 4 field goals, one safety, 44 first downs, 20 incompleted passes, and 129 yards in penalties.

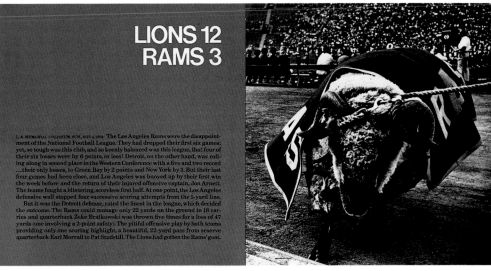

LIONS 12
RAMS 3

L.A. MEMORIAL COLISEUM, SUN. NOV 4, 1962: The Los Angeles Rams were the disappointment of the National Football League. They had dropped their first six games; yet, so tough was this club, and so keenly balanced was this league, that four of their six losses were by 6 points, or less! Detroit, on the other hand, was rolling along in second place in the Western Conference with a five and two record ...their only losses, to Green Bay by 2 points and New York by 3. But their last four games had been close, and Los Angeles was buoyed up by their first win the week before and the return of their injured offensive captain, Jon Arnett. The teams fought a blistering, scoreless first half. At one point, the Los Angeles defensive wall stopped four successive scoring attempts from the 1-yard line.

But it was the Detroit defense, rated the finest in the league, which decided the outcome. The Rams could manage only 22 yards on the ground in 18 carries and quarterback Zeke Bratkowski was thrown five times for a loss of 47 yards (one involving a 2-point safety). The pitiful offensive play by both teams providing only one scoring highlight, a beautiful, 22-yard pass from reserve quarterback Earl Morrall to Pat Studstill. The Lions had gotten the Rams' goat.

while fullback Joe Marconi keeps his quarterback from having seconds, with the help of a well-placed shoulder block.

Preston Carpenter will gladly yield this football. He's just snagged a Bobby Layne pass, good for 17 yards.

tives. The main text was written by the CBS staff. The captions describing the action were composed by an ex-pro-football player who reconstructed the plays from local newspaper accounts of the game.

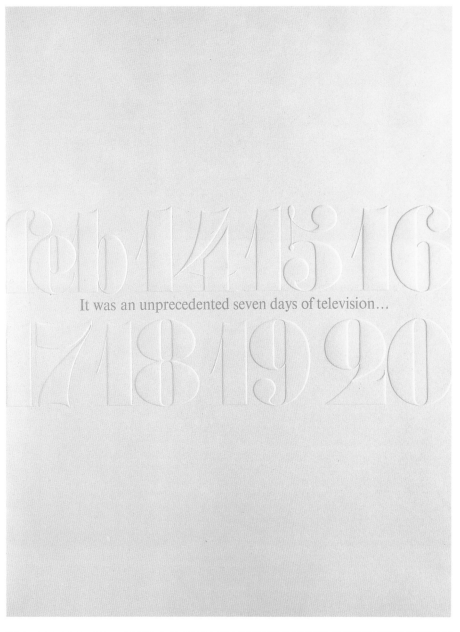

It was an unprecedented seven days of television…

Wednesday, February 14, 1962, 10 pm. As the columns of the White
emerged on the screens of some 21 million homes across the nation, the
of CBS News correspondent Charles Collingwood could be heard
"For the next hour Mrs. John F. Kennedy invites you to visit the Pres
house and see some of the restoration she has made in its interior."
that next hour the American people experienced a luminous sense of

ment in position, producer Perry Wolff, director Franklin Schaffner and
News correspondent Charles Collingwood "walked through" the
program, scene by scene, using one of their researchers as a stand-in fo
Kennedy. The next day, when the First Lady stepped in front of the car
at 11 am every contingency that could possibly be foreseen had bee
sidered. She took one "practice" walk down the corridor of the East Ha

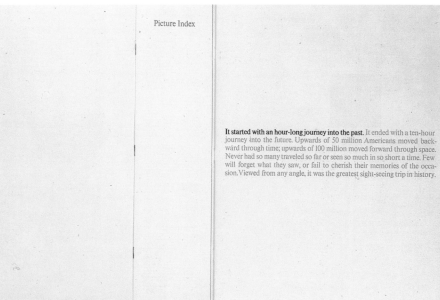

Picture Index

It started with an hour-long journey into the past. It ended with a ten-hour
journey into the future. Upwards of 50 million Americans moved back-
ward through time; upwards of 100 million moved forward through space.
Never had so many traveled so far or seen so much in so short a time. Few
will forget what they saw, or fail to cherish their memories of the occasion. Viewed from any angle, it was the greatest sight-seeing trip in history.

253.

<u>Double-header</u>
In the course of a single week, two events prompted CBS news specials. One was an unprecedented
CBS Television tour of the newly refurbished White House, with First Lady Jacqueline Kennedy as guide. The other
program covered the first manned orbit of the earth by John Glenn. The two seemingly unrelated broadcasts were recapitulated
in a single brochure under the theme "historic journeys." The text developed the idea of the White House
tour as a journey into the past, and the John Glenn tour as a journey into the future.

...e and identity. They watched Mrs. Kennedy recount with reverence, ...h and fascinating detail the memorable history of the White House, ...the television cameras caught the glitter of rare glass, the glow of ...e, the sheen of old furniture and fine fabrics—and in some mysterious, ...ensory way, the hallowed atmosphere and spirit of the nation's past. ...who watched it said: "He must be a callow and insensitive American

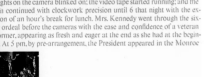

...ights on the camera blinked on; the video tape started running; and the ...on continued with clockwork precision until 6 that night with the ex-...ion of an hour's break for lunch. Mrs. Kennedy went through the six-...e ordeal before the cameras with the ease and confidence of a veteran ...ormer, appearing as fresh and eager at the end as she had at the begin-...e. At 5 pm, by pre-arrangement, the President appeared in the Monroe

in the Atlas which was then holding at T-minus-84. **At 9:47 am it happened.** From Mercury Control Center, NASA's chief information officer, Col. John Powers, could be heard uttering the critical words: "Lift-Off!" And then: "It looks like a good flight!" On the screen the great white missile seemed to tremble momentarily as it rose into the sky; then majestically assumed its orbital arc, diminishing gradually into a fiery ball as it disappeared from

view. Some thirteen minutes later, at precisely 10:00:05, one of the electronic miracles of the age took place as the muffled sound of Glenn's voice could be heard from outer space, reporting: "Capsule in good shape. Cabin pressure holding. All systems go. Capsule turning around. View is tremendous!" For the next 4 hours and 42 minutes the eyes of the nation's viewers were fixed on their television screens as they heard with a mixture of incredulity

Interlude: the extraordinary drama of the two broadcasts that opened and closed the seven-day period obscured much of what had happened on television in between. The night after their trip through the White House the nation's viewers were taken on "CBS Reports" to the Eisenhower farm in Gettysburg where the former President described his personal impressions of many of the world leaders he had known. Twenty-four hours later,

watching the CBS News program "Eyewitness," the television audience found itself touring Japan and Indonesia with United States Attorney General Robert Kennedy and his wife. On Sunday, the fiftieth anniversary of his election to Congress, Senator Carl Hayden of Arizona was interviewed on "Washington Conversation," and later that day "The Twentieth Century" presented a pictorial biography of the famous architect Frank Lloyd Wright.

253. The cover of the brochure led off with the sentence, "It was an unprecedented seven days of television."

The dates February 14, 15, 16, 17, 18, 19, 20, in blind embossing, surrounded the words.

The White House broadcast was documented with photographic details that provided a sense of his-

tory. The Glenn orbit was dramatized in storyboard fashion, with a sequence of action frames.

The theme of historic continuity carried through graphically with a band of type continuing across the pages and covers.

Worth | Repeating

"The Columbia Broadcasting System turned in a superb journalistic beat last night, running away with the major honors in reporting President Johnson's election victory. In clarity of presentation the network led all the way…In a medium where time is of the essence the performance of C.B.S. was of landslide proportions. The difference…lay in the C.B.S. sampling process called Vote Profile Analysis …the C.B.S. staff called the outcome in state after state before its rivals." THE NEW YORK TIMES (11 4 64)

"…VPA is now the most modern of election reporting techniques. It enabled CBS to demolish its competition Tuesday night. In 1962, and again in 1964, CBS has proved superior." CHICAGO DAILY NEWS (11 5 64)

"Long before 4:03 a.m., when Walter Cronkite breathed 'good night,' it was apparent that for quick, comprehensible, interesting reporting and projecting of the night's returns, neither NBC nor ABC had matched CBS." NEWSWEEK (11/16/64)

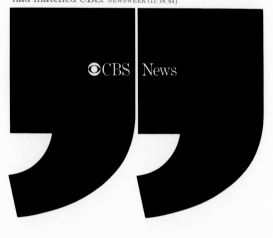

⬤CBS | News

"In the area of network performance the honors, this time, must go to CBS's Cronkite and his team of Eric Sevareid, Harry Reasoner, Roger Mudd, Robert Trout and Martin Agronsky." THE CHICAGO SUN-TIMES (11 5 64)

"…CBS, it seemed to me, did the superior job in the coverage. Walter Cronkite in the driver's seat was crisp, direct, objective and seemed confident and sure in reporting each move…thoughtful remarks of Eric Sevareid, couched in his measured prose and always with an eye toward historical perspective, seemed particularly valuable." LOS ANGELES TIMES (11 5 64)

"If we must choose our national favorite we…give our vote to Walter Cronkite…He was far and away the best of the lot." THE BOSTON HERALD (11 64)

"On Tuesday night it was the turn of the Columbia Broadcasting System News Department to ride the crest in a stunning achievement of organizational planning that provided much the clearest report of the Presidential contest." THE NEW YORK TIMES (11 8 64)

"It was easiest to know what was happening on CBS, which featured the simplest and clearest scoreboards and made the best use of computer projections… Cronkite…was skillfully in control at all times, and Eric Sevareid's interpretative comment was invariably interesting." THE PHILADELPHIA INQUIRER (11 5 64)

"…we became convinced over the exhausting hours of the full election night that Walter Cronkite turned in by far the finest job…" NEW YORK JOURNAL AMERICAN (11 4 64)

CBS News contacts New York State vote collection from the Hilton Hotel tabconv, sends totals to Network Election Service central for distribution to all media. NES vote tabulation is the fastest and most accurate ever.

254.   255.

Coverage of a news event

How do you promote your company's performance when every other major network carries the same show? Dorfsman relied on the time-honored technique of quoting an impartial expert. On election night, 1964, Jack Gould reported in *The New York Times*, "CBS demolished the competition with its Voter Profile Analysis."

predictions. The estimates were early, accurate and revealing. In a few cases where early NES tabulated vote totals appeared to contradict VPA estimates, later NES figures confirmed VPA.

As generally predicted, the presidential contest was far from close; it lacked the dramatic uncertainty of the 1960 Kennedy-Nixon election. In 1964, interest centered on the size and character of the Democratic landslide—and it was here that VPA data, dealing with the performance of identifiable groups of voters rather than mere lump totals, was most revealing. And as a tool for quick and clear evaluation of the senatorial and gubernatorial contests VPA again proved its superiority to previous systems of election reporting.

But the analytical material was the most impressive product of Vote Profile Analysis. In it could be found the main lines of political decision—and division—among various groups of the electorate—geographical,

It all started on November 3 at 6:02 p.m....

analyses, the "hows" and "whys" of the election story. At CBS News, this meant increased emphasis on VPA, the recruiting of nearly 2,000 vote reporters for the model precincts, the training of hundreds of key personnel.

It also meant facing and solving some difficult communications problems. NES would provide vote totals for all statewide and congressional elections. At the same time, VPA data would be developed for 107 major contests. This meant that a rapid flow of information would have to be reported quickly and clearly. And, of course, visual as well as editorial clarity was essential in a medium as dependent upon the eye as the ear.

Studio 41, Broadcast Center, was the laboratory in which the solutions were found. To avoid visual clutter, correspondents and cameras were elevated several feet above the heads of dozens of editors, writers and analysts, hurried messengers and harried secretaries. Also unseen, though by no means unsung, was the

residential, economic, ethnic and religious. To examine this data in detail is to realize that the revolution in election reporting has only begun.

The deeper meaning of every national election is something to be pondered and argued for a long time. But in 1964 the main facts, the major statistics, the raw material for understanding were right there in Studio 41. And the nation shared them, in broad outline, before the network finally said goodnight.

That au revoir came at 4:01:35 on the morning of November 4, which happens to be Walter Cronkite's birthday. The home audience, fortunately perhaps, did not witness the concluding performance from Studio 41, a ragged but happy rendition of "Happy Birthday."

But it was a beginning, not an ending. In ten hours CBS News had opened the electronic age of election reporting. The Election Unit, which started it all, is now working toward 1966 and 1968.

"Within an hour after the polls had closed in the Far West, the Vote Profile Analysis method of projecting results produced figures, nationally and regionally, that are proving accurate within a fraction of a per-centage point." THE NEW YORK TIMES (11 5 64)

"The record will show that...CBS ran away with the honors...for those viewers who wanted to know what was happening, CBS was the network to watch. Analysis and evaluations by such CBS commentators as Eric Sevareid, Martin Agronsky and Roger Mudd gave fuller meaning to the story than was provided by the other networks." CHICAGO DAILY NEWS (11 4 64)

"Walter Cronkite, Harry Reasoner and Roger Mudd made a pleasant and efficient troika of anchormen with a boundless supply of analysis and interpretations." THE EVENING BULLETIN (PHILADELPHIA) (11 4 64)

"The CBS margin was due mainly, I think, to its more clearcut manner of presentation, which enabled it to pinpoint the various state triumphs more directly than its competitors—often by more than a matter of minutes." THE BOSTON GLOBE (11 4 64)

"Cronkite took off like a screaming rocket last night, snatched the lead in reporting returns, then jovially maintained his control through the evening...In addition to his usual articulateness and accuracy, he was supremely confident of the CBS system of vote projection and witty as he obviously was aware he had the situation in control." THE INDIANAPOLIS TIMES (11 4 64)

...and ended on November 4 at 4:02 a.m.

254. The quotation and punctuation marks were turned into graphic devices for the front and back covers of a follow-up brochure promoting CBS's election night coverage.

255. The inside pages re-played the CBS broad-cast like a dramatic event. Details of the broadcast were strung out in storyboard fashion, as seen by TV viewers at home. Against the small clips, panoramic shots of CBS election head-quarters displayed the sophisticated equip-ment and extensive personnel involved in the event.

151

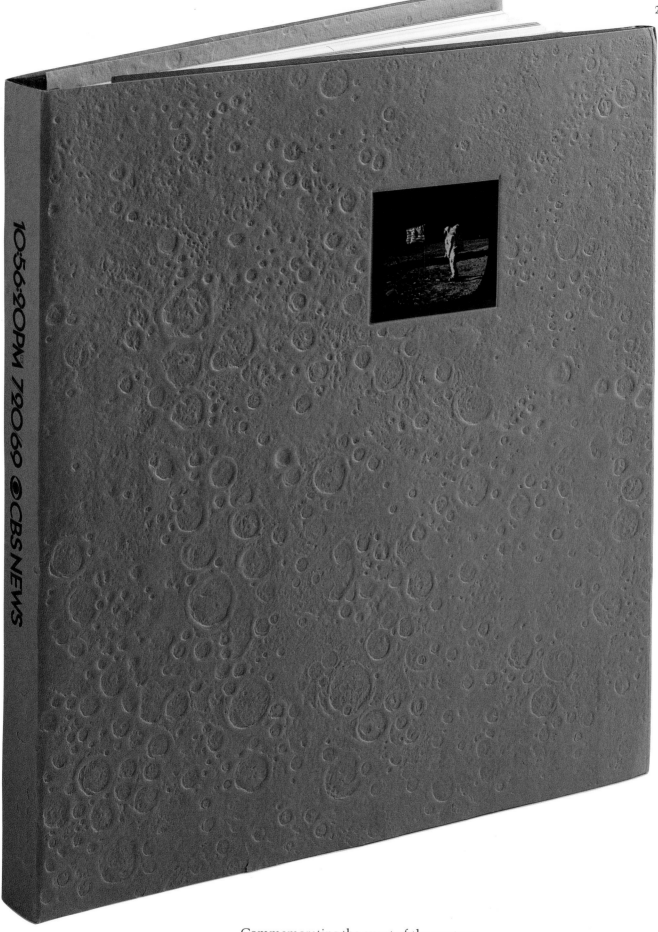

Commemorating the event of the century

Frank Stanton proposed the book; Dorfsman designed and produced it. Of all his labors on behalf of CBS, none so completely epitomized Lou's fantastic integrity as the book commemorating man's trip to the moon. Twenty thousand copies were published in hardcover. They were distributed to CBS clients, stations and affiliates; to government agencies, advertising agencies, educational institutions, school and public libraries. The quality of the book from concept to cover was another tangible testimonial to CBS's eminence as a communications institution.

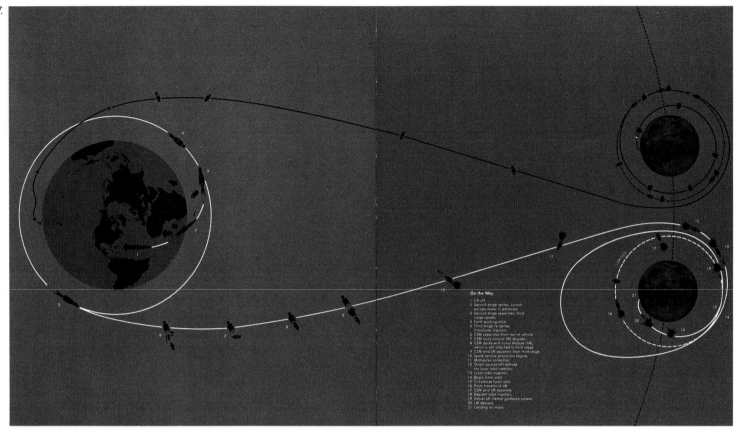

On the Way

1 Lift-off.
2 Second stage ignites. Launch escape tower is jettisoned.
3 Second stage separates; third stage ignites.
4 Earth parking orbit.
5 Third stage re-ignites. Translunar injection.
6 CSM separates from rest of vehicle.
7 CSM turns around 180 degrees.
8 CSM docks with Lunar Module (LM), which is still attached to third stage.
9 CSM and LM separate from third stage.
10 Ignite service propulsion engine.
11 Mid-course correction.
12 Orient spacecraft attitude for lunar orbit insertion.
13 Lunar orbit insertion.
14 Begin lunar orbit.
15 Circularize lunar orbit.
16 Pilots transfer to LM.
17 CSM and LM separate.
18 Descent orbit insertion.
19 Adjust LM inertial guidance system.
20 LM descent.
21 Landing on moon.

10:56:20PM ^{EDT} 7/20/69

The historic conquest of the moon as reported to the American people by CBS News over the CBS Television Network.

256. The jacket is a blind embossed replica of the precise area of the moon where the astronauts landed. A plaster model was made of the area, based on a NASA map. From that, the brass embossing die was cast. The textured paper was made to match the color of moon fragments brought back by the astronauts. The color photo, tipped on each book by hand, marks the exact landing site.

257. The first two pages contain a 'road map' of the trip, from lift-off to landing, indicating all rocket adjustments, mid-course corrections, separation of the lunar module and the final landing.

258. The title page bears the time and date to the exact moment Neil Armstrong set foot on the moon. The subtitle established CBS's involvement in reporting the event to the American people.

same for these kids. I don't think the past means anything to them. This is all very natural to them.

Cronkite: *I've noticed in the reporting that those under 16, who've really grown up with space since its first memorable moments—when they were four or so and the space thing was just coming into being— understand it and want more detail in our reporting. They want to know about escape velocity and they want to know about the lunar trajectory velocity, and those over 30 or so say, "Don't tell me all that, I just don't understand. Tell me when we get there."*

Sevareid: *Furthermore, this is not a romantic era, not a poetic era. The beauty the young find is in the things themselves. All the imagery and the words will come later, but we really don't have a language to describe this thing.*

As we sit here today, what are the words you use? I think the language is being altered, many new words and phrases and concepts are being added, and, I think, some language is being eliminated. How do you say "high as the sky" anymore, or "the sky is the limit"—what does that mean?

Cronkite: *Maybe it's that we have been so busy, so many things crowding in on us, we haven't had time for language.*

Sevareid: *There's always a great cultural lag on these things. It takes a long time for a new language to emerge.*

Many of the spectators had never witnessed the launch of a manned Apollo mission. For them, the moment of lift-off was an extraordinary one.

Treated pretty much like rookies who are about to play their first major league baseball game, they were regaled with stories of how they were about to witness one of the most awesome sights known to man. They were told that the man-made explosion is second only to that of the atomic bomb, that the roar at lift-off is deafening and the flames blinding, and that you can actually feel the sound waves slap against you as the Saturn V climbs the tower.

14

These descriptions aren't far from wrong. On a good, clear day one can see the "bird" some two and one-half minutes into its flight, two and one-half minutes that seem like twice that long to even the most casual observer. It seems that it takes a minute before the rocket starts to move, and an hour before it starts to climb the tower, and then streaks off into the sky spitting a white flame back at those on the ground.

You wait for the word that everything is going as planned. Then it comes from the astronaut serving as capsule communicator (CAPCOM) in Houston.

Capcom: **This is Houston, you are go for staging.**

Apollo 11: **Inboard cutoff.** [The inboard engines on the first stage have been shut down.]

Capcom: **Inboard cutoff.**

Apollo 11: **Staging and ignition.** [Astronaut Neil Armstrong tells the ground that the first stage of the rocket has fallen away and that the engines of the second stage have ignited on schedule.]

Capcom: **11, Houston, thrust is go all engines, you are looking good.**

Apollo 11: **Roger. Hear you loud and clear, Houston.**

Everyone reacts differently during these moments. Common symptoms are a sudden cold feeling in the chest and tears in the eyes, even for those who have lived the experience before. Eric Sevareid admitted that his eyes filled with tears when he saw Apollo 11 leave the launch pad. Dr. Ralph Abernathy, who led a poor people's march to the area to protest the huge expenditures of money in space that he believed should be spent on eliminating poverty, told CBS News Correspondent Ed Rabel that for a few moments he forgot why he was there.

Abernathy: *There's a great deal of joy and pride. For that particular moment and second I really forgot that we have so many hungry people in the United States of America. But now I remember that we will have to go back to business as usual in trying to really launch a pro-*

15

259. The text provided a detailed account of the moon shot and the telecast, interspersed with actual recorded dialogue between the astronauts, NASA officials and technicians, CBS co-anchors Wally Shirra and Walter Cronkite, and other CBS newsmen. The complex text provided a fascinating experience in typography. The book is set entirely in the Century typeface family. But to differentiate between speakers, variations of the typeface were used, i.e., CBS journalists' words appear in Century Expanded Italic; the astronauts speak in Century Bold; and editorial comments are in yet another weight.

260. A 48-page pictorial essay provides a full-color record of the voyage. Cameras locked on closed circuit monitors had recorded the action second-by-second. The actual landing was photographed by a camera

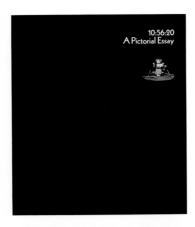

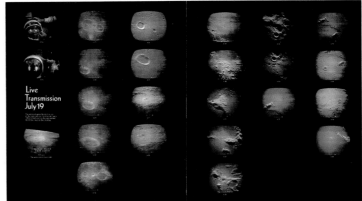

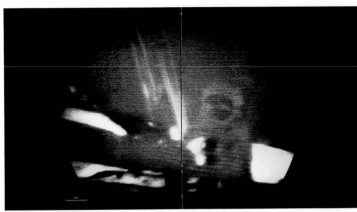

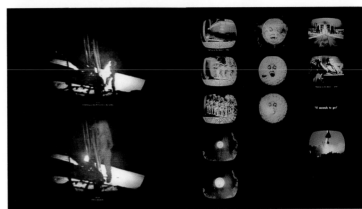

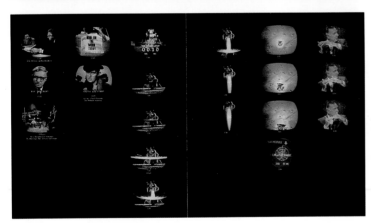

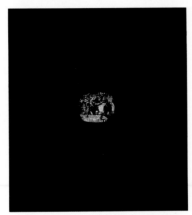

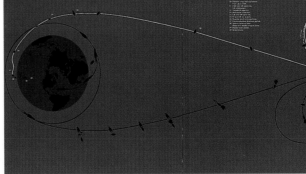

261.

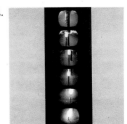

262.

dismounted from the capsule. Out of thousands of off-screen pictures, 400 were selected for the book. To enhance the quality of the off-screen photos, they were masked off in the shape of TV frames and washed over with clear varnish. The surrounding black paper was treated with a matte varnish to resist fingerprints and damage from repeated handling.

261. The final two pages contained a diagram of the return voyage to Earth, indicating all stages from lift-off to splashdown.

262. The Moon Book was distributed in a plain brown corrugated box sealed with a wrap-around photo of the lift-off.

263.

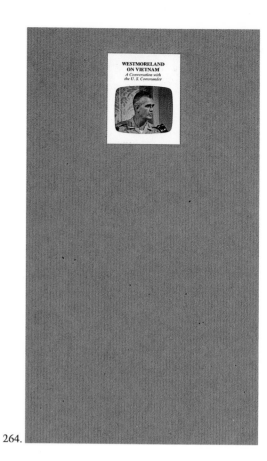

264.

265.

<u>Follow through</u>
One-time news specials were given
secondary lives with this package that summarized five
memorable CBS broadcasts of 1966.

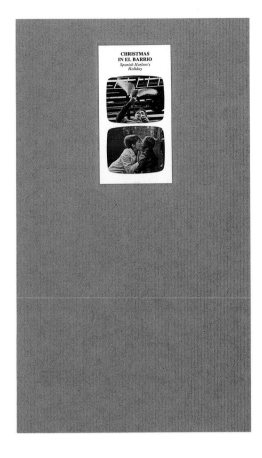

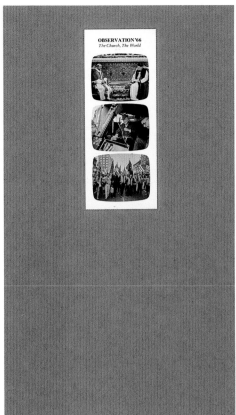

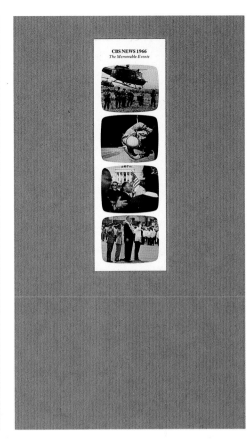

263. The mailing package consisted of a black cloth fold-out box that tied with a string at the side. Blind embossed on the cover were the words: "1966, A Year of Movement, A Year of Hope, A Year of Controversy."

264. Each brochure recapitulated one of the news specials. On the covers, color photos set in TV frames, identified the broadcasts. Shown here, from left to right, General Westmoreland in Vietnam, Christmas in El Barrio, The Church and the World, and Memorable Events of 1966.

265. Inside pages reproduced scenes and excerpts of the narration of each broadcast.

After they learn to spell C-A-T

Who's going to teach them to T-H-I-N-K?

A kid today can watch television and painlessly learn that a cat is spelled c-a-t, that it goes meow, and that if it now has nine kittens and then gets one more it has 10 kittens altogether.

All of which is pretty much kids' stuff.

Which is all it's supposed to be. Elementary. "See Dick. See Dick run" made into a motion picture.

It's television that's intended to help parents and schools teach kids the basics. A steady diet of this whimsy-cum-learning should be sufficient to equip most kids with the raw tools of learning. Reading. Writing. Counting. All the rote skills they need to know before they get to the heavier stuff.

And that brings us to a whole other level of children's programming. The heavier stuff. The hours devoted to helping kids learn how to think. How to make the connections from one area of living to another. How to abstract what has been learned from one subject and apply it to a totally new subject.

That's the incredibly big (and important) job that has been undertaken by the five CBS Owned television stations.

They deal with the many faces of knowledge. From A for aardvark to Z for zoology. In between, they touch lightly or probe in depth the limitless subjects of modern times, including science, art, the humanities.

Inside, you'll find a number of examples of the kinds of programs we're talking about.

It's a mixed bag. A kid who watched them all could learn a whole lot of things about a whole lot of things. Mostly important things. But it would include some information that he or she would delight in simply passing on to friends. (Immediately, a mind-bending program on how to crate an elephant comes to mind.) We know a big group of kids and adults who don't know what use they'll make of the facts they've learned, but they wouldn't have missed them for the world.

It includes a history of flying, from Icarus on down. And a new series called THE YOUNG REPORTERS, in which a bunch of nice, bright high school kids interview people like John Wayne and Walter Cronkite and ask the kinds of questions that

"IF YOU WANT CAPTAIN HOOK'S DREADFUL CAKE TO RISE, CLOSE YOUR EYES AND SAY, 'I BELIEVE.'"

There's a version of Peter Pan we know about that has to be the most breathtaking production of Barrie's classic ever performed.

Happily, it's ours.

It is quite an unusual piece of theater. The star is Breanna Buettow, a former hostess of "Romper Room," and she recites the story while she's telling and showing her audience how to bake a simply delicious and deliciously simple version of Captain Hook's Dreadful Cake.

And along the way she slips in some basic cooking instructions with particular emphasis on the aspects of kitchen safety and cleanliness.

And what happens when it's shown is that kids watch wide-eyed as Miss Buettow weaves her tale and bakes her cake. And they anticipate two spine-tingling climaxes.

Will Tinker Bell live?

Will the cake rise?

Tune in this delightful television special when it comes your way and find out for yourself.

THE STORYBOOK COOK

WHO IS THE MYSTERIOUS BLACK KNIGHT, AND WHY DID THE BEAUTEOUS REBECCA LOOK SO STRANGELY AT HIM? AND WHAT OF ROBIN HOOD? WHAT PLANS DOES HE HAVE AFOOT? TUNE IN TOMORROW AND HEAR ROWENA SAY...

Ivanhoe. If you liked the book, you'll love the BBC's 10-part production that we have incorporated into our children's programming.

What's more important, if you were forced to read it too early and didn't like it (something that happens all too frequently, e.g. Shakespeare), this might get you back for a more mature, understandable reading.

Because it's lavish, exciting theater. The cast is composed of Old Vic, Royal Shakespeare Company and Canterbury Repertory graduates, and they bring Sir Walter Scott's classic adventure tale vividly, startlingly to life.

It's a production that doesn't blind its audience to the somber aspects of the novel by the glittering romance of its high adventure. Explicit throughout the production are the grim realities of feudalism and the bloody power struggle between the Saxons and the Normans.

We won't ruin it for you by telling you who the Black Knight really was. But if you don't remember, it's because you didn't pay attention to IVANHOE when you were forced to read it as a kid.

That's a problem we don't have with our kids. They pay attention. Because they want to.

IVANHOE

HUGHES RUDD IN THE MORNING

IT'S LIKE RAISING A SHADE TO LET A LITTLE SUNSHINE IN

AS AMERICAN AS...

Up in Onondaga County, New York, some Kiwanis Clubs asked a fellow named Lister Benjamin to come up with some way to celebrate

Lights Went Out in Georgia," for instance. And as for post-operative care, how about "I've Got Tears in My Ears from Lyin' on My Back in Bed Crying over You"? Budding obstetricians could get a quick course in the mothering instinct by listening to "I Keep Asking Her What She Wants 'Em

Fer; She Just Smiles and Looks at Me and Says I Want A Little Baby." If the medical student plans to specialize in the care of alcoholics, "From the Bottle to the Bottom Stool by Stool" might help. And as for would-be gastroenterologists, well, all country music fans know all about gastroenteritis. Beer, chili and stale grease at Rosalie's Good Eats Cafe will do it to you every time. In short, that jukebox at the Albany medical school is a good idea whose time has come. Physicians in this country are woefully undereducated about the things that matter in Nashville. How many psychiatrists do you know who can sing all the verses of "Beneath a Neon Star in a Honky-Tonk I Fell in Love with You"? Most of 'em can't even hum it. Anyway, if you need a doctor, we hope you get one with Fritos and Dixie lager on his breath.

FOR THOSE WHO ARE ALL THUMBS...

People in this country are forever writing books about "What To Do Until The Doctor Arrives" —giving little tips about making the patient lie down or sit up or where to put the ice-pack and so on. But now there's a new book which seems to tell you just to twiddle your thumbs. It's called Nature's Rejuvenating Principles and in it the author, a Mrs. Valeska, says that if you get a headache, for instance, the way to cure it is to rub your thumbs with your forefingers, and if that doesn't work, rub your big toes with your thumbs.

In extreme cases, she says, press your thumb against the roof of your mouth. In case you come down with a cold,

Mrs. Valeska says the way to handle that is to grab hold of your tongue at the sides, stretch it out as far as you can and hold it there for five minutes. Of course, a cure like that's best undertaken in the privacy of your room. If somebody spots you doing that out in public,

To whom it may concern
Whether directed at the public, clients, affiliates, or employees, every graphic communication from CBS was treated with the utmost consideration and produced in a style that was relevant to its purpose.

266. A booklet designed to promote educational children's programs on the five CBS-owned stations. Each page was devoted to a review of a CBS children's show. The imaginative drawings by John Alcorn set the tone. The text is sincere and highly readable, with short paragraphs and open-spaced typography.

267. A brochure promoting the Hughes Rudd morning show was written in the breezy, vernacular style of the broadcasts, and illustrated with appropriate wit and humor by Jerome Snyder.

268. A series of pamphlets detailing employee benefit plans treated such somber topics as accidents, life insurance, disability, illness, old age, and death with light-hearted illustrations by John Alcorn to dispel the gloom and doom.

269. Another series of pamphlets were illustrated by R.O. Blechman.

268.

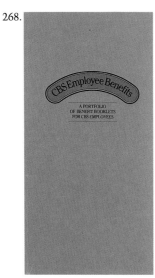

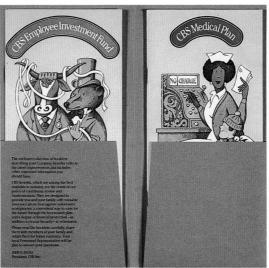

AN EXPLANATION OF THE
CBS TRAVEL ACCIDENT PLAN
FOR ELIGIBLE CBS EMPLOYEES

269.

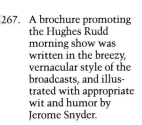

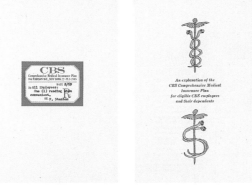

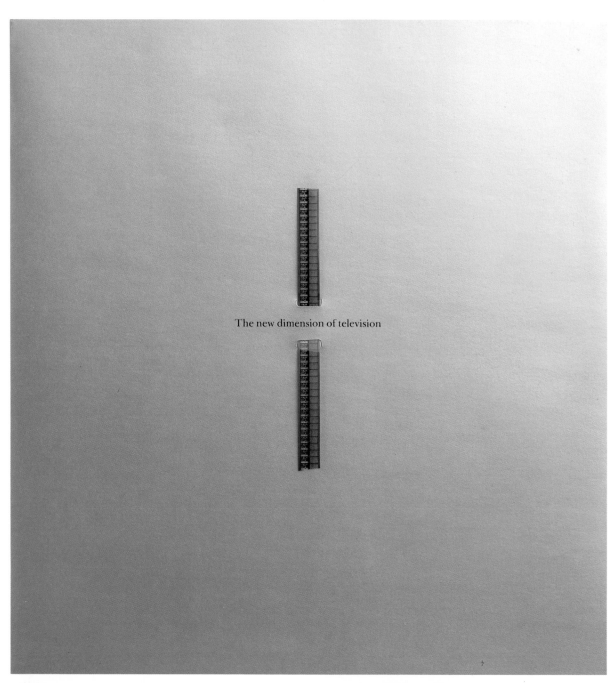

The new dimension of television

Cover of a book prepared for CBS Labs to introduce their Video Cassette Recorder— the first ever offered for sale. Along with the words, "The New Dimension in Television," the cover also held a strip of the actual film threaded through die-cut slots. Such details—die-cuts, hand-tipped-on photos, blind embossing— enriched and distinguished CBS promotions.

Interior spreads described the CBS Labs' innovation which combined film and electronic technology and was a precursor of the contemporary all-electronic unit.

In the same way that a long-playing record stores sound conveniently, inexpensively and with high fidelity on a record for selective play on standard phonographs, the EVR System stores pictures with sound for playback of consistently high resolution through any standard television receiver.

Both motion picture film and video tape can be recorded for distribution in EVR Cartridges.

There are three elements to the EVR System:

1. The thin EVR Film is less than ⅜ of an inch wide and is divided into two parallel channels, each with its own magnetic sound track. The monochrome version utilizes these two channels for separate programming, one program on channel A, the other on channel B. EVR color uses one channel for luminance (image information) and the other for chrominance (color information). The film is the same material whether for black and white or color display.

in fact, enroll in formal correspondence courses to sharpen and extend their skills.

Whether young or old, a high school or college graduate, an individual must study to keep up, to adapt, to increase his competence. Since more than 96 percent of America's 63 million homes have television sets, the EVR System is the logical key to home study. Wherever in the world they may be, the most inspired educators and other leading authorities in their fields will now be able to appear on film and give the student the next best thing to face-to-face lectures. And he will be able to study at his own pace— in the calm and privacy of his own home.

When not being used for home study, an EVR Player and Cartridge will also provide hours of exciting and stimulating recreation. Before that Saturday morning round of golf, the owner can insert a cartridge into the player and get a quick lesson. Or he can settle down for an evening of seeing and hearing Hamlet or some other selection from his

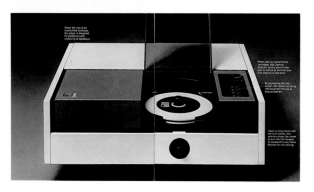

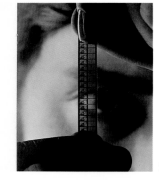

Dorfsman-designed logos
Some designers leave their fingerprints on
everything they do. What is most consistent about Dorfsman's designs are their
inconsistency in style, and their relevance to each particular purpose.

1963

Diaries

Unlike the promotional kits, brochures and books which were pure business, CBS also mailed an annual gift to clients and business associates. It took the form of a diary/calendar for the coming year. While Dorfsman went to great lengths to make these diaries entertaining and handsome, they were not entirely without a commercial tinge. All the illustrations, subtly or blatantly, promoted the CBS Television Network. Dorfsman also cloned illustrations from the diaries for spin-off trade ads, thus effectively amortizing his production costs.

A TELEVISION NOTEBOOK

with satirical drawings by Tomi Ungerer

CBS TELEVISION NETWORK
1963

Monday / 14 JANUARY		Saturday / 19
Tuesday / 15		day / 20
Wednesday / 16		
Thursday / 17		
Friday / 18		

Monday / 17 JUNE		Saturday / 22
Tuesday / 18		Sunday / 23
Wednesday / 19		
Thursday / 20		
Friday / 21		

Monday / 23 SEPTEMBER		Saturday / 28
Tuesday / 24		Sunday / 29
Wednesday / 25		
Thursday / 26		
Friday / 27		

272.

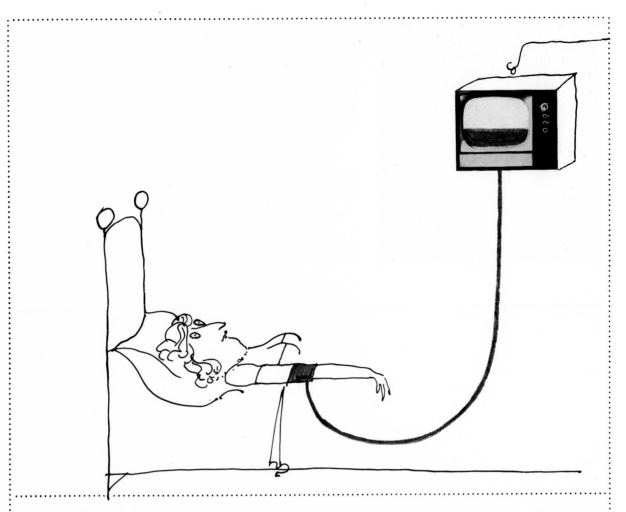

Some women can't live without it. Indeed, our daytime line-up is such a vital part of their lives that the 9 most popular programs are all ours. Of our 16 daytime programs, 12 are in the Top 15. The ladies have taken us to their hearts. CBS Television Network ◉

273.

We're all set with the ladies—attracting 57% bigger daytime audiences than the next network, 106% more than the third—and leading for the sixth straight year. The beauty part is that it may be permanent. CBS Television Network®

Here are the latest results, straight from the horse's mouth. Our Nielsen average audience rating for the season to date is 19.9. The second network is two lengths back at 17.9. The third network comes in at 15.5. Needless to say the smart money is on the winner. CBS Television Network®

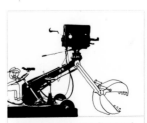

Digging around, we've discovered that of all the shows in television's Top 40 four years ago only 10 are still there today. And the big scoop is this: all 10 are ours. You can build another good season on a foundation like that. CBS Television Network ◉

At night we're really lowering the boom. Just to fill you in: of the 40 programs reaching 10 million or more homes, we have 21. While the second network has ten and the third network nine, we have more than both combined... and it doesn't hurt a bit. CBS Television Network®

A
Television
Notebook

including a glossary of television terms
artfully interpreted by John Alcorn
CBS Television Network / 1964

Cut in. (a) Commercial insert carried on a part of the
network. (b) Secondary image inserted in the picture.

Friday 17 / April

Cut'ting Room. A specially-equipped room in which
film elements are edited and prepared for broadcast.

Saturday 18 / April

Sunday 19 / April

In·te'ri·or Sounds. The sounds of an object, such as a
train, as they would be heard from within the object.

Friday 10 / July

In·ter·lac'ing. Process in which successively scanned
lines are interspersed to form the television picture.

Saturday 11 / July

Sunday 12 / July

Trap. An opening in the stage floor which permits
the performers to make their entrances and exits.

Monday 21 / December

Trick shot. To create an unusual situation with a
mirror, superimposition or other technical devices.

Tuesday 22 / December

274. The 1964 diary was
built around television
terminology. The
everyday vocabulary of
the television studio
and television viewing
was interpreted with
deliberate ingenuous-
ness by illustrator John
Alcorn.

275. A full-page, spin-off
trade ad composed of
all the Alcorn illustra-
tions created for the
1964 Diary.

274.

A Glossary of Television Terms

Some illustrations of recent additions to our lexicon as striking as the changes in our nation's habits: last year the average American television family spent more time viewing than ever before — 5 hours and 17 minutes a day.

All Out. When a picture previously superimposed on another is removed from the original picture.

Eye Cam'er-a. A camera specially designed to simulate the movement of the eyes on a reading surface.

Juic'er. Any television electrician who is especially trained and equipped to work with heavy power lines.

Nut. As applied to television, the complete cost of producing a program. Also called, "the whole nut."

Town Cri'er. A slang expression which refers to a vocalist who is noted for exceptional strength of voice.

Au'di-o. That portion of a television transmission pertaining to sound as opposed to the picture (video).

Fish Bowl. An observation booth, sometimes overlooking the studio, which contains television monitors.

Jump. The elimination of a previously planned scene from a film, which requires the film to be respliced.

One Shot. (a) Single show as opposed to series. (b) One installment script. (c) Subject which fills screen.

Trap. An opening in the stage floor which permits the performers to make their entrances and exits.

Ba'by Spot'light. The smallest of the incandescent spotlights which utilizes 100-watt or 150-watt bulbs.

Flood. A light which projects a broad, well-diffused beam on a set, encompassing all subjects in a scene.

Key'light. The principal source of directional illumination which falls upon a given object, area or scene.

Out'line. The synopsis or initial written account of a proposed television program. Also called scenario.

Ve-ne'tian Blind. A video tape displacement of lines in a band, causing a sawtooth vertical picture edge.

Bull'frog. The slang expression for a television performer with an exceptionally deep, resonant voice.

Gal'lows. An open frame which supports drapes and allows the cameras and equipment to pass through.

Kill. To order the elimination of any production element, including scene, set, action or the entire show.

Pan. To follow the action of any scene to the left or to the right by the gradual swinging of the camera.

View'er. (a) Person watching a television program. (b) Machine used to study film for editing purposes.

Cam'er-a Hog. A performer who monopolizes camera action to the exclusion of other persons in a scene.

Ground Cloth. A large section of waterproof canvas used as a protective or decorative cover for the stage.

Lick. An ad-libbed musical phrase which does not appear in the score. An ad lib in jazz is a "hot lick."

Per'i-scope. A special arrangement of mirrors which permits making camera shots not normally possible.

Wings. Entrance and storage area immediately offstage concealed from the camera or studio audience.

Core. The plastic or metal center section upon which film is often wound for storage or shipping purposes.

Hand Props. Movable materials of any description which are used or carried on stage by a performer.

Lock'jaw. (a) A performer who delivers lines without expression. (b) A vocalist who lacks inspiration.

Ride it. An instruction to the orchestra members on a television program to improvise or ad lib the score.

Woof. The word sometimes spoken into a microphone to check amplitude or to synchronize timing.

Dis-tor'tion. A picture change produced deliberately for special effect, or caused by equipment failure.

Hiss. A disturbing sound appearing at random in the audio frequency range of a television broadcast.

Me-chan'i-cal An-i-ma'tion. Drawings of inanimate objects given movement through a device called a rig.

Roll. A television picture which flips up and down due to improper synchronization of power source.

Zoom. Effect created by variable focus lens to make the subject appear to move to or from the camera.

Drop. Scenery which is suspended from metal framework or grid near the studio roof and is not framed.

Ink'er. Artist who traces the animator's drawings on celluloid sections which are later photographed.

Min'i-a-ture. Models of large objects (houses, automobiles, props) which appear as normal on camera.

Slide. A transparent frame of film which is mounted between two pieces of glass for use in a projector.

Ex-po'sure. To subject photographic film to the light in order to produce a hidden image on the emulsion.

In-te'ri-or Sounds. The sounds of an object, such as a train, as they would be heard from within the object.

Net. An abbreviation for network or multiple television stations linked by coaxial cables or microwaves.

Slow Mo'tion. To photograph at faster than normal rate so that the projected action will appear slower.

Lead'er-ship. The quality invariably associated with the CBS Television Network. e.g. 1. Biggest average daytime audiences for six consecutive years. 2. Biggest average nighttime audiences for nine years. 3. Specifically, this season* CBS delivers one million more homes, both day and night, than the second network; two million more than the third. 4. Since 1954, this Network has been the world's largest single advertising medium. CBS Television Network®

276.

276. With the 1970 Diary, for a change of pace Dorfsman switched from illustration to photography, and from whimsy to a more serious presentation of the CBS story. The cover was silver mylar; CBS and the logo were blind-embossed on the front, 1970 on the back.

277. The photographs spotted throughout the diary were reminders of the ramifications of the television medium. Photos showed receivers in living rooms, kitchens, recreation rooms, boats, hospitals, nursing homes, fire stations, hotels — all demonstrating the pervasiveness of TV and its potential as an advertising medium.

1970

6 FRIDAY
FEBRUARY

7 SATURDAY
FEBRUARY

8 SUNDAY
FEBRUARY

3 MONDAY
AUGUST

4 TUESDAY
AUGUST

25 FRIDAY
DECEMBER

26 SATURDAY
DECEMBER

27 SUNDAY
DECEMBER

277.

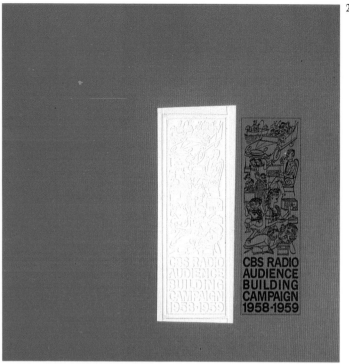

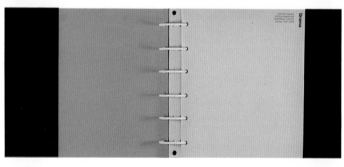

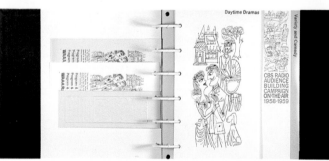

Packaging the promotions

For every show the network offered in the '50s and '60s, it produced comprehensive promotional kits to help sponsors and stations build local audiences. The packages contained background information about the shows and the stars, proofs of network advertising in support of the programs, mat ads for local advertising, photos, publicity releases, film strips, etc.

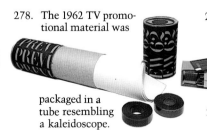

278. The 1962 TV promotional material was packaged in a tube resembling a kaleidoscope.

279. Cover for a CBS Radio audience building campaign 1958-1959. The red loose-leaf binder came with an actual ad mat tipped on the front.

280. Inside pages contained summaries of radio

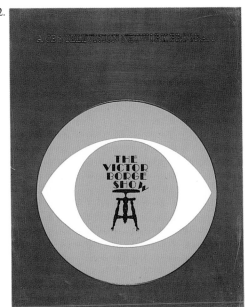
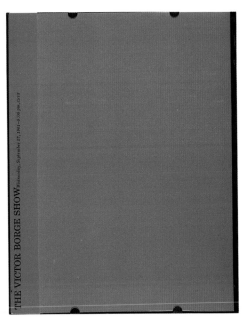
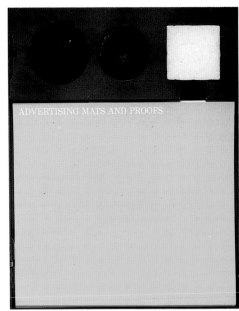

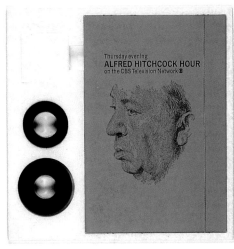

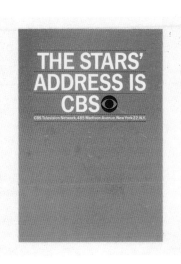
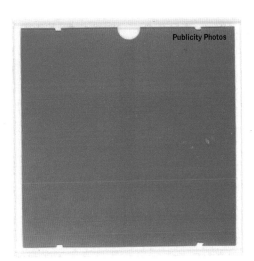

shows, with commercials, ad mats, photos, and press releases pertinent to each program. Brightly colored dividers separated the sections.

281. In 1963-64, all the promotional material for CBS daytime television programs was packed into this compact file cabinet. Inside was a box containing 10 and 20-second film strips for on-air promotions, as well as materials for print advertising in folders.

285.

282.-285. Dorfsman experimented with boxing promotional materials in expensive-looking packages. At first he used high impact styrene, but found later that styrofoam was less expensive and equally esthetic and functional. Each box contained promotional material sorted into file folders according to category. The bottom of the box had "nests" to accommodate slides and 16mm film strips in two lengths for on-air TV promos.

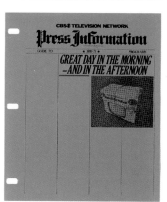

286.

287.

To the media
Aside from their enormous expenditures on
advertising and promotion, networks pursue all the free publicity they can get.
To that end newspaper and magazine editors are provided with newsworthy information about the
networks' activities, including reviews of new shows, information about sponsors, directors,
producers, network personnel, and bios and photos of the stars. In this area, as in others,
CBS efforts went beyond the expected in organization and esthetics.

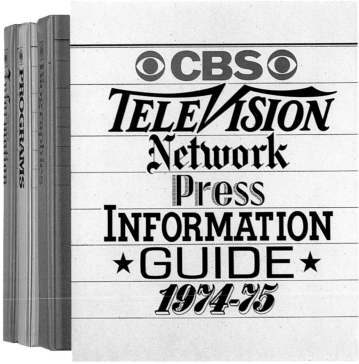

288.

289.

286.-287. Examples of CBS press kits packaged in convenient loose-leaf binders. The information was presented as hot-off-the-press news items, a refreshing departure from the usual, dull, no-frills printed sheets of data.

288.-289. It would be hard to ignore press kits packaged in these substantial, expensive-looking boxed sets.

290.

291.

292.

293.

290.-293. Dorfsman, who doesn't usually like to repeat himself, did so with purpose in this 1956 series of election-related promotional kits. All three packages contained materials to help CBS stations publicize their convention coverage (290), the candidates' campaign activities (291) and election night returns (292). The outer flaps, all uniform in design, opened to an inner gate-fold (293) which secured the promotional materials. The consistency of format throughout the campaign multiplied the impact of CBS support for its stations.

294. The 1968 TV election promotional kit was mailed in a fold-out box, circled with a decorative band which, step-by-step, reproduced the animation of the '68 campaign logo.

294.

Election coverage
The quest for election news audiences starts early in the summer before the national nominating conventions, and the competition among the networks reaches fever pitch by Election Day in the fall. Networks vie for listeners by promoting their news teams, their analysts, their sophisticated technology, and their superior experience. To support its stations and affiliates in attracting listeners, CBS prepared elaborate kits with complete sets of promotional tools: ad mats, press releases and photos for local newspapers; slides and film promos for on-air announcements. The kits were deliberately designed to look distinctive and authoritative to reinforce the local stations' confidence in its affiliation with such a dynamic network.

295. The 1972 promotional kit took the form of an elaborate die-cut box which folded up to read "72" and fastened with a snap. The logo for that election year was animated for on-air promotion. (157.)

296. The 1976 election kit was designed with two overlapping covers. The first flap illustrates an amorphous galaxy of stars. On the inside flap, the stars coalesce toward the center. On the inside pocket, containing the promotional materials, the stars have aligned themselves into the CBS election-year logo.

295.

296.

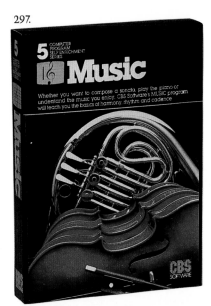

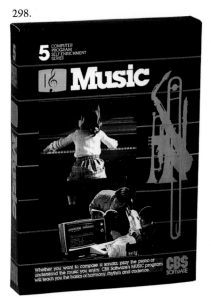

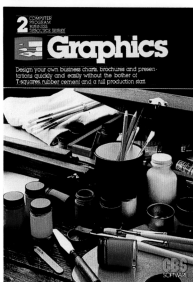

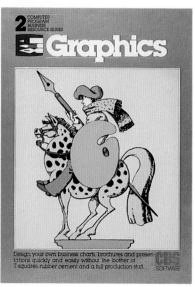

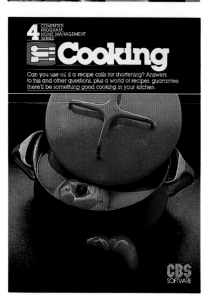

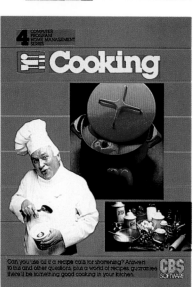

Package designs
As Creative Director of Advertising and Design
for all of CBS Inc., Dorfsman has been called upon to advise and suggest solutions
for graphic problems in divisions other than Broadcasting.

WIZARD OF WOR

Burwors, Garwors, Thorwors, Worluk and Wizard await you in the Dreaded Dungeons

WIZARD OF WOR

For use with the Atari® Video Computer Systems™

CBS VIDEO GAMES

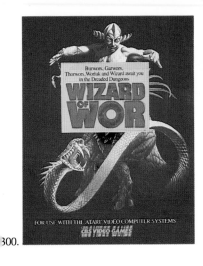

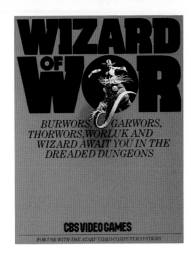

297-299. A series of suggested design solutions for video cassettes.

300. Comps of five possible package designs for an electronic video game.

301.

302.

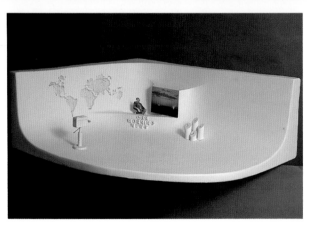

Drama in the news room

Although it was obvious to the networks, even in the early days
of television, that soap operas, variety and comedy shows, and other forms
of entertainment required appropriate stage sets, the news division was completely
neglected in that area. News anchormen and reporters were just talking heads seated at a
desk in front of a blank wall or curtain. The exhibit-designer in Dorfsman could not suppress
the urge to improve the newsmen's environment. News and weather reports could now be
augmented with meaningful maps, visual aids and all the new technological facilities
that were becoming available. In 1965, before anyone else conceived of 'a news set',
Dorfsman initiated plans and had models built to demonstrate the possibilities.

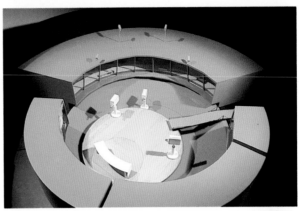

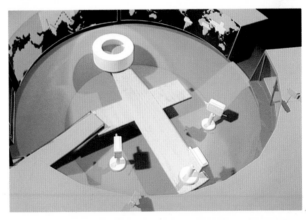

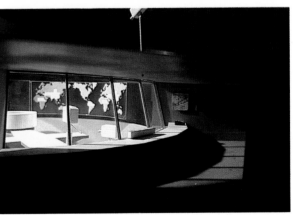

303.

301. Actual set designed and constructed for CBS-TV Channel 2 in New York City. It includes weather maps, charts, and space for visual aids and props, in an up-to-date setting.

302. Models of suggested studio environments for the CBS network morning news broadcasts.

303. A projected changeable set for CBS-TV News included seats for a live audience, electronic maps, motorized equipment, and special hardware and software for space-related broadcasts. Models, showing variations of the basic set design, were constructed in collaboration with Herb Rosenthal Associates of California.

304.

305.

306.

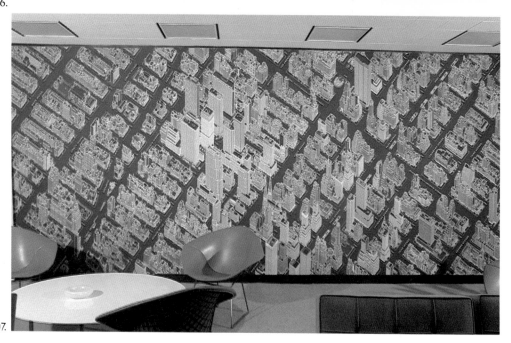

307.

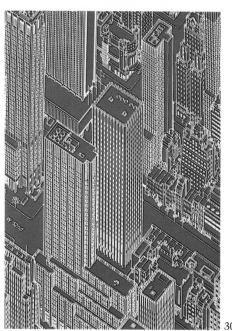

308.

Interior designs

Dorfsman contributed numerous interior design ideas for CBS headquarters,
as well as for other CBS properties. Such entrance areas and interiors, accessible to the public,
telegraph a good deal about the imagination, inventiveness
and stability of a company.

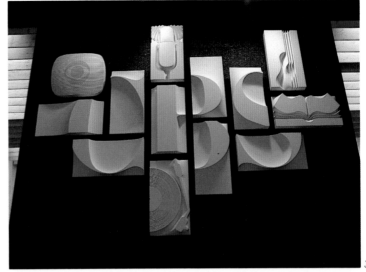

309.

310.

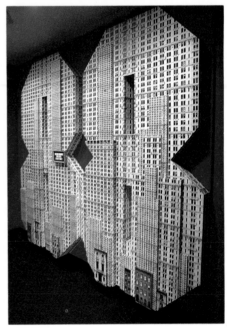

311.

312.

304. Relief map on wall of Columbia Records board room.

305. Reception area, Columbia Records International.

306. Design for a mural for a CBS affiliate in Philadelphia. The all-music FM station had no funds for the project. Dorfsman's plan was to have the mural executed by students from a Philadelphia art school.

307. CBS Cafeteria. At the end of the room opposite his "gastrotypographical assemblage," Dorfsman installed an enlarged isometric drawing of the area surrounding the CBS building.

308. Close-up of the CBS building in the drawing.

309. Wall decoration for lobby of the CBS Broadcast Center on 57th Street in New York City featuring the insignia of the CBS "Sunday Morning Show."

310. Wall design for the lobby of CBS headquarters. Three dimensional letters and design elements are covered over with stretch fabric.

311.-312. WCBS Newsradio 88 reception area. The station numbers '88' are cut out of an enlarged photomontage of New York City building facades. A tiny illuminated billboard on the first digit reads: THE BIG NUMBER FOR NEWS IN NEW YORK.

179

Annual reports

Once upon a time, a company's annual report to its stockholders and potential investors consisted mainly of figures, charts and graphs indicating the health of the business. The preparation of the report was primarily the job of the accountants. But about the same time that corporations became self-conscious about their building facades, interior design, corporate art collections and public image, the preparation of the annual report fell into the hands of designers. Now the hard core facts and figures are embellished with radiant photographs, elegant typography and design details that amplify the image of the company. The esthetics of the report have become as much a tool for projecting the sagacity of the corporation as the dollars-and-cents figures within.

Dorfsman frankly admits he has a love-hate relationship with annual reports. The subject is always the same. Every division of the company must be treated even-handedly. Generally, he is confined to using stock photos from the CBS library. The project can become a strait jacket for a staff designer. On the other hand, all the inherently limiting factors add up to a powerful challenge: how do you treat the same material, year after year, and make it look different and exciting each time?

Beyond the specific graphics, Dorfsman concerns himself with a basic psychological problem: how to represent the company's financial health without making stockholders nervous? If you've had a better-than-expected year and are tempted to produce a prosperous-looking annual report, they may be contentious about the undue expense. If the company has had a bad year financially, you certainly shouldn't squander funds on a showy job, but neither do you want to rub the bad news in stockholders' faces by going cheap. This is the kind of subtle but serious thinking that occupies Dorfsman, along with decisions about size, photos, typography and paper.

Even within the limited scope of the annual report, Dorfsman and CBS staff designers Ted Andresakes and Ira Teichberg have made some daring innovations. "Actually, the real credit for several breakthroughs in design goes to Tom Wyman," Lou explains. "It's easy enough for a designer to say 'to hell with tradition,' but for the chief executive officer of the corporation to approve a radical change in policy, as he did in a couple of annual reports, takes far-sightedness and guts."

31

180

CBS/83

ANNUAL REPORT TO THE SHAREHOLDERS

Among the Company's successes in 1983 was Michael Jackson's album Thriller. *More than 27 million copies have already been sold, making it the largest-selling album by a single artist in recorded music history.*

314.

313. (Overleaf)
1983 was a record-breaking year for the Columbia Records Division of CBS Inc., and it provided Dorfsman with a reason to break one of the rigid rules established for annual reports. Traditionally, no one division of the corporation may be singled out for special attention on the cover. But when Michael Jackson's album *Thriller* sold 27 million copies, the greatest number by a solo artist in recording history, Dorfsman persuaded Tom Wyman, who was then Chief Executive Officer, to feature the singing star on the cover. The only other time an individual appeared on an annual report cover was in 1982, the year William S. Paley, founder of CBS, retired.

The 1983 CBS Annual Report was also distinguished by its reduced size. The 6½" × 10" book was a departure from the usual 8½" × 11" format favored by most companies. The smaller size not only elicited extra attention, it saved on paper, printing and mailing costs. (Those are always worthy objectives, according to Lou, "if accompanied by good design.")

315.

314-315. Very few special photographs are commissioned for CBS Annual Reports; most are selected from the CBS library of photos.

However, the way they are cropped, scaled and paired, with regard to tonality and size, invests the page with visual excitement.

CBS 1968

ANNUAL REPORT
TO THE
SHAREHOLDERS OF
COLUMBIA
BROADCASTING
SYSTEM, INC.

316.

The dramatic flight of Apollo 8 lifted the nation's spirit, brought pride to all Americans and earned the admiration of the world. CBS News alone devoted more than 30 hours to its radio and television coverage of the flight, and carried the story to an estimated 65 million viewers and to millions more who listened on radio. As poet Archibald MacLeish wrote: "To see the earth as it truly is... is to see ourselves as riders on the earth together, brothers on that bright loveliness in the eternal cold—brothers who know now they are truly brothers."

The assassination of Senator Robert F. Kennedy followed, by only nine weeks, the murder of the Reverend Martin Luther King, Jr., and left the nation shocked and stunned. In its coverage, CBS News devoted nearly 74 hours to the news of the Kennedy shooting, the funeral services at St. Patrick's Cathedral in New York City and the burial at Arlington National Cemetery.

Big Brother and the Holding Company signed with Columbia Records in 1968 and won a Gold Record for their first album, Cheap Thrills. Leonard Bernstein, who records on the Columbia Masterworks label, emerged as the year's Number One conductor on the classical best-seller lists, with 13 albums appearing a total of 249 weeks.

316. Pages from the 1968 Annual Report demonstrate the awesome effect of closing in on a small detail or bleeding a full panoramic photo across a double-page spread. The immense scale and quality of the reproductions subliminally confirmed the company's commitment to the best of everything.

TO OUR SHAREHOLDERS:

Financial Results

CBS net income for 1968 was $58 million on net sales of $988 million, a 6 percent increase in earnings on a 7 percent increase in revenues. Earnings per share advanced from $2.08 to $2.20 despite the 10 percent Federal surtax of 23¢ per share.

All four of our operating groups participated in this record sales year, which saw improvement in all of the major businesses in which we are engaged. The fourth quarter was particularly strong; and the momentum—directly related to the resurgence of the national economy—has carried into 1969, giving us reason to anticipate further improvement during the year at hand.

Diversification and Expansion

Over the past five years, from 1963 through 1968, CBS net sales have risen from $565 million to nearly $1 billion. Part of this increase has come from expansion of existing operations and part from the acquisition of new businesses. Among those joining forces with CBS during this period were, in chronological order, the New York Yankees, Fender Musical Instruments, V. C. Squier, Electro Music, Rogers Drums, Creative Playthings, Bailey Films, Film Associates, Holt, Rinehart and Winston, and W. B. Saunders Company.

These new activities have given us important new sources of revenue. But they have done more. They have provided a measure of diversification which we believe to be strongly conducive to a healthy rate of growth in the future. And they have assured us a variety and range of managerial talent—always a matter of the highest priority to your Company. A significant factor in developing this talent, we believe, is our method of operating new acquisitions: our policy is to provide substantive backing without intruding upon the

5

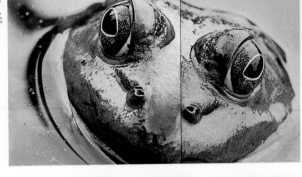

The Vladimir Horowitz concert at Carnegie Hall, carried by the CBS Television Network, was sold by CBS Enterprises Inc. in more than 20 countries and —as a Columbia Masterworks release —became one of the record industry's best-selling classical albums of the year.

W. B. Saunders Company, the nation's foremost medical publisher, which joined CBS in 1968, keeps doctors abreast of developments in the swiftly changing field of medicine. This past year, Field & Stream had its best year in the magazine's 73 year history. Typical of the rising caliber of Holt's college-textbook authors is Dr. Grant R. Fowles, of the University of Utah, author of Holt's popular new Introduction to Modern Optics (upper, far right). Bailey Films and Film Associates have sharply expanded their production and sales of educational films (lower, immediate right), since joining CBS in 1967. Hand puppets, designed by Creative Playthings, help develop a child's imagination and coordination.

The electronic video recording (EVR) system, developed by CBS Laboratories and demonstrated publicly for the first time in 1968 by the CBS Electronic Video Recording Division, enjoys a potential market as vast as that of television itself. The system consists of three basic components: the ultra-thin, high-density EVR film, the circular EVR cartridge which holds the film, and the EVR player which projects the film images through a standard television receiver. To operate the system, a viewer simply clips a lead wire from the player to the antenna terminals of his receiver, inserts an EVR cartridge into the player, pushes a button and switches on his television set.

185

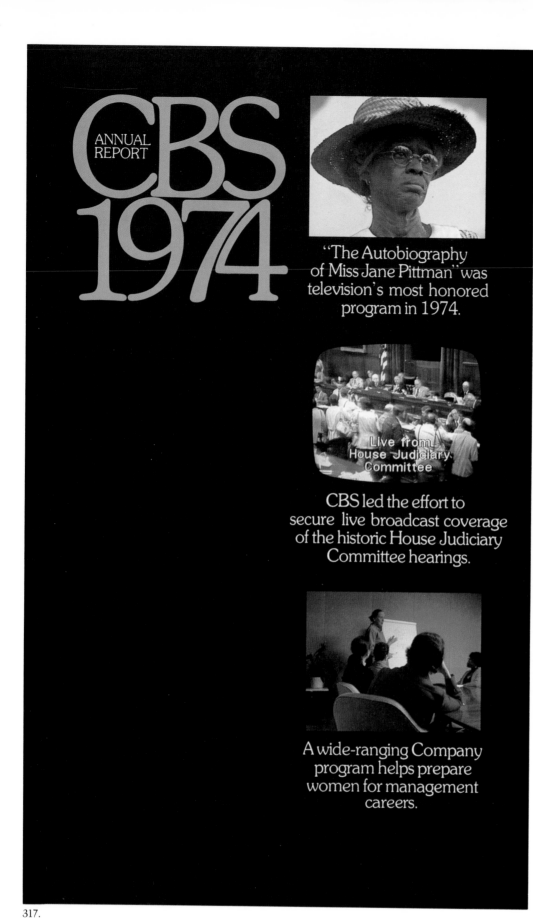

ANNUAL REPORT

CBS 1974

"The Autobiography of Miss Jane Pittman" was television's most honored program in 1974.

CBS led the effort to secure live broadcast coverage of the historic House Judiciary Committee hearings.

A wide-ranging Company program helps prepare women for management careers.

CBS Records artists encompass the full range of music styles and tastes, from Charlie Rich (1), who has eme as the nation's leading country music star, and the contemporary sound of Loggins & Messina (2), to Pie Boulez (3) conducting the New York Philharmonic, a distinctive voice of Barbra Streisand (4).

Art Garfunkel (5) and Paul Simon (6) now appearing individual performers continue to attract new audienc does Neil Diamond (7), whose first release for Colum *Jonathan Livingston Seagull*, became one of the faste selling albums of 1973.

The new rhythm and blues sound of Earth, Wind and (8) has added another dimension to the CBS Records catalogue; and Roberto Carlos (9), Brazil's most popular singer, is one of many important artists recording for the CBS Records International Division

317.

317. The vitality of television was conveyed in print in the 1974 Annual Report. Page after page was loaded with photos, with quick cuts from close-ups to long shots, and abbreviated copy blocks. The irregular photo grids also helped to activate the pages.

Entertainment, news and information are the essential elements of broadcasting: excitement and immediacy in live local news coverage through ENG—Electronic Newsgathering—at CBS Owned television station KMOX-TV (1); laughter and tears shared by millions viewing the CBS Television Network's *All in the Family* (2), *The Waltons* (3), *M*A*S*H* (5) and *Rhoda* (6); the spine-chilling tales of the *CBS Radio Mystery Theater* (4) with such fine performers as Mercedes McCambridge; distinguished drama in the Television Network's presentation of *The Autobiography of Miss Jane Pittman* (7); coverage of the historic events of the House Judiciary Committee Hearings, anchored by CBS News Correspondent Walter Cronkite (8), and the Television Network's fact-filled tribute to the nation's 200th anniversary, *Bicentennial Minutes* (9).

The many accents of the universal language of music are heard in performances of CBS/Records Group artists throughout the world: the continental rhythms of Italy's Gigliola Cinquetti (1); the country tones of Charlie Rich (2) and Mac Davis (3); American composer Charles Ives' classical genius (4); Barbra Streisand's compelling voice (5); Chicago's driving sound (6); the colorful popular songs of Japan's Momoe Yamaguchi (7), and the contemporary beat of Britain's David Essex (8).

The fine quality of such CBS Musical Instruments as Rogers drums (1), Steinway pianos (2) and Fender guitars (3) has brought them outstanding public acceptance.

The demand for tapes (4) is a significant factor in the growth of the Columbia Record and Tape Club, the world's leading organization in its field. Hobby/craft activities such as X-acto (5) and National Handcraft Institute (6) are also important to the future of Columbia House.

Unique display facilities (7) attract many customers to Pacific Stereo stores.

Imaginative toys such as the Indoor Gym House (8) are a hallmark of Creative Playthings.

CBS Inc. 1975
Annual Report

1 In 1975, a year of record financial achievement, the performances of the many businesses that constitute CBS today were marked with impressive highlights: All in the Family remained the most popular series on television,

2 as the CBS Television Network enjoyed its 22nd year as the world's largest advertising medium and completed two decades of primetime audience leadership. The CBS Evening News with Walter Cronkite again led

3 its competition as CBS News continued to be the nation's principal source of broadcast news and information. The CBS/Records Group, at a historic sales peak, released albums by Earth, Wind and Fire and by Chicago

which sold nearly two million copies each. The world's largest producer, manufacturer and marketer of recorded music, it also introduced many new artists to the music-buying public in the United States and abroad. **4**

5 The Columbia House Division reached the highest membership enrollment in the history of its Columbia Record and Tape Clubs and had outstanding sales of record and tape packages through broadcast promotion.

CBS Musical Instruments Division **6** products such as Steinway pianos, Fender guitars and Gulbransen organs sustained their excellent quality reputations as they outperformed an industry pressed by recession.

7 Strong sales performances in both school and college textbook fields brought Holt, Rinehart and Winston its largest share of the educational publishing market since its acquisition by CBS more than eight years ago.

The CBS Consumer Publishing **8** Division's six major special-interest magazines, led by Field & Stream, achieved both record circulation levels and the highest advertising revenues in their histories.

1975 Masters Golf Tournament, led the Network to plan the most extensive golf coverage in its history in 1976—including not only the Masters but 12 other Tournament Players Division contests.

CBS Television Stations Division The five CBS Owned television stations, WCBS-TV New York, KNXT Los Angeles, WBBM-TV Chicago, WCAU-TV Philadelphia and KMOX-TV St. Louis, had a banner year in 1975. The Division's strong performance reflected progress in both business and creative areas.

A new emphasis on market development for national spot television advertising (the time bought by national advertisers on local stations) attracted some 100 new clients in 1975. The Division established a highly innovative test market program at KMOX-TV in St. Louis, the nation's 12th largest market, at costs comparable to what advertisers would pay in traditional test markets half the size. Retail sales departments were expanded at all five stations to accelerate the trend toward increased local retail advertising on television.

Division program development efforts have been highly productive. Originally produced by the Division, Dinah!, hosted by Emmy Award-winning star Dinah Shore, has attracted large audiences and advertiser support in the CBS markets where it is seen. At year-end the Division began development, with the Independent Television Corporation, of a primetime, family-oriented series featuring Jim Henson's puppets, The Muppets. It is planned for broadcast beginning in the fall of 1976.

The new electronic newsgathering (ENG) system installed at KMOX-TV, utilizing remote live and tape mobile units, has brought significant efficiencies and improved news coverage capability. WBBM-TV is converting to a similar total ENG system and expects it to be fully operational in 1976. Other CBS Owned television stations have partial ENG capability and plan to complete their systems over the next few years.

Local programming at the CBS Owned television stations was impressive in 1975. Several news and documentary programs generated national attention and stimulated positive change at the local community level. A KNXT special about breast cancer, Why Me?, featuring Lee Grant, received the Alfred I. duPont-Columbia University Award and was

CBS/Records Group

(Dollars in Millions)	1975	1974	1973	1972	1971
Net Sales	$484.3	$420.4	$349.5	$312.3	$276.2
Income	56.3	44.8	47.8	49.8	43.2

The CBS/Records Group had the highest sales and income in its history in 1975. The growth for the Group, which is the world's largest producer, manufacturer and marketer of recorded music, resulted from gains in both domestic and international operations.

The domestic CBS Records Division, which was affected by the economic problems experienced by the entire U.S. recording industry in the early months of 1975, made a dramatic turnaround in the second half to finish the year with record sales and income. Improvement in profit margins throughout the Division reflected the impact of operational and cost efficiencies instituted during the past two years.

The CBS Records International Division achieved new highs in sales and income, despite the effects of the more sluggish recovery from the recession evident in many international markets.

The excellent sales of new and established artists, in the U.S. and abroad, were the key factors throughout 1975 for both divisions of the Group. This outstanding creative performance brought the Group into the new year with considerable momentum.

CBS Records Division In 1975 the CBS Records Division continued to provide the nation with outstanding recorded music of great diversity, ranging across the complete musical lexicon from rock, popular and jazz to rhythm and blues, country and classical. The Division's recording artists, on its own Columbia and Epic labels and on labels distributed by CBS Records, won 32 Gold Records representing sales of at least one million units for a single or 500,000 units for an album. This success reflected not only the high quality of the Division's artists and its strength in creative production, but its effective and sophisticated marketing techniques—tailored to each artist's unique attributes.

Among the record industry's best-selling albums in 1975 was That's

---

Year in, year out, annual reports contain the same basic information and elements. The problem for Dorfsman and Art Directors, Ira Teichberg and Ted Andresakes, who are responsible for the design, is to make the book look new and exciting each time.

318. They alternate between tight grid layouts and open-spaced arrangements. They also vary the sizes of photos and the shapes of copy blocks page to page.

319. In 1976, the year of CBS's 50th anniversary, Dorfsman commissioned a special photo of vintage CBS microphones for the front and back cover of the year's annual report. Most of the relics were borrowed from William Paley's personal collection. Lou ferreted out the remainder by sending out a call on ham radio to oldtime CBS engineers who, he correctly deduced, had retired with antique mikes as souvenirs.

CBS/BROADCAST GROUP

CBS TELEVISION NETWORK DIVISION

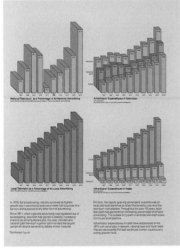

319.

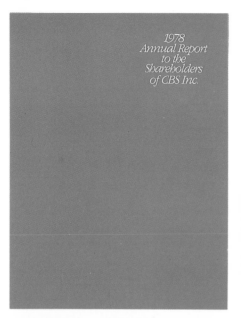

1978
Annual Report
to the
Shareholders
of CBS Inc.

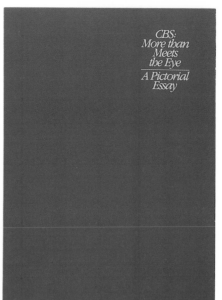

CBS:
More than
Meets
the Eye

A Pictorial
Essay

The CBS/Publishing Group and each of its four divisions, serving the educational, consumer, professional and international markets, achieved record revenues in 1978.

Profits for the Group increased by 45 percent over 1977 as a result of the outstanding performances of the Educational and Consumer Publishing Divisions, and a reduction in the amortization of costs related to the 1977 acquisition of Fawcett Publications.

The Educational Publishing Division performed particularly well in 1978, outpacing the moderate growth of the textbook publishing industry. The Division's elementary and secondary school textbook sales, which account for over half its business, were especially strong.

Industrywide magazine advertising revenues and paperback book sales increased significantly during the year. The Consumer Publishing Division, which serves these areas, matched market growth, with magazine advertising revenues—the largest revenue component—achieving the highest dollar gains.

Although the Professional Publishing Division was adversely affected by a softening of the market for medical and health science texts, overall Division revenues were slightly above 1977 levels. The International

Publishing Division, which distributes and translates U. S. products and publishes indigenous materials in foreign languages, had record revenues resulting primarily from the strength of its Spanish, Portuguese and English language operations.

CBS Educational Publishing Division

The CBS Educational Publishing Division is composed of Holt, Rinehart and Winston, one of the nation's foremost textbook publishers, and BFA Educational Media, a leading producer and distributor of audiovisual and printed supplementary material for elementary and high school students.

Despite a decline in the number of school-age children, sales of Holt's elementary and secondary school tests reached all-time highs in 1978.

U.S. Publishing Industry Sales of Textbooks and General Books

The increased emphasis educators and parents on development in schools continued to favor Holt p which stress these educa damentals. In the elemer product line, strong sales mances by the Holt Scho matics Program—which is used by one out of every school children in grades through eight—and the s sales growth of the revise Reading System contribut tially to the Division's ove gains. In addition the Divi strengthened its leadersh in the school science textb ket with the introduction successful new tests inclu Life Science, Holt Earth Sc Holt Physical Science

Although full-time colli ments have flattened in re Holt's College Departmen tinued to expand and to in sales largely as a result of book list. Participation in c cation by older students v suing a college degree or basis and by individuals w specific professional care the traditional college fra continues to grow. These led to a more diffuse coll tional market which requi only a greater variety of te targeted toward specializ study, but also a greater v marketing techniques de sell the Division's product

Edward R. Murrow, William Eric Sevareid, Charles Coll Robert Trout, Cecil Brown, LeSueur and others reportir the front lines of Europe an

As television emerged as entertainment medium in radio shifted its emphasis to information, music and sp 1971, CBS introduced Spec daily radio series for the pr of identifiable and opposin view on important current problems. Then in 1974, aft absence of more than a dec brought back radio drama wide audiences with the ri Radio Mystery Theater. The stations have allowed a new tion of Americans to enjoy programming format that h an integral part of their par

Today the CBS Radio broadcasts a full rang gramming to more t affiliated stations around th In addition, the seven CBS AM stations (WCBS New Yo Los Angeles, WBBM Chicago Philadelphia, KMOX St. Lou San Francisco and WEEI Bo vide 24-hour specialized ne oriented service. The seven Owned FM stations—locate same cities—offer their liste highly popular music form Television broadcasting, gral part of CBS for more th decades, has assumed incre

We are unique among companies our size in deriving virtually all of our revenue from human creativity rather than material resources—from what people write, what they compose and what they perform—and from products which further human expression and development.

CBS

THE CBS ORGANIZATION

CBS is a broad-based entertainment and communications company headquartered in New York City. Since its founding in 1927, CBS has grown from a small radio broadcasting service to a thriving, diversified operation with thousands of shareholders and a worldwide work force that numbers well over 35,000.

At the core of the CBS organization are four operating groups: Broadcast, Records, Columbia and Publishing. Through its six divisions, the Broadcast Group comprises all broadcast activities of CBS—news, sports and entertainment programming, the five CBS Owned television stations and 14 CBS-Owned AM and FM radio stations. In addition, the Group's Television and Radio Networks distribute programming to hundreds of CBS affiliated television and radio stations.

The Records Group is the world's largest U.S.-based producer, manufacturer and marketer of recorded music. The domestic CBS Records operations include the Columbia, Epic, Portrait, ARC/Columbia, Odyssey and associated labels in addition to a growing number of manufacturing and distribution facilities. CBS Records also repackages and distributes previously recorded music and is engaged in music publishing, while its International Division sells recorded music in virtually every country in the world.

The four divisions of the Columbia Group offer a broad range of consumer products including musical instruments, toys, and mail-order records, tapes and books. The Columbia Group also operates two chains of retail stores which sell the finest in stereo components and other audio products.

The Publishing Group, through its four divisions, publishes and distributes hardcover and paperback books and magazines for educational, consumer and professional markets. In addition, its international operation markets original publications as well as adaptations of CBS/Publishing Group products worldwide.

The CBS corporate staff aids in establishing and implementing overall Company policy, helps coordinate matters of common interest and supervises central operating functions. This includes Administration, Finance, Law, Planning, Corporate Affairs, Economics and Research, Acquisitions, and Industrial and Governmental Relations. The Planning section of the corporate staff also oversees the operations of the CBS Technology Center in Stamford, Connecticut, which conducts advanced research and development for the CBS groups.

CHAIRMAN PRESIDENT

CBS/BROADCAST GROUP
CBS/RECORDS GROUP
CBS/COLUMBIA GROUP
CBS/PUBLISHING GROUP

CBS TELEVISION NETWORK DIVISION
CBS ENTERTAINMENT DIVISION
CBS SPORTS DIVISION
CBS NEWS DIVISION
CBS TELEVISION STATIONS DIVISION
CBS RADIO DIVISION
CBS RECORDS DIVISION
CBS RECORDS INTERNATIONAL DIVISION
COLUMBIA HOUSE DIVISION
CBS MUSICAL INSTRUMENTS DIVISION
CBS SPECIALTY STORES DIVISION
CBS TOYS DIVISION
CBS EDUCATIONAL PUBLISHING DIVISION
CBS CONSUMER PUBLISHING DIVISION
CBS PROFESSIONAL PUBLISHING DIVISION
CBS INTERNATIONAL PUBLISHING DIVISION

320.

320. In 1978, the CBS Annual Report was issued in two sections. Though the covers were identical in design, each section had its own special purpose. One book was devoted to financial information for shareholders. The other, a pictorial essay, recounted the history of CBS and the functions of its various divisions. Apart from the Annual Report, the essay was designed to be used as a promotional mailing throughout the year.

CBS International Publishing Division

...opportunities in this changing marketplace, the College continued to realign its efforts and also develops of textbooks for a specialized professional business, education...

General Book Department. The best sales performance by Edith Holden's *The Diary of an Edwardian Lady*... remained on national bestseller lists throughout the year... important sellers for the book Department included *Rock's Greatest Hits* by Garry... *The Power Look* by Egon... and the critically... *A Place for Noah* by Josh...

...competition for limited audiovisual funds made 1978 a key year for 16mm films. ...sional Media responded to ...product mix by continuing ...which teach basic education ...for the primary and ...school market. This strategy ...with increasing success and ...for these kits resulted in ...sales growth. During the ...produced several new ...line including *The ...dge*, an individualized

program designed for students who need special training in beginning reading skills, and *Writing Skills Workshop*, which teaches fundamental writing skills.

CBS Consumer Publishing Division

Sales in the consumer magazine and paperback book industries continued to climb in 1978 and CBS Publications, as the Division is known in the trade, maintained its position as a major factor in these fields. Established in 1971, the Division now ranks among the top publishers in magazine advertising revenue, average paid circulation and paperback sales.

Over 90 percent of the Division's revenues in 1978 came from magazine advertising, subscriptions and retail sales of magazines and books. During the year each of these sources

achieved record revenues.

For the third consecutive year, U.S. magazines reached advertising revenue peaks and, for the second year in a row, magazines led all other media in percentage of advertising revenue growth. In 1978, continuing a four-year trend, CBS Publications outpaced the field, with each of the Division's eight major publications achieving advertising revenue records.

The Division is organized into five operating units: three for its various magazines, one for paperbacks and one incorporating the publishing service activities of worldwide single-copy distribution and subscription fulfillment.

The Women's Magazine Group consists of *Woman's Day*, the Division's flagship publication. An average issue is read by over 17 million adult women, and in single-copy sales *Woman's Day*'s eight million average circulation ranks third among all magazines in the world. In 1978 *Woman's Day* set a record in total number of magazine copies sold. Following a plan formulated in 1976 when, after extensive research, a 15th issue was published, *Woman's Day* put out a 14th issue in 1978. Consumer demand has continued to be strong and *Woman's Day* will publish 15 issues in 1979.

The Men's Magazine Group is composed of *Field & Stream* and *Mechanix Illustrated*. With a 1.7 million circulation, *Mechanix Illustrated* is the fastest-growing

19

14

15

News also has produced critically acclaimed special reports and documentaries focusing on such diverse subjects as teenage smoking, migrant workers in America, the business of sex, the national judicial system, the Panama Canal treaty, baseball as a business, arson in the South Bronx, learning and energy.

Certainly no discussion of CBS News would be complete without *60 Minutes*, the news magazine of the air, which has proved that broadcast journalism can be competitive with primetime entertainment programming. Viewed by an average of 33 million people every Sunday evening, *60 Minutes* has the distinction of being the most popular program in broadcast history. It is usually one of network television's top 10 programs and has been the recipient of virtually every important award in the field of broadcast journalism.

CBS brings the exciting world of sports into America's living rooms for millions to enjoy.

...over the years. The Company... inaugurated the first regular... of television broadcasts in 1931. As television set... increased, the CBS Television... became to millions of... spectrum of comedy,... personal drama, sports and... CBS has brought into... coast to coast such... series as *Playhouse 90*, *The ...Show*; *I Love Lucy*; *Gun...*; *the Beverly Hillbillies*, *The ...*; *The Carol Burnett Show*; *...Tyler Moore Show*; *All in the ...*; and *M*A*S*H*. ...there have been...cultural contributions to...life through such award...television programs as...*for a Heavyweight*, Barbra ...'s *My Name Is Barbra*; *Do...onto into That Good Night*,...*Hour*'s *J.T.*, *Danny ...In at the Metropolitan ...Autobiography of Miss ...*; the series *The Body... The Defection of Simas...* and *Loney: A Circle of Chil-...*.

...programming for children ...been innovative. For over ...the Emmy and Peabody ...running *Captain Kangaroo* ...standard as the only daily ...preschool youngsters on a ...cial television network.

9

2

electrical recordings in which microphones, rather than acoustic horns, were used in the studios. Recordings of famed cellist Pablo Casals were released as early as 1915, and the first complete set of recorded Beethoven symphonies in 1927.

In 1948, CBS researchers were responsible for the most revolutionary innovation in the recording industry's history—the 33⅓ rpm long-playing disc. In the following decade, these CBS researchers developed the first low-cost, mass-produced, high fidelity phonograph, the model "360."

CBS Records' vast contributions in the area of repertoire extend to all areas of music. It made the earliest jazz recordings, introducing such jazz giants as Billie Holiday, Louis Armstrong, Duke Ellington and Artie Shaw. It made the first American recordings of serious contemporary compositions by such composers as Bartok, Stravinsky and Schoenberg on a major label. The first blues recordings in America were released through Okeh Records, an early subsidiary label. Original Broadway cast recordings of such musicals as *My Fair Lady*, *South Pacific*, *West Side Story* and *A Chorus Line* are part of

The flat disc familiar to everyone today as a phonograph record—and shown here in the early production stage—is a far cry from the cylinder played by our grandparents.

23

1. Technicians study the lighting in a CBS studio. The stars of some hit shows on the CBS Television Network. 2. Ed Sullivan (*The Ed Sullivan Show*). 3. Lucille Ball (*I Love Lucy*). 4. Alan Alda (*M*A*S*H*). 5. Jean Stapleton and Carroll O'Connor (*All in the Family*). 6. Bob Keeshan of *Captain Kangaroo*, a program which has delighted children for many than 20 seasons.

1

58

Physics and Modern Biology—a volume which has been used by more than half of all U.S. secondary schools since its introduction in 1921. Similarly, the *Holt School Mathematics Program*, the *Holt Basic Reading System* and the *Holt Databank System* for social studies each maintains a significant position in the educational community.

Dryden Press in Chicago and Praeger Publishers in New York are units of Holt's College Department. Dryden Press concentrates primarily on business and economic texts, while Praeger publishes scholarly monographs in international politics,

economic development and the social sciences.

Another acquisition which has helped make CBS one of the nation's preeminent publishers took place in 1968 when the Company purchased the W.B. Saunders Company of Philadelphia. Since 1888 Saunders has been a world leader in the medical and related health sciences publishing fields, and it has been said that it is impossible to go through medical school or practice medicine today without using a Saunders book. The *Kinsey Reports* on American male and female sexuality were first published by Saunders in 1948 and 1953, respectively; and Dorland's classic *Illustrated Medical Dictionary*, now in its 25th Saunders edition, is one of the best-selling reference volumes of its kind ever printed.

Besides medical texts, Saunders also publishes college textbooks on a variety of subjects in important areas of science, mathematics, social and human studies, health and physical education, and business administration. In addition Saunders "Clinics"—serial publications containing original articles by physicians and professors in particular subject areas—are exceptionally popular with individuals interested in the specialized medical disciplines.

Along with leading educational materials, CBS also publishes hardback books through Holt, Rinehart and Winston's General Book Department. Celebrated writers associated with Holt over the years have included Thomas Hardy, Robert Louis Stevenson, Herman Hesse, John Stuart Mill, William James and Robert Frost. Today Holt's offerings range from the powerful social commentary of Dee Brown to the pungent satire of Garry Trudeau, and from the gripping adventure stories of Jack Higgins to the eternally

1977 CBS Annual Report: We are unique among companies of our size in deriving virtually all our revenue from human creativity rather than material resources—from what people write, what they compose and what they perform—and from products which further human expression and development.

The enjoyment of music, from the first drumbeats of primeval man through the symphonies of Beethoven, was confined to those few fortunate people present when it was played. Until a brief century ago, the majority of mankind never heard music. Then, the phonograph finally freed the genie from the bottle. Now the CBS/Records Group is the leader in producing the records and tapes that have made the enjoyment of music a universal experience.

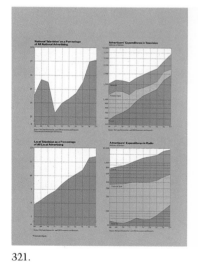

CBS/Broadcast Group

The CBS/Broadcast Group set sales and profit records in 1977 based on solid increases for both the CBS Television Network Division and the CBS Radio Division...

CBS TELEVISION NETWORK DIVISION

CBS ENTERTAINMENT DIVISION

Broadcasting is both the miracle of our age and its vernacular. At the twist of a dial, tragedy and comedy, personal drama and world events materialize from the ether. Before the eyes and ears of millions, the whole range of human experience and creativity unfolds. No one is excluded; the benefits of broadcasting are available to all. The CBS/Broadcast Group has led in developing broadcasting to its full potential, and today it sets the standard for the world.

321.

321.-322. After years of solemn, decorous covers for CBS Annual Reports, Dorfsman and Ted Andresakes made a design breakthrough.

In the 1977 and 1981 issues, they stirred up interest in the inside stories with teaser pictures and captions on the cover.

CBS 1981

ANNUAL REPORT

CBS/BROADCAST GROUP

CBS Television Network Division

CBS/RECORDS GROUP

CBS Cable Division

CBS News Division

CBS Television Stations Division

CBS Radio Division

CBS Records Division

322.

193

The infinite range of his activities at CBS notwithstanding, Dorfsman could never resist plum projects that beckoned from the outside. And CBS management, in its infinite wisdom, never interfered with Lou's extra-curricular activities. He has been a board member and chairman of the International Design Conference in Aspen, and trustee of both The Cooper Union and the New York Institute of Technology. He lectures, teaches and acts as a design consultant to schools and private organizations. He collaborated with Herb Rosenthal on a major exhibit on the rebuilt steel pier in Atlantic City. He designs letterheads and fanciful house numbers for friends; he does freebees for worthy community organizations. At the request of the parents of Andrew Goodman, he even designed a tombstone for the young civil-rights marcher who was killed during a voter registration drive in the South.

Beyond CBS, Lou's most conspicuous work has been for Dansk International Designs. Mr. Ted Nierenberg, founder of Dansk, described an early meeting with Lou regarding an advertising campaign for his "little company that was producing simple, well-designed, functional tableware for an emerging lifestyle." He reports: "At that first meeting, Lou started to ask some tough questions and he has been asking the same tough questions for 20 years. His national ads have helped build a great brand name and a very successful business for Dansk. The ads have won every award in the book, to say nothing of international acclaim. In ad after ad, Lou confirms the image of Dansk as the producer of beautiful, functional, affordable tableware."

When Lou finally retires from CBS Inc., there will be no dearth of projects to feed his voracious appetite for work. But what does this man, who has done almost everything in the field of visual communications, want to do next? "Well," Lou confesses, "I'd really like to fool around with film. I'd take a job for $50-a-week just to hang around Francis Ford Coppola or George Lucas."

Are you listening Francis?...George?

Consider the egg. Dansk® did. One of nature's most satisfying and useful forms, it signifies the beginning of things. The beginning of Dansk things was 10 years ago, when this first Fjord spoon was hand-forged. Its success egged us on to create a number of other fine objects. Tawny teakwood bowls. A candlestick crowned with twelve thin tapers. Dusky Flamestone cups. An enamelled casserole as bright as a sunflower. And linens with rainbows in their warp and woof. Today there are 493 Dansk designs. Every one made for daily use. And not an everyday piece in the lot. They all appear in a new 96-page book, a book with the good form to be absolutely free. Write Dansk Designs Ltd, Dept. O, Mount Kisco, N.Y.

Although red, yellow 324.
and blue were the three
basic colors of Dansk
Købenstyle casseroles,
Lou persuaded the
company president to
offer them in black and
white also. This full-
page ad of the late '60s
was headlined by an
epigram relevant to
the social revolution
of the times.

Two of a series of 325.-326.
full-page ads with a
compaign theme origi-
nated by Dorfsman:
"Expensive...By
Design." It subtly
connoted that Dansk
tableware was designed
to look more expensive
than it was.

Dansk photographs 327.
were portraits of the
products, posed and lit
with infinite artistry.
The copy was informal,
"you-we-they" in tone,
and informative. Such
ads affirmed the sense
of elite merchandise
intended for relaxed,
informal lifestyles.

The ad that introduced 328.
a line of Dansk stem-
ware manufactured in
France was headlined
"FRANSK." It made an
immediate connection
between France and
Dansk and took advan-
tage of the public's
association of France
with high style. Coin-
cidentally, "Fransk" is
the Danish pronuncia-
tion of "France."

Black is beautiful
White is beautiful

Købenstyle is beautiful. And has been
for years — in red, yellow and blue.
Now we introduce two new colors
—black, and white. The only two
colors as basic as the original three.
Notice how the natural color of food
is vividly enhanced against black
and white. Potatoes, tomatoes,
carrots, beef, (even boeuf), seem to
be more tempting in these pots.
If you like our black and white, just
wait until you see our full color
brochure of 596 tabletop classics.
Send 10¢ to Dansk Designs Ltd.,
Dept. BW, Mt. Kisco, N.Y. 10549.
DANSK DESIGNS LTD.

324.

Dansk Advertising
In his work for Dansk International Designs, Dorfsman consistently reflected the company's
policy of striving for handsome, unusual tableware design for everyday use. (Overleaf)
A Dansk ad designed for *The New Yorker* magazine. The same photograph was
repeated on a Dansk catalog cover. (334).

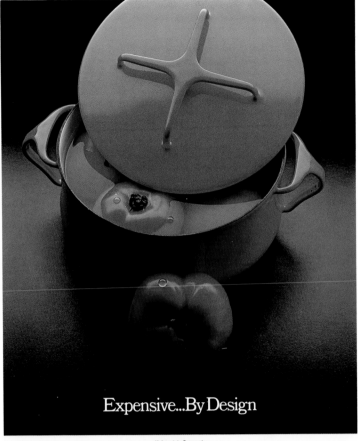

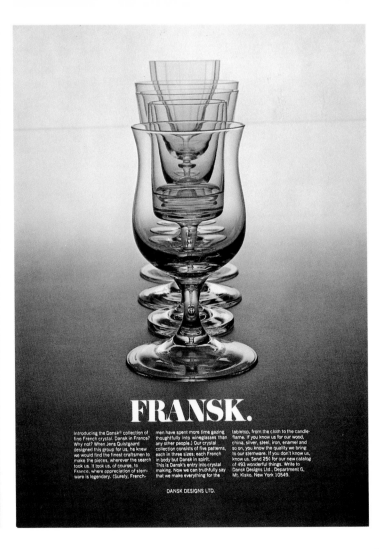
197

DANSK STARTS A REVOLUTION IN CHINA

About time.

For the last few thousand years, China has been thought of as necessarily pale, frail and fragile. Delicate eggshell stuff that you could see a candle's light through. Refined. Overly refined.

So much for the past.

Today we appreciate objects for the natural quality of their materials. We see beauty in the grain of oiled teak, the unbroken curve of a steel or silver spoon, the accidental texture of handwoven linen.

Now, to match this mood, Dansk commissioned famed designer Niels Refsgaard to create *unaffected* China.

The material itself makes its own surprises. Those specks, for instance, are left by minerals that kiln-firing burned from the clay. The irregular surface that catches the play of light is the mark of hand-throwing, hand-glazing. No two pieces can ever be identical.

This is the China that goes with the life you lead, from Saturday night to Sunday morning. And on through the week. China that can glamorize a knockwurst or understate caviar.

We call it Generation, because we think it might start something. Most Dansk Designs do. It costs $18.95 for a five-piece place setting. Also comes in four patterns, slightly higher in cost. We make all the serving pieces you could want. (When you see them you'll want them all.)

To start your own tabletop revolution, send 25¢ for our 96-page catalog of 493 ideas. Write to Dansk Designs Ltd, Department AR, Mt. Kisco, N.Y. ©MFG. TM DANSK DESIGNS LTD

Take our double duty pepper mills (they all have salt-shaker tops). We designed over 180. Built 96. Whittled the number to 20. After testing and time, we're down to nine we think are Dansk.®

On the other hand a design could be right, right off. Like Jens Quistgaard's classic ice bucket—so right it's in the permanent collection of six museums.

Then there are ideas that lead to ideas. Like our end grain blocks for trays and cutting boards. It's the butcher block concept Dansk was first to bring into the home. (End-grain won't dull your knives and knives won't dull its beauty.)

All told, our woodworkers turn out over 35 teak things. From hefty carving boards as tough as the keel of a Viking ship—to delicate Smorgasboards as light as a Thai fan.

But what really counts is not How Much but How Good.

To see how good, pick up a piece. Turn it over. The back is as beautifully finished as the front.

To see how much in woodworks (as well as goodworks in silver, steel, glass, china, stoneware, linen and candleware) send 25¢ for our catalog of 493 designs for your tabletop to Dansk Designs Ltd., Dept. W, Mt. Kisco, New York 10549.

DANSK DESIGNS LTD.

How Much Wood Would a Woodworker Work if a Woodworker Worked Wood for Dansk?

329.-330.

333.

329.-332. Typical full-page ads, each highlighting a line of Dansk merchandise. The products are glamorized in the photography, but de-mystified in down-to-earth, accessible copy.

198

The end of the plain white tablecloth.

You'll still see a few around. In old-timey hotels. Grandma's house. But, really, white has had it. Behind this shift to color is a finicky Finnish fabric designer named Ritva Poutila. She designed this collection just for us.
How do you design a solid-color fabric? By not making it solid. Ours are woven from two colors of yarn. (Pistachio, for instance, is gold and green.) You can't get rich, glowing colors like these by dipping white cloth in a dye-vat.

Curiously enough, only Dansk® makes yarn-dyed napkins and tablecloths like these.
We call them "Finnish Accent." You can mix them or match them in any combination you choose. Because they're designed that way.
There are 493 other designs for the well-dressed table in our 96 page catalog. For your copy send 25¢ to Dansk Designs Ltd., Dept. E, Mt. Kisco, New York 10549. And don't throw out your white tablecloths. They may be back in style some day.

Dansk Designs Ltd.

How to be graceful though short and fat.

Who would have thought a candle as high as it is wide could be as poised and pretty as this? Who but Dansk?
We pack them six to a box, each on its own vineyard green glass base, in subtle two-color combinations. Put one in front of each place setting. Group them in a glowing ring for a holiday centerpiece. Set them in the dimmer corners of an intimate party room. At only

$8.95 the package, you can act as if you had candles to burn.
Choose white and bronze, red and orange, or aegean and pine, all with green glass bases, handsomely gift-packed 6 to a box. For our new 96-page catalog showing 493 other Dansk 'Top of the Table' items, send 25¢ to Dansk Designs Ltd., Dept. A, Mt. Kisco, New York.

Jens Quistgaard gives crystal the heft of a tankard, the grace of a chalice. No wispy stems, no lifted pinkies. Instead, a hand-sized handhold on faceted or Doric-columned crystal. This pure lead crystal comes in six Quistgaard patterns, each in three

sizes. It's all part of the new tabletop architecture in our current color brochure. To get 576 more-or-less monumental ideas of this kind send a thin dime to Dansk Designs Ltd., Dept. 2, Mt. Kisco, N.Y. 10549.
DANSK DESIGNS LTD.

Put fine wine on a pedestal.
It's good for your skòl.

331.- 332.

333. Double-page spread ad introducing Dansk color-coordinated tablecloths and napkins. Photographs reminiscent of classic still-life paintings, established an aura of high art, tradition and elegance, while also presenting (for merchandising purposes) the full range of color combinations available.

10 years ago a new concept in tabletop decor was born. Just as the egg is nature's perfect form, so did Dansk Designs create beautiful forms. It began with this now-classic Fjord spoon and grew into 493 striking designs illustrated in this booklet.

FLUTED FLAMESTONE. Casseroles   48   FLUTED FLAMESTONE. Buffet server   49

Table Coverings
Dansk's sumptuous linen collection, created by Ritva Puotila in colors to inspire creative settings.

FINNISH ACCENT. Mats and napkins

Stainless Steel
Six museum-worthy table settings designed by Jens H. Quistgaard for both formal and casual dining. All are forged. All but Fjord are dishwasher safe.

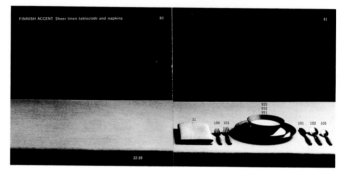

FINNISH ACCENT. Sheer linen tablecloth and napkins   80   81

SIAMESE TEAK. Trivets and bowls   38   SIAMESE TEAK AND RARE WOOD. Mills   39

Dansk Designs means rare wood trays, a 'great' salad bowl, dark flamestone cups, a candlestick with a spire-like candle and handforged stainless place settings. It means color, like linen table mats blending beautifully with the past, the present, the future...It means time-less beauty of good design.

334.

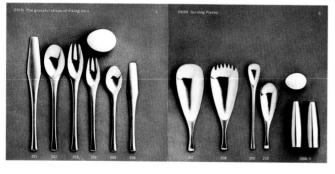

ODIN. The graceful shape of Viking oars   8   ODIN. Serving Pieces   9

Dansk International Designs
Catalogs were so much a part of the company's merchandising philosophy that every ad concluded with an offer for a free one. Since the enormous number of requests for catalogs put a strain on the advertising budget, Dorfsman designed a compact, 4″ × 4″ mailing to do the job. The reduced size saved enough on paper and postage costs to permit him to indulge in high quality photographs, paper and printing.

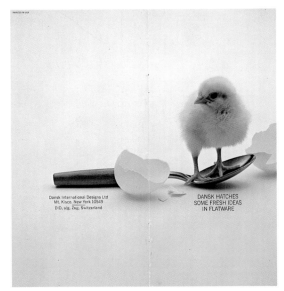

Dansk International Designs Ltd
Mt. Kisco, New York 10549
DID, a/g, Zug, Switzerland

DANSK HATCHES
SOME FRESH IDEAS
IN FLATWARE

VARIATIONS V
Designer: Jens H. Quistgaard

THISTLE
Designer: Jens H. Quistgaard

Dansk International Designs Ltd
Mt. Kisco, New York 10549

A NEW
GENERATION
OF DANSK
DINNERWARE

A Serving Platter
B Vegetable Bowl
C 3 Qt. Casserole with Lid
D Beverage Server
E Creamer
F Sugarbowl
G Coffee Cup
H Coffee Saucer
I Salad Plate
J Dinner Plate
K Tea Cup
L Tea Saucer
M Butter Plate
N Soup Bowl
Not Shown:
2 Qt. Casserole with Lid

334. The small size catalogs
-335. showed the design of
the merchandise
explicitly, but to indi-
cate the true scale of
the pieces, an egg was
introduced in each
photograph in one cata-
log, and a chick in
another.

335.

DANSK DESIGNS.
ADD SOME SPICE.
TO YOUR LIFE.

Dansk International Designs Ltd.
Mt. Kisco, New York 10549

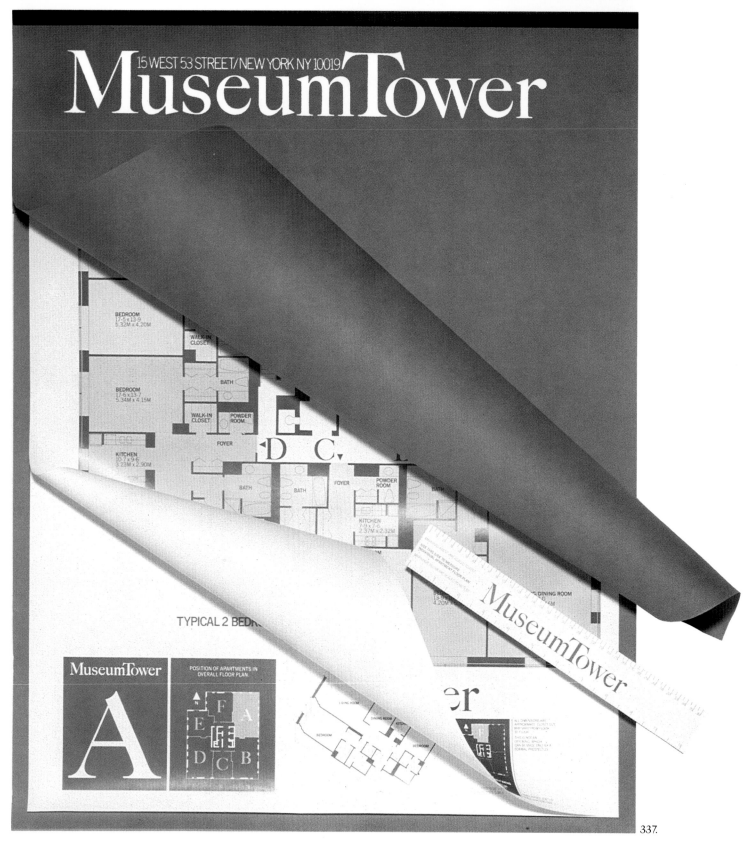

The Museum Tower
The Museum of Modern Art and CBS are
neighbors on 53rd Street in New York City, but they are united by more
than geography. William S. Paley is a trustee and board member of both. So it was more than
coincidental that Dorfsman was commissioned to create the graphics for the
apartment complex erected above the Museum.

338.

MuseumTower

Museum Tower is the 52-story New York City building above and overlooking The Museum of Modern Art. This rare residential building was conceived, designed and built to provide understated luxury. Surrounded by the resources of one of the world's greatest and busiest cities, the Tower offers quiet elegance.

With its entrance at 15 West 53rd Street, just west of Fifth Avenue, the Tower also looks on 54th Street to the north. Thus it is located in one of the few areas of Manhattan that remains residential in flavor and character, yet is close to prime office space, shopping, museums, galleries, theatres and concert halls. The condominium contains 44 residential floors, plus 2 service floors, situated above the Museum's own 6-floor expansion. It belongs to a distinguished and private old neighborhood, for its immediate neighbors are the Museum itself and the block of fine old town houses on 54th Street.

Architecturally the Tower is a work of distinction. The design is the product of collaboration between

Views of New York City from the top of the Tower

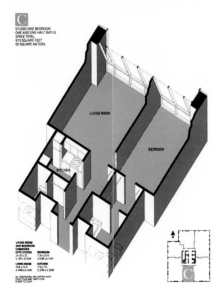

15West53Street

336.-337. The floor plan and carrying tube for distribution to prospective purchasers. The tube could also be used for mailing.

338. Front cover, inside spreads and back cover from the prospectus for Museum Tower. The isometric drawing was suggested by Dorfsman to aid prospective purchasers in visualizing apartment layouts.

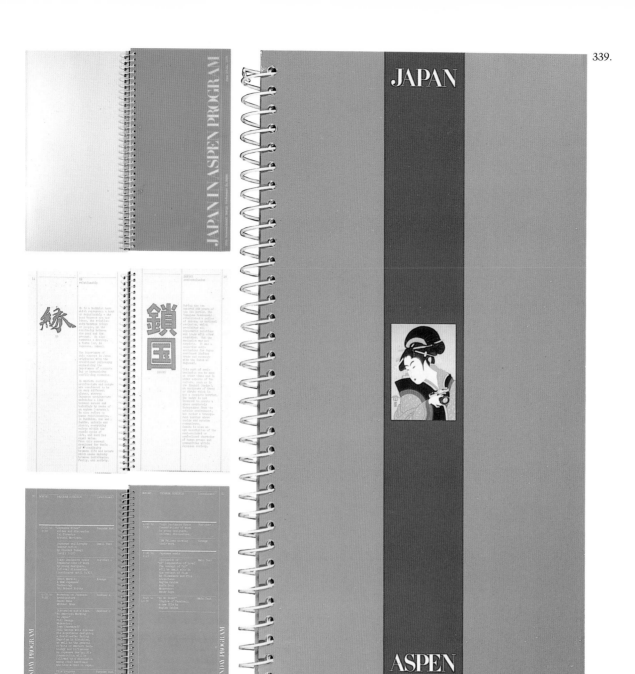

339.

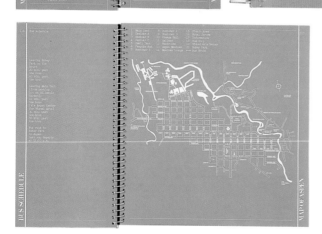

340.

<u>The Aspen involvement</u>
For many years, Dorfsman, along with Saul Bass, Ivan Chermayeff, Jay Chait,
Milton Glaser, George Nelson, Moshe Safdie, and Henry Wolf, has been a board member
and active participant in the International Design Conference held annually in Aspen, Colorado.
The purpose of the conference is to bring management executives and designers face-to-face,
to exchange ideas and build better understanding of each other's functions and goals.
It also provides a meeting place for designers from all over the world
and facilitates the cross-fertilization of ideas.

339. In 1978 Dorfsman served as chairman of the conference. In addition to setting the theme, *Japan in Aspen*, he designed the program and auxiliary graphics. The agenda focused on the culture, design, technology, and business methodology of Japan, past and present, as a source of inspiration for contemporary business and design people.

The program book for the conference included the schedule of events, maps of the conference area and a directory of information for visitors. The silver-colored cover was interrupted by a vertical purple band with an illustration spun-off from the poster.

340. The program book was presented to conference guests in a convenient plastic shoulder bag decorated with Japanese calligraphy which read: *Japan in Aspen*.

341. Poster designed for the 1978 conference. The illustration is by Heather Cooper.

341.

A SYNTHESIS OF CONTRADICTIONS

THE INTERNATIONAL
DESIGN CONFERENCE IN ASPEN
JUNE 17-22, 1979

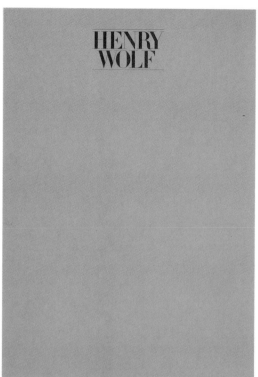

342. Design for Henry Wolf monograph.

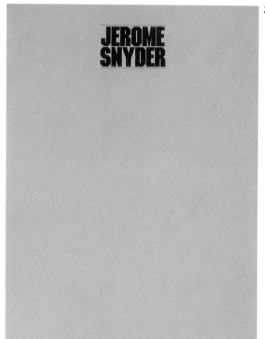

343. Design for Jerome Snyder monograph.

His extraordinary knowledge and his literary abilities became inexorably Intertwined and inseparable from his art. Because of this unique combination of skills, many clients faced with solutions to complex subject matter that called for superior intellect in illustrative interpretation sought his services. He had the rare gift of distilling abstract concepts down to intelligent clarity.

Wit, wisdom, breadth and scope are the ingredients found throughout the body of his work.

His artistry mirrored his personality as art invariably mirrors the artist. The multi-faceted skills and intelligence of Jerome Snyder are amply reflected in his whimsical, painstakingly careful paintings and drawings.

One sees in an earlier period of his work, drawings of rather abstract shapes and forms where the influence of Miro is visible. Invariably, they delineated humorous and decorative objects, figures, or both. Upon a closer look one notes larger forms are composed of a myriad mosaic of countless multi-colored smaller forms that are further made up of gemlike, multi-colored forms within multi-colored forms. A Snyder pointillism of sorts.

A delightfully squat shape is revealed a figure with a face somewhat flesh-colored. But upon closer observation skin tones turn out to be composed of triangular or square or rectangular shapes made up of bits of pink, yellow red, probably green, purple and blue. Jerome has invented a ruddy-faced (r quite cartoon-y) man. The sheer staggering effort of it all.

One notes that Jerome Snyder has not suffered the "flattery" of imitation very much. His work is simply too difficult a process to replicate.

Another side of Snyder is his delicate and extraordinarily meticulous line drawings. The absence of color provid him with the opportunity to demonstra his control of line, his studied draftmanship, and his thoughtfulness interpretation as well as a surprising ability for caricature.

A third aspect of Snyder's art is a rathe more recent development. A new mod evolves. Refreshing, naturalistic paintings of nature's bounty: fruit, fish, flowers, crustaceans, – a sudden beautiful realism executed with a sure lightness of touch, in color and renditic A demonstration of enormous technica facility combined with a poetic reality.

In short, Jerome Snyder leaves a legac of the picture and the word in vibrant unity...of the seminal artist, writer, teacher, whose perceptions were at once intellectual and aesthetic. His art line and language, exuding clarity and He moved his art from visually brilliant fantasies to neo-realistic nature studies—without dropping his 4H penc He accepted his talents, he mined his resources, and he used them both for lasting performance. Lou Dorfsman

The AIGA involvement

Each year the American Institute of Graphic Arts awards a medal to an outstanding individual in the field of communication arts. By consensus, it is the most prestigious medal awarded in the graphic arts community. Dorfsman received the award in 1978 and was subsequently honored with a one-man show. When designer Henry Wolf and illustrator Jerome Snyder were the designated recipients of the AIGA medal, Dorfsman was called upon to design the souvenir monographs.

When I first met Henry Wolf in the fifties, he seemed to be the most sophisticated person I'd ever known.

owned a Jaguar, was always in the pany of beautiful women and was dy clearly the best editorial designer e world. Not to mention a charming nese accent.

ough he matched many of my nal cliches for success and power e were some dissonances. For one g his jackets never fit right (years I learned that this characteristic is eric to a class of successful gners. The difficulty is usually centrated around the shoulders). For ther, he seemed to be without ension. Nevertheless he conveys effect of extraordinary elegance.

at one actually experiences from ry is his lack of capacity to accept second rate. It is a behavioral racteristic that is largely unspoken totally understood by anyone who known him for any length of time. I ress the quality negatively because demand for beauty extracts a price. e of Henry's favorite stories concerns meeting a girl who was carrying a sparent plastic handbag. The ning of the bag made it impossible him to be with the girl. "I think it's a rible thing to be bothered by and I e myself when I do it because maybe e was the nicest person I ever met, but cause of this…she was sort of shed."

The search for belief, cohesiveness and standards as a defense against life's disinterested disorder may be one of the roots of form making activities. In Henry's case the world he creates either as designer, art director or photographer, is characterized by an extraordinary clarity of form and literary content. We are convinced of its "rightness." Every element is the right size, the right shape and in the right place. The illusion is complete and hermetic. When I free associate about other artists whose perceptions of the world seem to share some quality with Henry, Vermeer and Mozart come to mind. Lucidity and the conspicuous lack of excess characterize all three.

In the sixties, Henry chaired a conference he called "Art, Love, Time and Money," a title which is about the most reductive expression for the totality of human experience I can think of. These four themes emerge as obsessive elements in most of Henry's work. Finally, what separates Henry from his peers is his special capacity to evoke the best from those who work with him. It is a rare and special gift. Milton Glaser

THE GREAT CRAFTSMEN

121 EAST 31
NYC 10016
PHONE 212
679-2755

$

344.

JEROME SNYDER ARTIST WRITER CRITIC GOURMET NOTARY PUBLIC

345.

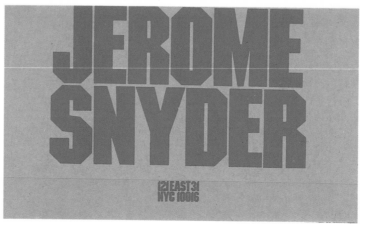

JEROME SNYDER

121 EAST 31
NYC 10016

346.

344. Front of billing form for friend Jerome Snyder.

345. Back of Snyder's billing form reflects Lou's sense of humor, as well as the multiple talents and credentials of Jerome Snyder. The bold typography was consistent with Snyder's portly physique and imposing mentality.

346. Back of envelope.

No job too small
For a perfectionist like Dorfsman, no job is insignificant.
Letterhead designs for friends, acquaintances and worthy causes were treated with the same deliberation and imagination as mammoth exhibitions.

Somoroff Photography inc., 421 East 54 Street, New York 22, Mu 8-2167

347.

347. Stationery for Photographer Ben Somoroff. The small die-cut hole (a typical Dorfsman touch) identifiable as the aperture of a camera.

348.

348. Just a few of the many letterheads Dorfsman has designed over the years.

349.

Atlantic City exhibit

When Atlantic City on the New Jersey shore made its comeback as a tourist attraction and gambling
center, several enterprising developers bought an old defunct pier and converted it into a triple deck shopping mall
and entertainment center in the guise of an ocean liner. Herb Rosenthal, the exhibit designer, and Dorfsman were engaged to
plan and produce the display and exhibition areas. Dorfsman's first contribution was to christen the place *Ocean One*
and to design the logo. His other major contribution was a gigantic wall sculpture, *The World of Sunken Treasure.*

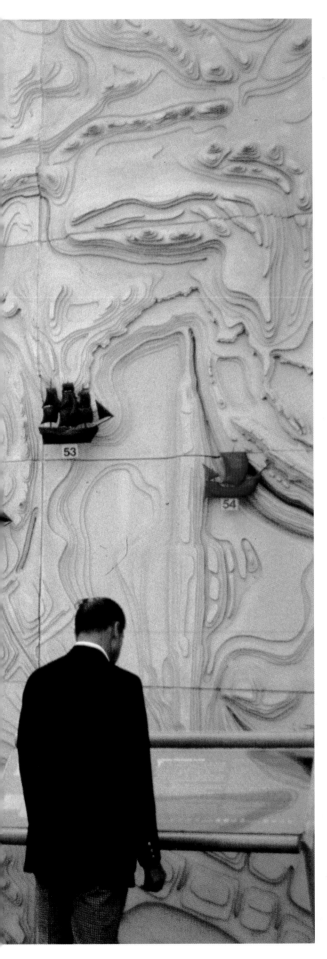

THE WORLD OF SUNKEN TREASURE

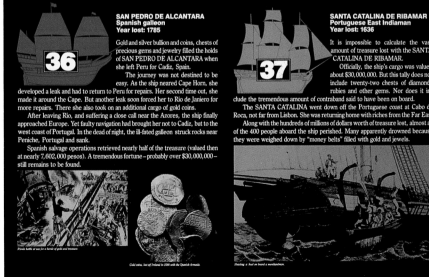

SAN PEDRO DE ALCANTARA
Spanish galleon
Year lost: 1785

36

Gold and silver bullion and coins, chests of precious gems and jewelry filled the holds of SAN PEDRO DE ALCANTARA when she left Peru for Cadiz, Spain.

The journey was not destined to be easy. As the ship neared Cape Horn, she developed a leak and had to return to Peru for repairs. Her second time out, she made it around the Cape. But another leak soon forced her to Rio de Janiero for more repairs. There she also took on an additional cargo of gold coins.

After leaving Rio, and suffering a close call near the Azores, the ship finally approached Europe. Yet faulty navigation had brought her not to Cadiz, but to the west coast of Portugal. In the dead of night, the ill-fated galleon struck rocks near Peniche, Portugal and sank.

Spanish salvage operations retrieved nearly half of the treasure (valued then at nearly 7,602,000 pesos). A tremendous fortune—probably over $30,000,000—still remains to be found.

SANTA CATALINA DE RIBAMAR
Portuguese East Indiaman
Year lost: 1636

37

It is impossible to calculate the vast amount of treasure lost with the SANTA CATALINA DE RIBAMAR.

Officially, the ship's cargo was valued about $30,000,000. But this tally does not include twenty-two chests of diamonds, rubies and other gems. Nor does it include the tremendous amount of contraband said to have been on board.

The SANTA CATALINA went down off the Portuguese coast at Cabo da Roca, not far from Lisbon. She was returning home with riches from the Far East.

Along with the hundreds of millions of dollars worth of treasure lost, almost all of the 400 people aboard the ship perished. Many apparently drowned because they were weighed down by "money belts" filled with gold and jewels.

349.- Combining the nautical
350. theme of *Ocean One* with the get-rich-quick dreams of Atlantic City gamblers, Dorfsman hit upon the idea for his exhibit. It is a vast sculptured fiberglass map, 100 ft. across and 20 ft. high, of all the continents and ocean floors of the world. On it, he located 54 historic shipwrecks with known sunken treasure. Each one is marked by a model of a sailing ship, color-coded to the country under whose flag it sailed.

351. The legend of each shipwreck, plus scientific data about the oceans, is provided in an illuminated case which runs the length of the exhibit. It also serves as a protective guard rail.

USA, LAND OF OPPORTUNITY

USA, LAND OF PLENTY

USA, LAND OF LIBERTY

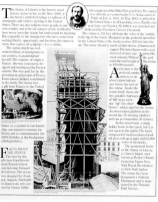

USA, LAND OF COMFORTS AND CONVENIENCES

USA, LAND OF INGENUITY

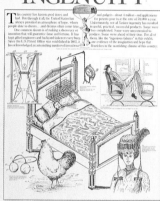

USA, LAND OF IMMIGRANTS

Unless he or she is an American Indian, every person in the United States is an immigrant or a descendant of immigrants!

The first 105 foreigners arrived here in 1607. They came from England and settled in Jamestown, Virginia. Boatloads of immigrants followed, establishing colonies of every major country of Europe. And from Africa, slave traders brought in more shiploads of "foreign born" men and women. There is no way of knowing the exact number of immigrants who have come to this country, since no records were kept until the year 1820. But since then, according to U.S. Government statistics, we have received close to 50,000,000 legal immigrants—more than any other country in the world. They came from more than 50 countries of Europe, Asia, Africa, the Americas and also Australia and New Zealand. They represent every race, color and religion.

From the beginning, people flocked to this country for three basic reasons: to escape religious persecution, to escape political repression, to find a better way of life. The United States Constitution had built-in guarantees of religious and political freedom. The young expanding country also needed skilled and unskilled hands to help develop its agriculture and industry and to expand its frontiers.

Tales of jobs, land, prosperity, free education, reached the depressed and oppressed populations of Europe, where wars, famine and political unrest made life hopeless. The promise of a secure and more hopeful future encouraged people to leave their homelands for the new, young, "golden" country.

Ship owners whose craft were returning to America with half-empty holds also encouraged migration from Europe by offering low fares to the poor. The trip was made economically sound for the passengers and the ship owners.

Immigrants have come from different countries, at different times for different reasons: 1820-1889: Poor harvests, revolutions and political unrest brought refugees from Germany, Ireland, Canada, Sweden and France in response to U.S. offers of open farmland in undeveloped areas of the country. 1890-1919: Industrial development in the U.S. offered opportunities for jobs and a higher standard of living; it brought laborers from Italy, Austria-Hungary, Russia, Britain and Ireland. 1920-1959: While Europe was devastated by two World Wars on her soil, the United States was supplying the world with agricultural and industrial products. Workers flocked in from Italy, Great Britain and Mexico. Religious and political refugees streamed in from oppressive totalitarian governments in Germany, Italy and European countries. 1960-PRESENT: Refugees fled war-ravished countries of Southeast Asia and political oppression in South and Central America.

USA, LAND OF PERPETUAL PROGRESS

USA, LAND OF GROWTH AND CHANGE

USA, LAND OF GIVERS

352. Posters for each section of the exhibition provide informative text that is easy to read and digest.

353. For the section paying tribute to American inventors, Dorfsman and Rosenthal created a giant, free-standing light bulb with famous inventors' names spelled out in neon tubing.

The American Celebration
Another exhibit at the *Ocean One* mall was a collaborative effort involving Herb Rosenthal, Dorfsman and a number of other designers, artists, photographers and craftsmen. The exhibit pays tribute to individuals and systems that are uniquely American, and that account for the growth and prosperity of the country.

1918	*Born April 24, New York City.*
1935	*Graduated from Roosevelt High School, The Bronx, N.Y.*
1938	*Asst. Exhibit Designer, New York World's Fair.*
1939	*Graduated from The Cooper Union School of Art and Architecture, BFA Degree.*
1942	*Designer/Artist, U.S. Navy Training Films.*
1943	*Inducted into the U.S. Army.*
1944	*Chief Designer, U.S. Armed Forces traveling exhibits.*
1944	*Awarded first and second prizes in National Army Arts Contest.*
1945	*Associate Art Director, Reiss Advertising, N.Y.C.*
1946	*Joined CBS as Assistant to Art Director, Bill Golden.*
1951	*Art Director, CBS Radio Network.*
1954	*Associate Creative Director, CBS Radio Network.*
1956	*Awarded citation from The Cooper Union for outstanding professional achievement.*
1956	*One-man show in Japan.*
1959	*Vice-President, Advertising and Promotion, CBS Radio Network.*
1960	*Creative Director, CBS Television Network.*
1962	*Awarded the Philadelphia Printing Gold Medal for Best-of-Year Design.*
1963	*Awarded the Augustus St. Goudens Medal, The Cooper Union's highest award.*
1964	*Director of Design, CBS Inc.*
1965	*One-man show, Tokyo.*
1966	*One-man shows in Munich, Frankfurt and Amsterdam.*
1968	*Vice-President, Creative Director of CBS Broadcast Group.*
1970	*One-man show in Tokyo.*
1974	*Elected to Board of Trustees, New York Institute of Technology.*
1974	*Visiting Lecturer in Tokyo, Osaka, for Nainichi Broadcasting Co.*
1975	*President of New York Art Directors Club.*
1975	*Visiting Professor, Syracuse University.*
1976	*Visiting Professor, The Cooper Union.*
1976	*Elected to Board of Trustees, The Cooper Union.*
1976	*Elected to Board International Design Conference in Aspen.*
1978	*Senior Vice President, Creative Director, Advertising and Design, CBS Broadcast Group.*
1978	*Awarded American Institute of Graphic Arts Gold Medal.*
1978	*One-man show, American Institute of Graphic Arts.*
1978	*Chairman, International Design Conference, Japan and Aspen.*
1978	*Inducted into the Art Directors Hall of Fame.*
1980	*Vice-President, Creative Director, Advertising and Design, CBS Inc.*
1984	*Awarded Honorary Doctorate in Fine Arts, Parsons School of Design, N.Y.C.*
1984	*Conducted seminars at Syracuse University, N.Y. and University of Kansas.*

Awards: *13 Gold Medals, New York Art Directors Club; 22 Awards of Distinctive Merit, New York Art Directors Club; Fifty Ads-of-the-Year Awards; Several Clios and an Emmy for TV Graphics; Honored by the New York Type Directors Club, Poor Richard's Club and the Philadelphia Art Directors Club.*

Publications: *Featured in* American Artists, CA *Magazine,* Fortune, Graphis, Graphic Design *(Japan),* Gebrauchsgraphik *(Germany),* Idea *(Japan),* Industrial Design, Mademoiselle, Pagina *(Italy),* Penrose Annual, Print, Ten Designers *(Japan),* Type Talks.

Personal: *Lou Dorfsman is married to Ann Hysa, a Cooper Union alumnus, who is a weaver and currently Keeper of Wall Coverings at The Cooper Hewitt Museum, New York City. They live in Great Neck, New York and have three grown children, Elissa, Mitchell and Neil.*

A Creative Director, like an orchestra conductor, is nothing without the players. There are other art directors, designers, writers, photographers, illustrators, staff secretaries, and clients I must thank for their major solo contributions as well as their ensemble playing. To assign specific credits for work done over a 40-year period would tax my memory and invite errors of attribution and omission. Therefore, in alphabetical order, these are the people to whom I owe many thanks.

— Lou Dorfsman

JOHN ALCORN
RICHARD ALCORN
TOM ALLEN
AL AMATO
RALPH AMMIRATI
CAL ANDERSON
GERRY ANDREOZZI
TED ANDRESAKES
NAOMI ANDREWS
CAROL ANTHONY
HERMAN ARONSON
VINCENT ASHBAHIAN
GORDON AUCHINCLOSS
RICHARD AVEDON
JOEL AZERRAD

IRV BAHRT
RUDI BASS
SAUL BASS
BOB BATSCHA
ALAN BEAVER
STAN BECK
BUD BENJAMIN
BILL BERNBACH
R.O. BLECHMAN
GARY BLOWERS
ALLEN BOORSTEIN
RONALD BOROWSKI
PETER BRADFORD
CHUCK BRAVERMAN
DICK BRESCIA
GEORGE BRISTOL
ROLF BRUDERER
MICHAEL BURKE
AARON BURNS

RALPH CAPLAN
KEN CHANDLER
IVAN CHERMAYEFF
SEYMOUR CHWAST
ADRIENNE CLAIBORNE
BILL CONKLIN
HEATHER COOPER
JOAN COSTA
TOM COURTOS
RICHARD COYNE
JERRY CRAW
WALTER CRONKITE
MIKE CUESTA

MIKE DANN
ANNE DAVIS
PETER DEROW
NEIL DERROUGH
CHRIS DESANTIS
JOE DEVOTO
PHOEBE DORIN
RAY DOWDEN
JULES DUNDES
JIM DURFEE

HAROLD EGAN
NAIAD EINSEL
BOB ELLIOT
TONY ESPARZO

DICK FARSON
NICK FASCIANO
GENE FEDERICO
DOROTHY FIELDING
CARL FISCHER
KARL FISCHER
STEVE FRANKFURT
FRED FRIENDLY
DAVID FUCHS

SID GARFIELD
MEG GATES
CHARLES GILLETT
RALPH GINSBURG
PHIL GIPS
MILTON GLASER
LEN GLASSER
STANLEY GLAUBACK
RUDO GLOBUS
IRWIN GOLDBERG
BILL GOLDEN
HARRY GORDON
STEVE GORDON
DENNIS GOTTLIEB
SHEILA GREEN
AL GREENBERG
MARILYN GREENBERG
SHARON GRESH
LARRY GROSSMAN

STANLEY HARRIS
LOUIS HAUSMAN
ART HECHT
DAVID HERZBRUN
DICK HESS
WALTER HICKEY
AL HIRSCHFELD
JOHN HITE
BOB HOSKING
FAITH HUBLEY
JOHN HUBLEY
GERARD HUERTA
DON HUNSTEIN

DICK JACKSON
RAY JACOBS
GENE JANKOWSKI
VANCE JOHNSON
JIM JORDAN

KIYOSHI KANAI
NURIT KARLIN
ART KANE
PETER KATZ
JOE KAUFMAN
TERI KERNER
BURT KLAPPER
BOB KLEIN
TANA KLUGHERZ
RAY KOMAI
CHARLES KORBETT
YASUO KUBOTA
KISHO KUROKAWA

JANE LANDER
DON LAWSON
TOM LEAHY
ED LEE
MITCH LEIGH
BILL LEONARD
JOHN LEPREVOST
RICK LEVINE
DAVID LEVY
ARNE LEWIS
DICK LOEW
GEORGE LOIS
TONY LOVER
JOSEPH LOW
HERB LUBALIN
SALLY LUDLOW

GEORGE MCGINNIS
PAUL MAC COWATT
JAY MAISEL
PHIL MARCO
PACY MARKMAN
HARRY MARKS
LOUIS MASACHIO
BARRY MASON
E.K. MEADE
TOM MEANS
SOL MEDNICK
MITZI MELNICOFF
TOMOKO MIHO
LARRY MILLER
ALAN MITTLEMAN
ANDREW MORIMOTO
MARION MULLER
TOBY MULLER
LOU MYERS

TED NIERENBERG
GEORGE NELSON
PETER NORD
SHAD NORTHSHIELD
DAVID NOVEMBER

ROBERT OSBORN

EMILIO PACCIONE
ONOFRIO PACCIONE
WILLIAM S. PALEY
KATHY PALLADINI
TONY PALLADINO
PETE PALAZZO
FRED PAPERT
DAVID PARKER
IRVING PENN
CHUCK PFEIFER
GIERARD PIEL
JONATHAN PIEL
MARTY PURIS

GEORGE RADKAI
BOB RAFAELSON
LOU REDMOND
TOM RINALDI
BEN ROSE
MIL ROSEMAN
BONNIE ROSENFELD
HERB ROSENTHAL
PAUL ROSENTHAL
MORT RUBENSTEIN
DICK RYAN

RICHARD SALANT
JACQUES SAMMES
ED SAXE
CHARLES SAXON
JOE SCHINDLEMAN
HARVEY SCHMIDT
JACK SCHNEIDER
JOHN SCHNEIDER
DAN SCHWARTZ
TONY SCHWARTZ
IRWIN SEGELSTEIN
IZZY SEIGAL
AKIHIKI SEKI
ISADORE SELTZER
IRA SHAPIRO
CHARLES SHAW
JIM SHEFCIK
JIM SHUMAKER
ED SIDE
KAREN SILVER
MARTY SILVERSTEIN
FRANK SKORSKI
BOB SMALLHEISER
DICK SMITH
JOHN SMITH
BILL SNYDER
JEROME SNYDER
MIKE SOLURI
BEN SOMOROFF
WARREN SPELLMAN
FRANK STANTON
BOB STRUNSKY
DAVID SUH

IKKO TANAKA
ZANE TANKEL
MYLES TANENBAUM
DAN TAYLOR
IRA TEICHBERG
JOHN TITIMAN
JOE TOLE
JACK TOM
SALLY TOMLINSON
TED TRINKUS

JIM UDELL
GRACE UHLIG
TOMI UNGERER

BOB VERNO
ALAN VOGEL

TODD WALKER
ANDY WARHOL
ROBERT WEAVER
KURT WEIHS
BILL WEINSTEIN
JAMES WINES
GARY WINOGRAND
MARTIN WINTER
FRED WITZIG
BURT WOLF
HENRY WOLF
ROBERT D. WOOD
RICK WURMAN
BILL WURTZEL
TOM WYMAN

TOM YEE
TADASHI YAMAMOTO

LINDA ZARBA